Health and Health Services

Health and Health Services

An Introduction to Health Care in Britain

John R. Butler
Health Services Research Unit
University of Kent at Canterbury

Michael S.B. Vaile
Maidstone Health Authority, Kent

Routledge & Kegan Paul
London, Boston, Melbourne and Henley

First published in 1984
by Routledge & Kegan Paul plc

14 Leicester Square, London WC2H 7PH, England

9 Park Street, Boston, Mass. 02108, USA

464 St Kilda Road, Melbourne,
Victoria 3004, Australia and

Broadway House, Newtown Road,
Henley-on-Thames, Oxon RG9 1EN, England

Set in IBM Press Roman 10/11 pt
by Columns of Reading
and printed in Great Britain
by T.J. Press (Padstow) Ltd, Padstow, Cornwall

Library of Congress Cataloging in Publication Data

Butler, John R.

Health and health services.
Includes index.
1. Medical policy–Great Britain. 2. Medical care–
Great Britain. 3. Health services administration–Great
Britain. 4. Great Britain–National Health Service.
I. Vaile, Michael S.B. II. Title . [DNLM: 1. Health
services–Great Britain. 2. Delivery of health care–
Great Britain. 3. State medicine–Great Britain.
4. Great Britain–Ministry of Health. W 275 FA1 B97h]
RA395.G6B88 1984 362.1'0941 83-27031

British Library CIP data also available

ISBN 0-7100-9902-9 (pbk.)

Contents

Acknowledgments

We gratefully acknowledge the various contributions made towards this book by many friends and colleagues. We are particularly indebted to the following for their help: Lynn Browne, Colin Cannon, Vic George, Rose Knight, Robert Lee, Tina Martin, Jan Pahl, David Perkins, Jill Relton, Michael Warren and Shirley Woodward. They bear no responsibility at all for any errors, inaccuracies or imperfections.

Data in the following tables are reproduced by kind permission of the Controller of HMSO and/or © Crown copyright: 3.1, 3.2, 3.3, 3.4, 3.5, 3.6, 3.8, 3.9, 3.10, 3.12, 4.1, and figures 3.1 and 4.1. Data in table 3.3 are reproduced by kind permission of Sir Richard Doll and The Royal Society of Medicine. Table 3.7 is reproduced by kind permission of the Royal College of General Practitioners. Figure 3.2 is reproduced by kind permission of Routledge & Kegan Paul. Table 3.11 is reproduced by kind permission of the Office of Health Economics.

Chapter 1

An organising framework: the health services system

Since its introduction in 1948, the National Health Service (NHS) in the United Kingdom has frequently been the focus of intense national scrutiny, debate, conflict and passion. It has been prodded, poked and analysed by politicians, doctors and nurses, trades unionists, voters, academics and patients' organisations. It has engaged the attention of top-level commissions and committees of enquiry. It has been praised as the most noble and unselfish institution created in post-war Britain, and it has been criticised as cumbersome, bureaucratic and inefficient. Those who use the service appear, for the most part, to be satisfied with the care they receive, while those who work in it present what a former minister of health has described as 'a deafening chorus of complaint'.[1] Against a background of growing concern about a financial crisis in the NHS, the service has steadily consumed more and more of the nation's resources.

This book aims to explore some of the issues underlying these reactions. What are the patterns of health care needs in the United Kingdom and how do they arise? What is the balance in the health service between the prevention and treatment of disease? What are the social and political forces in society that create the kind of health service we have? How much money is spent on the NHS, and how has it changed over time? Are we spending too much or too little? What determines the amount of money that is spent? How is the money raised, and what scope is there for raising it in different ways? Is a tax-funded health service better than an insurance-based service? What happens when the demands made upon the health services exceed the resources available to meet them? Who decides, and on what basis, how the resources in the NHS are shared out among different parts of the country? Who decides which forms of care will be given to different groups of people – the old and the young, the handicapped, the chronically sick and the acutely ill? What organisational structures exist for making these decisions? How is the NHS actually organised and managed? How are policies formulated? Is policy-making in the NHS a rational or an arbitrary activity? What does the NHS achieve? How can the products of the service be defined and measured? How can the service be made more effective and more efficient – indeed, what do effectiveness and efficiency actually mean? How can the NHS be evaluated, and what happens when things are found to be unsatisfactory? Who is accountable to whom, and for what?

These are the kinds of questions with which the book is concerned. It tries to clarify and illuminate issues as much as to provide answers, for there are no easy or simple answers to be had. And it makes no claim to comprehensiveness. Each one of the themes of the book is vast in its implications and each has been the subject of many other books and articles. Our aim is to summarise some of the more important contemporary ideas and arguments about the health service, to set out some of our reflections about them, and to point the way towards some of the relevant literature. In doing this, we have tried to write in a style that is free of unnecessary jargon and that will be intelligible to readers with different intellectual and occupational backgrounds. The book deals principally with the health services in the United Kingdom (UK), and makes only occasional reference to the health services of other countries. Within the UK, the NHS operates in somewhat different ways in England and Wales, Scotland and Northern Ireland, and we have endeavoured always to be clear about the constituent parts of the kingdom with which we are dealing.

The book is organised loosely around the concept of the health services as a system. The word 'system' has come to acquire a fairly precise, technical meaning in several different contexts, but it is used in this book in the more general way suggested by the *Oxford English Dictionary's* definition as 'a set or assemblage of things connected, associated or interdependent, so as to form a complex unity; a whole composed of parts in orderly arrangement according to some scheme or plan'.[2] As though anticipating the application of this definition to a complicated organisation such as the NHS, the OED adds that it is 'rarely applied to a simple or small assemblage of things'.

The main elements of the health services system are set out in a simple form in figure 1.1.

The first point to note is that the system (bounded by the broken line) is set in an environment that is characterised by a number of salient features, and in order to understand the system itself we must understand its relationship to the environment. The NHS cannot be seen as analogous to a foetus, largely isolated and protected from the outside world in an administrative amniotic sack; rather, it should be regarded as an integral part of the social structure, shaped by it

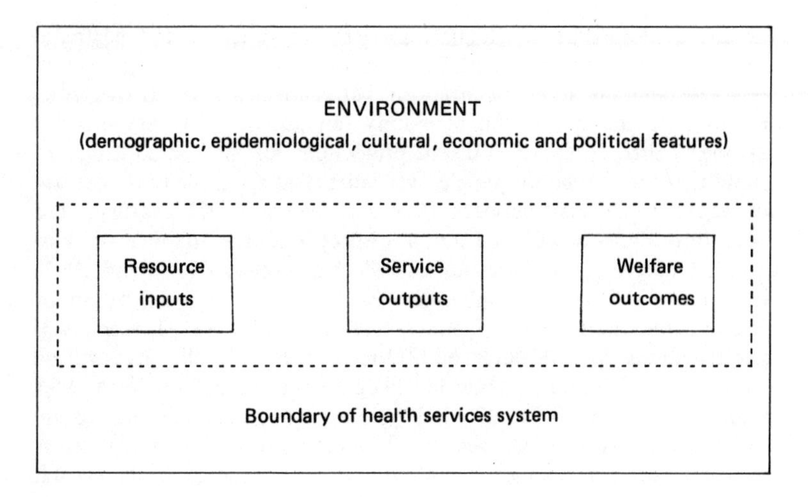

FIGURE 1.1

and contributing to its continuously changing contours. Health services do not come ready-made, and governments cannot choose a particular system from an international catalogue of approved models. As Maxwell has put it, 'no pattern of health service organisation and administration is for export, since each country's traditions and values are sufficiently different to make it uncomfortable with solutions developed elsewhere.'[3] The health services system is subject to continuous change and development in the light not only of evolving patterns of need and of developments in the technology of care, but also of shifting social and political values, cultural aspirations and economic vicissitudes.

Figure 1.1 draws attention to five features of the environment that impinge upon the health services system in different ways. First, there are demographic features. Demography is the study of human populations, particularly their size, structure and development, and demographic features and trends are bound to exert an influence over the pattern of health service provision. The young and the elderly usually experience more ill health than people in their middle years, and the single, the widowed and the divorced suffer higher rates of disease and death than the married; but the age and marital structures of the population are changing all the time, with consequent changes in the volume and nature of the demands that are made upon the NHS. For seventeen years following the inception of the NHS in 1948 the crude birth rate in the United Kingdom (that is, the number of live births per 1,000 total population) increased, focusing attention particularly on the development of adequate services for antenatal and postnatal care and the care of children. Between 1966 and 1977 the crude birth rate fell, and the focus of attention began to shift towards the growing number and proportion of elderly (and particularly very elderly) people in the population. Current projections for the United Kingdom show that the number of people over retirement age is likely to increase by about 20 per cent between 1980 and the end of the century,[4] and that this increase will contain a disproportionate number of non-married people. It has been estimated that, between 1976 and 1991, the number of single people over the age of 65 will fall by about 121,000 but the number of elderly widowed and divorced people will rise by about 287,000 and 166,000 respectively.[5] In all, there will be about 332,000 more non-married people over the age of 65 in 1991 than there were in 1976. If elderly non-married people continue to use the health services more heavily than their married counterparts, as they have done in the past,[6] then these projected changes in the marital structure of the population will further intensify the demand for services, in addition to the pressures resulting from an increase in sheer numbers. Indeed, it is likely that the needs of the growing number of elderly people will be the most important single concern of social policy over the next twenty-five years, with far-reaching consequences for the health and personal social services.[7] It has been estimated that, merely in order to maintain the same level of services for elderly people, expenditure on the NHS must increase in real terms (that is, after allowing for the effect of inflation) by 1 per cent per year,[8] but resources that are used to maintain the level of services for the elderly are unavailable for improvements and developments elsewhere. Choices have to be made about priorities. We discuss the prospects for the future funding of the NHS in chapter 4, and we consider different aspects of the allocation of resources in chapters 6 and 7.

Next, the environment in which the health services system is located is characterised by epidemiological features. Epidemiology is the study of diseases among populations – the way they are distributed and spread and the factors that are implicated in their onset and natural history.[9] As the word suggests, epidemiologists were concerned originally with the outbreak and spread of infectious diseases, but modern epidemiologists are equally concerned with non-infectious diseases and their distribution and causes. Epidemiological features of the environment are likely to have an important influence on the objectives and priorities of any health services system that tries to be responsive to the needs of those it serves. A simple illustration is seen in the contrast between what are conventionally called developing and developed countries. Developing countries are typically characterised by high birth rates, high infant mortality rates, high death rates from infectious, parasitic and nutrition-deficiency diseases, and a low proportion of elderly people.[10] Health services in these countries that are responsive to the needs of their populations would therefore be producing rather different patterns of care than those in developed countries, where the emphasis is on the chronic and degenerative diseases of old age and on diseases associated particularly with an affluent, urban industrialised life style – coronary heart disease, liver cirrhosis, vascular disease, psychoneurotic disorders and accidents. Even within the United Kingdom there are differences in rates of death and ill health between different regions that might lead to different emphases in the provision of health care. Epidemiological evidence ought therefore to be an important ingredient in planning health services,[11] and might also be used as a yardstick against which to assess the impact of health services.[12] After all, health services exist to maintain and enhance people's health, and their effectiveness ought therefore to be reflected in improvements in the health status of the population. But in practice things are not quite as straightforward as this. Ill health is notoriously difficult to define and measure, and the links between the provision of health services and the health of the community are not always clear to see. We tackle some of these issues in chapters 2, 3, 10 and 11, where we discuss different ways of measuring the health of communities, the influences of health services on health, and ways of thinking about the effectiveness of health services.

Third, there are cultural features in the environment that carry implications for health services. Patterns of behaviour, attitudes, beliefs and mythologies run deep in societies, shaping the health experiences of people and influencing the ways in which they cope with them.[13] Many of these ways of thinking and behaving are harmful to health, requiring the health services to use a considerable part of their resources in providing care for conditions that might never have arisen in the first place. For example, the preliminary report of a study by the Royal College of Physicians of London into the causes of death among hospital in-patients aged between 1 and 50 showed that, among the first 250 cases included in the study, ninety-eight patients had contributed directly to their own deaths by overeating, drinking too much alcohol, smoking, or not complying with medical treatment.[14] Similar results have been reported in an American study of 136 patients admitted to general hospital care, 44 per cent of whose admissions were judged avoidable if their personal behaviour or life styles had been different.[15] These studies suggest that aspects of individual behaviour which are threatening to health, and to which the health services are required to respond, are deeply rooted in notions of social acceptability and may be reinforced by powerful social and commercial interests. Draper has put the point in these vivid terms:

> The pinnacle of achievement in health has come to be equated with the spectacle of men and women becoming overstressed and under-exercised, indulging in excessive consumption of food, cigarettes, and alcohol . . . before being rushed to an intensive care unit and submerged in expensive medical technology only when acute symptoms have prevented them from indulging in further consumption.[16]

Another illustration of the influence of the cultural environment on health is seen in the greater degree of social equality that women have secured in many countries in recent years. Whilst full equality has not yet been attained, women have made significant gains in their struggle to live on equal terms with men, but at the cost of a tendency to die on equal terms with men.[17] Female death rates in both the United States and the United Kingdom, from such conditions as coronary heart disease and lung cancer (which are assumed to result in part from life styles that have in the past been the prerogative of men), are now rising closer to the male death rates from these conditions. In the case of lung cancer, Stolley has drawn attention to the commercial pressures that have been exerted on women in recent years to smoke.

> As women have become more self-sufficient with more disposable income, the cigarette manufacturers have intensified their effort to induce them to smoke by developing cigarettes designed especially for women and by advertising messages calculated to equate smoking with independence and freedom from the domination of males.[18]

We take up some of these themes in chapter 2, where we examine different ways of explaining the causes of ill health and the different implications they have for coping with disease.

The general state of the economy is another important feature of the environment in understanding the health services system, for economic vicissitudes affect both the health of people and the level of spending on health services. It has long been known that economic depression and long-term unemployment are bad for health,[19] but interest in the relationship between the national economy and health has increased recently with the work of an American economist, Brenner.[20] Through the use of statistical models, Brenner has examined the relationship between periodic fluctuations in the economy and various measures of ill health and death. He has claimed to demonstrate that periods of economic recession and high levels of unemployment affect the least skilled and the lowest paid much more severely than those higher up the occupational ladder, and that such erosion of economic security engenders stress, weakens the protective effects of social and family structures, and is manifest for many years subsequently in enhanced rates of death and chronic illness. Brenner's work has been criticised, particularly for its failure to account convincingly for the time lags between peak periods of economic recession and subsequent levels of death and ill health in the population as a whole,[21] but it is not surprising to find evidence at the individual level that the costs of prolonged unemployment are to be counted in terms not only of lost earnings and impaired self-esteem, but also of personal and family ill health, chronic disease and increased rates of hospital admission.[22]

The link between the economic performance of a country and the level of spending on health services is remarkably consistent between different countries, whatever the methods by which health care is financed: the higher the productivity of a country (relative to its population size), the more it spends on health services. Indeed, the general prosperity of any country appears to be one of the best predictors of its expenditure on health care.[23] We examine this relationship more closely in chapter 4, but it is sufficient to note here by way of illustration that the increasing economic difficulties of the United Kingdom since the sharp increase in world oil prices in 1973 have led to cut-backs in the level of public spending as a whole and in spending on the NHS. There has been a widespread belief among both the major political parties when in government that the restraint of public expenditure is a necessary pre-condition of economic recovery, and that without such recovery there can be no significant increase in spending in the public sector.

The environment in which the health services system is located is also characterised by political features. Politics is concerned with the conflicts and disagreements that exist in society and the way they are resolved or contained. Any group of people, whether a family or an entire community, is bound to generate a divergence of opinion about the way things should be done, and mechanisms or institutions must emerge for coping with such diversity. Opinions on fundamental issues about the way society should be organised and the relationships that individuals should have to the social and economic processes of society provide convenient benchmarks against which to evaluate the policy choices made by government and other public agencies. The social services in general, and the health services in particular, are no exception to the pervasive influences of political thought and action.[24] For some, the provision of social services by the state is politically suspect, supposedly fostering irresponsibility and undermining individual initiative and autonomy; for others, the social services are both necessary and intrinsically desirable in combating the malign effects of a competitive, market-oriented society. Such views fit readily into the bundles of attitudes and values that characterise the right and left wings of the British political spectrum. Titmuss, for example, has drawn attention to what he calls the 'institutional' and 'residual' models of the social services.[25] The institutional model regards the social services as a vital part of government action to maintain social justice through the provision of public services to all who are in need of them. The residual model, by contrast, sees the social services as a minor appendage, catering only for those who will not or cannot provide for their own and their families' welfare. Reflected in this brief summary of the two models can readily be seen a divergence of political views about several important aspects of social life: the role of the state in the lives of individuals, the merits of market forces in the allocation of goods and services, the virtues of individual thrift and self-sufficiency, and the nature of social justice. And because the health services system is located in an environment in which these political tensions and ideologies exist, it too is caught up in ideas and aspirations that have their political roots in much wider fields than the provision of health care. Consider, for example, the perennially contentious matter of private practice both within and outside the National Health Service. The existence of private (pay) beds within NHS hospitals has generated a political tension out of all proportion to its probable impact on the NHS,[26] and arguments about the growth of private hospitals outside the NHS have, in the words of two commentators, been characterised more by political rhetoric than by hard-nosed actuarial calculations.[27] Yet that is not really surprising. Private practice has become a symbol, for both those who are for and against it, of wider political conflicts, and those who believe that the NHS should be taken out of politics have misunderstood the essential interrelationship between the service and its environment. We look in chapters 5 and 7 at some of the political arguments about different ways of financing health care and of allocating the goods and services that are produced from the NHS.

So much, by way of introduction, for the environment. Turning now to the health services system itself, the first point to note is that it is bounded. The boundary (depicted in figure 1.1 as a broken line) emphasises the importance of careful definitions. It circumscribes the collection of institutions that are generally regarded as comprising the health services of any country or community – institutions, that is, which have been created and which function principally to maintain and improve the health of individuals and communities. There are, however, other institutions and processes in society which, whilst not being concerned *principally* with the maintenance of health, nevertheless have *incidental* implications for health. The health *services* system can therefore be distinguished from the broader concept of health *care*, which includes not only the health services themselves, but also a wider array of institutions that have implications for health. Policies for housing, the control of environmental pollution, the elimination of child poverty, and health and safety at work all have implications for health care, though they do not fall within the boundaries of what is normally regarded as the health services. The focus of this book is mainly on health services, although the health services system is only a part (albeit an obviously important part) of the wider concept of health care.

The system itself is made up of resource inputs, service outputs and welfare outcomes, though, as will be seen, there is a good deal of imprecision in the application of these terms to the analysis of health services. The resource inputs represent the raw materials that are used in the provision of care. Resources may be classified in various ways, but a common classification would distinguish between manpower resources (doctors, nurses, physiotherapists, accountants, engineers, record clerks, porters, laboratory assistants, etc.); capital resources (buildings and other big things that can usually be seen from the road); durable goods (such as equipment or machinery that have a reasonable length of life but eventually wear out or become obsolete); and consumption goods that are actually used up (drugs, dressings, fuel, food, stationery and the like).

Resources are costly; that is, they have a price and must be bought for use in the health services system, and the cost of purchasing any particular resource is the variety of other resources that cannot then be bought with that money. It follows, then, that even when decisions have been made about the total amount of money that will be available for spending in the health services each year, difficult choices still remain about the things to be bought with it. How much of the total sum is to be spent on buildings and maintenance, how much on equipment, how much on different categories of manpower, and how much on consumption goods? Of course, these choices need not (indeed cannot) be made from scratch each year. The existing pattern of service provision and staffing levels will automatically determine the expenditure of a very large proportion (perhaps over 95 per cent) of the next year's allocation of money, and spending on certain kinds of capital resources will generate inevitable consequences for spending on a whole range of other resources.[28] If a new hospital is built, or even if a new piece of equipment is bought, staff will be needed to operate it and a variety of other resources will be required in order to use the equipment to its full potential. But there may be room for manoeuvre in the medium term (for example by changing expenditure priorities and reallocating money from one service area to another), and there is usually scope also for substituting one kind of resource for another. It may be possible, for example, to revise traditional ways of working so that things which have previously been done by doctors are transferred to less highly qualified staff. If there is no dilution in the amount or quality of the services produced as a result of this reallocation of work, the system is likely to become more efficient because doctors are usually a more costly resource than other staff. We discuss the concept of efficiency in greater detail in chapter 11.

The output of services refers to the large variety of activities that take place through the use of all the different resources bought into the system. The distinction between resource inputs and service outputs is important, for the capacity to plan sensibly and to evaluate the worth of the health services system is limited if attention is concentrated exclusively upon the inputs.[29] For example, in 1980 the National Health Service in England used some £10,000 million of resources: it had about 360,000 hospital beds and it employed about 40,000 doctors and dentists, 370,000 nurses and midwives, 105,000 administrative and clerical staff, and 172,000 ancillary staff. This volume of resource inputs appears at face value to be quite impressive, but it would be difficult to draw any conclusions about how well the service was working, or whether it was providing value for money, from these figures alone. In order to evaluate the service, further information would be needed about the amount of care produced from the resources. Doctors, nurses and hospital beds have little inherent value in themselves, and it would be naive on the basis of the numbers alone to say whether there were too many or too few of them. The real value of these resources comes when they are used to provide services for patients who need them, and no sensible evaluations can be made about the workings of the system without taking account of the production or output of services.

The measurement of service outputs is by no means straightforward, and more will be said about it in chapters 10 and 11. For the present, two of the more obvious measures of output may be noted by way of illustration. First, it is possible (though not always easy) to count the number of people who pass through the different parts of the NHS. In the case of hospitals, for example, counts may be made of the number of people admitted as inpatients or seen in outpatient clinics; in general practice, the number of surgery consultations and home visits may be counted; in the field of prevention the counting may be of the number of people screened for the early signs of disease or immunised against infections. If the statistics are good enough, they can be further analysed by age, sex, social class, area of residence and so on, in order to show the coverage and scope of the service outputs. A second obvious measure of the output of services is the quantity of actual treatments given to people. Measures of the physical output of services might include such things as the number of surgical operations performed, the number of teeth extracted, filled or crowned, the number of diagnostic tests carried out, the number of courses of immunisations given, the number of prescriptions written, and so on.

The last part of the system carries the label 'welfare outcomes'. As with the distinction between inputs and outputs, that between outputs and outcomes is conceptually important, though sometimes blurred. Suppose, for example, that the mythical man in the street is given certain information not just about the resource inputs to the National Health Service (beds, manpower, equipment, etc.), but also about the service outputs produced from those resources. He might be told, for example, that in 1980 just over 5½ million hospital admissions and about 35 million outpatient attendances took place in England, that some ¾ million surgical operations were performed, that about 150 million consultations occurred between GPs and their patients in which some 300 million prescriptions were written. If invited to pronounce upon the merits of the NHS on the basis of this information about outputs, the man in the street might reply that, whilst many impressive things were indeed being produced by the service, he would nevertheless like to know what *good* was being achieved from this flurry of activity. He might point out, for example, that the real reason for having a health service is to keep people well, to cure them when they fall ill, and to provide care and comfort to those whose diseases cannot be cured; and that therefore the input of resources and the output of services (though important) are ultimately no more than the means to those ends. In short, the health services system exists to maximise people's health and wellbeing, and it is to be judged by its achievement in doing just that.

The measurement of outcomes presents considerable problems, both conceptual and methodological. What is 'welfare', and even if we can recognise it, can we be sure that it is a consequence of health services? We examine these problems in chapters 2, 10 and 11, but for the moment two possible approaches to the outcome of health services may be noted by way of illustration. First, outcomes may be thought of in terms of beneficial changes in the health of individual people, whether that is the curing of disease, the relief of pain, the restoration of normal functioning, the reduction in the risk of future ill health, or the minimisation of anxiety and discomfort. The question to be asked here is whether the different dimensions of the health of individual people have improved as a result of their encounter with the health services. Second, outcomes may include some notion of benefit to the health of the community as well as of the individual. Whilst there is an obvious sense in which the health of the community is no more than the sum of the health of the individuals comprising it, it is nevertheless true that some services confer a more general benefit upon the community as a whole. Immunisation is an obvious example. Each individual person who is immunised receives a personal benefit in the form of a reduced risk of contracting the disease, but he or she simultaneously confers a benefit on others by increasing the level of immunity in the population and hence reducing the risk that others will contract the disease. There may be occasions when the welfare of the individual conflicts with the welfare of the community.[30] When the incidence of an infectious disease is low, there may be a greater threat to the health of the individual from the vaccine itself than from the risk of contracting the disease; but each individual who refuses immunisation for his or her own supposed benefit is thereby enhancing the risk that others may contract the disease. Similarly in the field of mental illness, the law provides that people may, under certain closely defined circumstances, be deprived of some personal liberties through compulsory detention in hospital for the sake of the protection of others.

Chapter 2

Health, health services and politics

In his book *Beyond the Magic Bullet*, Dixon has recounted a drama that occurred in a farmyard at Pouilly-le-fort, in France, on 5 May 1881.[1] Assembled in the farmyard were a group of farmers, scientists, veterinary surgeons, senators of the republic, and forty-eight sheep. Into this mixed throng limped a professor of chemistry at the University of Lille, Louis Pasteur. Pasteur had claimed to be able to protect sheep against anthrax, an awful and usually fatal disease; and this theatre of the farmyard was to be the demonstrative act. The sheep were divided into two groups of twenty-four each, one group of which was injected with a weak solution of anthrax bacilli – the microbes causing the disease. The other group received no injection. Everyone then departed. Twenty-six days later the spectators reassembled, and on this occasion all the forty-eight sheep were injected with a lethal dose of live anthrax bacilli. Again, everyone departed. Two days later the assorted crowd assembled yet again. Pasteur's entry was greeted with tumultuous applause, for of the twenty-four sheep that had *not* received the initial weakened solution of anthrax bacilli, twenty-two lay dead and two were in the last throes of anthrax, with blood oozing from their mouths and noses; whilst of the twenty-four that *had* received the initial injection, all were alive and well, peacefully munching the grass.

What Pasteur had done was to stage a dramatic demonstration of the principles of immunisation. By exposing half the animals to a weakened dose of an infective organism (in this case the anthrax bacillus) he had stimulated the build-up of antibodies to the point where they conferred protection on the animals when later exposed to a normally lethal dose of the organism. The principle of immunisation is now readily accepted, and it is perhaps difficult, a hundred years later, to understand the stir caused by Pasteur's theatrical demonstration. But the point in telling the story is that the work of Pasteur and other nineteenth-century scientists advanced our understanding of the cause of the disease by a quantum leap, and laid the foundation for important advances in the medical treatment of disease.

Early attempts to explain the origins of disease relied heavily upon the magical and religious concepts of pre-scientific cultures, although some shrewd insights were made by individual observers.[2] In about 400 BC Hippocrates had accurately recorded the environmental conditions associated with particular disorders, and the general facts of infection and contagion had been worked out during the Black Death in the fourteenth century. It was not until the work of Leeuwenhoek in Holland in the seventeenth century, however, that microbes were first seen and described, and a further 150 years elapsed before they were firmly associated with disease. Pasteur's particular contribution was the demonstration that microbes could *cause* disease, and towards the end of the nineteenth century Robert Koch in Germany worked out a set of rules or postulates that could reliably be used to identify the specific microbes causing particular diseases. Between 1879 and 1900 the specific aetiological agents of at least twenty-two infections were identified, and the search began for the chemical substances (the so-called magic bullets) that would combat the effects of these agents.[3] The first big breakthrough came in 1911 when Paul Ehrlich, working in Berlin, synthesised the drug salvarsan, which had some effect against syphilis. It was the first drug that acted specifically against a particular causal agent. Others followed, including most notably the family of drugs based on sulpha compounds that offered treatment for pneumonia, meningitis, puerperal fever, gonorrhoea and various bowel infections. The golden age of the magic bullet arrived in 1941, when Howard Florey and Ernst Chain succeeded in turning Alexander Fleming's chance discovery of penicillin thirteen years earlier into a usable drug. Penicillin was the first antibiotic, and others developed in the next forty years have included streptomycin (for the treatment of tuberculosis), chloramphenicol (for typhoid), tetracycline (a wide spectrum antibiotic used in the treatment of a range of bacterial infections) and many others.

The identification of microbes as the causal agents of infectious diseases, and the subsequent development of drugs to knock them out, are representative of a philosophy and practice of medicine that has had a powerful influence on western culture. It is variously described as the theory of specific aetiology,[4] the mechanistic model,[5] and the medical model. It postulates that disease can be understood as 'something that has gone wrong with the individual human organism', that diseases have a specific cause or causes, and that, once discovered, the causes can be attacked by appropriate medical or surgical intervention. It is a view that emphasises the importance of medical care in maintaining people's health through the treatment of disease, and it sees the health services (as the organisational channels for the delivery of medical care) as a major factor in the improvement of the health of the western world in recent times. The treatment of infectious diseases has provided obvious evidence in support of this view, but other diseases have also been consistent with it. As the twentieth century progressed, causal agents were implicated in equally specific ways with other types of disease. Vitamin deficiencies were identified as the specific cause of rickets, scurvy, beri-beri, pellagra and some forms of anaemia. Genetic defects were found to cause mongolism, sickle cell anaemia and phenylketonuria. The deficiency of a hormone (insulin) was identified as the cause of diabetes. All of these categories of disease appeared to sustain the theory of specific aetiology: they have specific, identifiable causes, and in the case of the vitamin- and hormone-deficiency diseases they can be corrected or ameliorated through medical intervention by replacing the deficient substances in appropriate quantities.

Because of the critical stance taken towards this model of disease in some of the contemporary literature,[6,7] it is important at this point to stress the positive benefits it has produced. The critics of the medical model argue that poor environmental factors (in such matters as pollution, sanitation, housing, warmth and diet) are of paramount importance in the onset and spread of many diseases, and that the advances in health resulting from their declining importance have owed much more to improvements in these factors than to the beneficial effects of medical intervention and specific therapy.[8,9] They argue that health services have made a much smaller contribution to health than is generally assumed. We examine these arguments more closely in chapter 10, but wish to emphasise here the importance of distinguishing the level of argument about the causation of disease and the different possibilities for action at each level. At one level, for example, it is perfectly correct to say that tuberculosis is caused by exposure to the tubercle bacillus. Without exposure to the bacillus there is no disease, and in this sense the theory of specific aetiology is right. Moreover, modern drugs, beginning with streptomycin in 1944, offer a specific and effective therapy against tuberculosis, and other drugs are equally effective against other infectious diseases. Dollery has noted in this context that

> some of the early achievements in the treatment of infections were so miraculous as almost to surpass belief . . . they literally changed the world . . . antibacterial chemotherapy made the cure of such scourges (as pneumonia, osteomyelitis and pulmonary tuberculosis) almost a matter of routine.[10]

With the gradual control of the major infectious diseases, the goal of medical intervention shifted somewhat away from the simple preservation of life towards the improvement in its quality, and here too there have been successes. Beeson has concluded from a comparative study of the recommended treatments for a very large number of diseases in both 1927 and 1975 that

> substantial advances have been made along the whole frontier of medical treatment. A patient today is likely to be treated more effectively, to be returned to normal activity more quickly, and to have a better chance of survival than fifty years ago. These advances are independent of such factors as better housing, better nutrition, or health education.[11]

Morris has also drawn attention to the achievements of medical intervention in situations where effective prevention is not yet possible.

> In the host of chronic conditions that we do not know how to prevent (many of the disabilities of aging for a start) treatment today may be able to make all the difference to the quality of life – that is, to health. Maintenance, repair and restorative medicine in an aging population are still 'prevention', even if late. Arthroplasty (reconstruction) of the hip can offer relief from suffering and greater wellbeing, functional improvement and social independence (that is, better health) to many old people.[12]

Dollery's verdict on the charge that much of medical practice is irrelevant to people's health was that the case had been overstated.[13]

Yet whilst acknowledging the great contribution that the medical model has made to the sum of human health and happiness, it is only partially satisfactory as an explanation of the causes of disease and as a pointer to action. Indeed, Pasteur was always aware of the limitations of an exclusively microbiological account of the causes of infectious disease, insisting that an adequate explanation had to take account of the 'terrain' in which the microbes worked as well as the microbes themselves; and his view was vindicated dramatically in a bizarre experiment in 1892. Max von Pettenkofer, a Bavarian chemist, swallowed a mixture containing what in ordinary circumstances was regarded as a lethal dose of cholera bacilli, and suffered no more than mild diarrhoea. Deeply impressed, other members of his staff did likewise, and also survived unscathed.[14] Whilst Pasteur had shown that microbes were a *necessary* condition for infectious diseases to occur, von Pettenkofer had demonstrated that they were not a *sufficient* condition. Other conditions had to be met as well. The view that disease is the result of multiple causal factors, interacting in complex ways, is now part of the conventional wisdom of medicine, although it is a significant departure from the earlier belief that each disease has a single and specific cause. It explains why many of the laboratory results achieved by the nineteenth-century scientists could not be replicated with the same degree of exactitude in the real world,[15] and it also explains why, in spite of the impressive achievements of medicine in the twentieth century, the problem of disease in the last quarter of the century is more daunting than Pasteur, Koch and Ehrlich might reasonably have expected. Many of the common diseases in modern industrial societies (such as heart disease, mental disorder, cancer and arthritis) have no single and simple cause, and they are not always amenable to treatment by magic bullets. Their causes are multiple, complex, and deeply rooted in the social and even the economic and political fabric of society; and strategies for coping with them must likewise be multi-faceted and far-reaching. The contributions of medical care and the health services are important, but they cannot be seen as the only weapons of attack.

A topical example of the implications that different levels of explanation about causality have for different courses of action is that of lung cancer. It is the commonest form of cancer in both the United States and the United Kingdom,[16] accounting for some 45,000 hospital admissions each year in England and Wales.[17] It is, however, a serious disease, and the prospects for those who contract it are poor. No more than 10 per cent of those who are diagnosed are still alive after five years, and this proportion has not changed appreciably over the last twenty-five years.[18] Only about 10 per cent of those who are found to have lung cancer are suitable for surgical treatment, and of these, the five-year survival rate is between 25 per cent and 30 per cent.[19] The use of cytotoxic drugs as a supplement to surgery is probably no more beneficial in increasing the survival rate than a placebo (inert) drug.[20] Moreover the early detection of lung cancer through regular X-ray screening has not been shown to have any appreciable effect on survival in those afflicted by the disease.[21] Yet lung cancer is largely preventable. The key factor is smoking. Although some non-smokers do contract the disease, it has been estimated that of the 95,000 deaths from lung cancer in the United States in 1978, between 80,000 and 85,000 were attributable to smoking,[22] and in the UK the corresponding figure would be between about 30,000 and 32,000. About a quarter of all regular cigarette smokers are killed before their time by tobacco, but those who stop smoking before the onset of cancer or serious heart or lung disease avoid nearly all their risk of dying from tobacco.

These statistics suggest that future effort might be directed more effectively towards changing the behaviour of established smokers and discouraging potential smokers than in extending the search for more effective chemotherapy. But how is this to be done? The answer lies partly in the assumptions that are made about the reasons why people smoke – assumptions, that is to say, about the causal links farther back in the chain. A common assumption is that smoking is a purely personal habit, reflecting a weakness of will in the smoker's personality.[23] Most health education programmes in the UK have been based on this individualistic approach, aiming to change the behaviour of individuals through exhortation, fear, encouragement or incentive. There have been warnings of the dangers of smoking, increases in tobacco duty, the use of popular comic heroes to dissuade young children from smoking, the promotion of healthy life styles among adults, and other similar approaches.[24] Such efforts have produced beneficial changes in people's smoking habits, particularly those in the higher socio-economic groups,[25] but by focusing mainly upon the individual's responsibility for his or her own behaviour, attention is diverted away from those aspects of the social environment that create and sustain the individual's need for cigarettes. As Doyal has put it, 'we can only really understand the use of nicotine as a dependence-producing drug within the context of the prevailing social climate which encourages smoking much more strongly than it discourages it'.[26]

Another approach, then, to the problem of altering people's behaviour would be through regulation of the activities of the tobacco companies and their advertisers. Considerable sums of money and a good deal of talent are invested in the promotion of tobacco products. In contrast to the Health Education Council's annual budget of some £6 million in 1980, the tobacco companies were estimated to have spent more than £100 million on advertising, much of it through the sponsorship of sporting and cultural events.[27] The companies tend to argue that the effect of their advertising is to persuade established smokers to switch from one brand to another, not to encourage new smokers; but there is evidence that the sophisticated promotion of cigarettes, with the promise of social status and sexual attractiveness, does have an effect on people's behaviour.[28] Various controls exist over the advertising and marketing activities of the tobacco companies, both in the United Kingdom and elsewhere,[29] but it has proved difficult to increase their effectiveness. Attempts to introduce legislative controls in the UK have proved to be politically impossible in the face of a strong parliamentary lobby in favour of the industry,[30] and any such controls would in any case be politically unacceptable to governments favouring a free market economy. As a minister of health in the Conservative government of 1979 remarked, 'my government does not welcome the use of regulatory or legislative measures in order to control ... the legitimate commercial freedom of tobacco companies.'[31] Because of these kinds of political considerations, coupled with the fear of governments of the loss of excise duty revenues, the companies retain a good deal of freedom to pursue their interests, unhampered by serious constraints. In 1982, for example, the minister of sport announced that the sponsorship of sporting events would continue to be allowed, in spite of a warning from the Health Education Council that 250 lives a year would be lost as a result.[32]

The case of lung cancer is a particularly clear illustration of the way in which links in the causal chain of disease can be traced back deep into the political and economic fabric of society, offering possibilities for the promotion of health that are far removed from the traditional concerns of the medical model. But it is by no means an isolated illustration. Road traffic accidents claim between 6,000 and 7,000 lives each year in Great Britain and cause about 80,000 serious injuries.[33] Between 45,000 and 50,000 people require hospital treatment for their injuries, and some 2,000 hospital beds are occupied each day by the victims of traffic accidents.[34] The costs of these injuries are to be counted not only in terms of the resources required to treat them, but also in terms of the lost earnings of their victims, the additional social and financial costs to the families involved, and the cost of whatever rehabilitative treatment is required. The causes of road traffic accidents vary from case to case, but they are likely to lie well beyond the scope of the health services system, requiring preventive action through other institutions in society. Accidents may be caused by the faulty behaviour of drivers (through alcohol, drugs, tiredness, incompetence or inexperience), by the faulty design or maintenance of vehicles, or by faults in the physical environment; and once an accident occurs, the damage caused to those involved in it may be exacerbated by weakness in the design of the vehicles and the failure of the occupants to wear seat belts. Action to minimise the effect of these causes would be wide-ranging, and would pose obvious threats to the interests and established practices of many groups and individuals in society.

Similar analyses might be made of the causes of diseases that are associated with the excessive consumption of alcohol and of foods that are rich in refined carbohydrates and fats and low in fibre content. Or again, the debate about the effects of lead concentrations in the environment on the health and intellectual development of children is as much a political as a medical debate.[35] And at the global level, the two most important contemporary threats to health are the risk of nuclear war and the existence of widespread poverty. The risk of nuclear war is probably the greatest affront to health that has ever existed,[36] and it is becoming increasingly clear that the health services would be rendered virtually impotent by the explosion of nuclear devices in urban areas.[37] The only option for health is prevention, and whilst medical institutions can and do press the case for prevention,[38] the means for effective action lie in the hands of politicians, not doctors. The global effect of poverty on health has been documented by the Brandt Report on the rich and poor nations of the world.

> There are countries in Africa where one child in four does not survive until its first birthday . . . . blindness from vitamin deficiency and water-borne infections afflict 30 to 40 million people in the Third World . . . . the number of people who are undernourished and hungry could be more than 500 to 600 million . . . . four out of five people in the rural areas of developing countries do not have reasonable access to unpolluted water . . . . between 20 and 25 million children below the age of five die every year in developing countries, and a third of these deaths are from diarrhoea caught from polluted water.[39]

Manifestations of ill health on this colossal scale require a response that is far beyond the capacity of the health services or even of the governments of developing countries. As the Brandt Report repeatedly stressed, they are inextricably linked up with food and nutrition, with employment and income distribution, with the world economic order.

Much of the recent literature on the social, political and economic origins of ill health has drawn attention to the effects of the production and consumption of goods in industrialised capitalist societies.[40,41,42,43] The success of such economies depends upon a method of producing goods or commodities that can be sold for more than the cost of the factors that are used in their production, and upon the willingness of sufficient numbers of people to buy the goods that are produced. The process of production and the creation or maintenance of demand may, however, generate threats to the health of both workers and consumers.

The most obvious relationship between the production process and the threat to health is seen in industrial accidents and diseases, but it is also manifest in various forms of industrial pollution, in the deleterious psychological consequences of repetitive and unstimulating work in noisy environments, and in the health risks arising from the enforced termination of employment.[44] Navarro, for example, has given three examples of the way in which aetiological factors in ill health can be traced back to the processes of production.[45] The alienation that many people feel from society, reflecting the lack of control they have over their lives and work in highly organised industrial societies, is responsible for a large part of the psychosomatic and psychoneurotic disorders in those societies; ill health and premature death from occupational diseases and injuries are caused in part by the priority given in capitalist forms of production to the maximisation of profit where this conflicts with the provision of safe working environments; and many causes of cancer are related to the uncontrolled pollution of the environment resulting from industrial processes. 'These are just three examples of the economic and political aetiology of disease', Navarro wrote, 'and this aspect is as apparent today as when our diseases were predominantly infectious ones.'

On the demand side, the pressure on people to consume more and more of the outputs of the production process, which is essential to the success of industrialised capitalist economies, produces harmful as well as healthy forms of consumption. The promotion of tobacco and alcohol products and of foods that are rich in refined carbohydrates and fats and low in fibre content has already been mentioned, and there are other commodities, the production of which is good for the health of the economy but potentially bad for the health of people. Among them may even be counted some drugs, which are advertised intensively among the medical profession, and which may cause more harm than good if prescribed excessively or inappropriately. The pressures towards the consumption of harmful products have even been aimed by companies in developed countries towards the expanding markets of the developing countries. For example, the consumption of cigarettes has more than doubled in some developing countries over the last twenty years;[46] the aggressive marketing of breast milk substitutes in Africa, Asia and South America has caused widespread concern;[47] and there is evidence that certain drugs in Third World countries are over-priced, over-promoted, inappropriate for the problems they are supposed to tackle, and carry inadequate instructions and warnings.[48]

All of these examples of the ways in which aetiological factors in ill health may be located deep in the social, political and economic fabric of societies, are in marked contrast to the emphasis placed in the medical model upon the individual as the appropriate focus for action to maintain health. Disease is seen as a fault in the individual human organism, and health is to be maintained through such activities as educational programmes to change personal behaviour, personal preventive measures such as immunisation and screening for the early signs of disease, and personal medical care when disease occurs. Of course, doctors have for long been aware of the importance of people's social and physical environment in maintaining good health, but not usually to the point of seeing political action to change the environment as a necessary and legitimate aspect of the practice of medicine. Yet, as we have seen, many potentially harmful aspects in the environment of both developed and developing countries are beyond the control of the health services system and those who operate it, residing instead in the hands of politicians and others who occupy positions of power. And whilst (as we have argued) the medical model has made a tremendous contribution to the sum of human health and happiness, there are many points at which it is impotent.

A forceful illustration of the way in which political power might be used to improve the health of the nation has been given by Lipton in the form of an imaginary speech delivered in the House of Commons by the minister of health of a newly elected government.[49] The speech outlines a fundamental change in government policies towards health in order to raise the level of the nation's health by 25 per cent in a context of limited economic growth and therefore of limited expansion in the real resources available to the health services. The key to the speech is the wide concept of prevention adopted by the minister, and the consequent emphasis on policies for *health* rather than policies for health *services*. The strategy has three prongs to it. The first is the use of fiscal mechanisms. The minister announces that direct incentives to ill health (through duty-free customs allowances for cigarettes and spirits) will be removed; that taxes and subsidies will be adjusted to encourage safer motoring; that people will be compelled to bear the full social cost of their health-endangering actions; that tax concessions will be available to employers for the provision of sports facilities; and that national insurance contributions will be adjusted according to the contributors' life styles. The second prong is that of restrictive legislation. Legislation will be introduced, the minister announces, to restrict smoking in public places; to prohibit smoking by pregnant women; to ban all advertising of cigarettes; to outlaw smoking by teachers, doctors and nurses in schools and hospitals; to restrict the use of saturated fatty acids in packaged foods; to limit the sugar content of prepared foods; to reduce the permitted blood alcohol level of drivers; to reduce speed limits; and to transfer from insurance companies to the individual the first £1,000 of personal injury charges to any injured person not wearing a seat belt. The third prong is that of public activities. In future, the minister says, all schoolchildren without physical handicap will be taught how to attain and retain reasonable levels of heart-lung fitness, and 5 per cent of National Health Service funds will be placed at the disposal of a new Division of Positive Health, whose task will be the translation of scientific knowledge about the causes of death and disease into active programmes to increase security against needless ill health and mortality.

Lipton was careful to conceal the political colour of the minister's party, observing merely that the speech is based on long-known facts and could have been made by an intelligent politician of the radical left or the radical right. The fact that it has not been made in reality is indicative partly of the disproportionate emphasis given in the British political context to policies for health services rather than policies for health, and partly to the constraints on the exercise of political power that exist in pluralist democracies. We return to this theme again in chapter 9.

Chapter 3

Some epidemiological trends in the United Kingdom

Health services exist mainly to meet people's needs for health care. In the course of doing this, secondary goals arise and other socially desirable aims are fulfilled; but the principal justification for the existence of health services is the need that people have for them. In the case of the National Health Service in the United Kingdom the justification is endorsed by act of parliament. Section 2 (2) of the 1973 National Health Service Reorganisation Act states that 'it shall be the duty of the Secretary of State to provide throughout England and Wales, to such extent as he considers necessary to meet all reasonable requirements . . . .'; and there follows a list of the services that the secretary of state must provide, including hospital and other accommodation; medical, dental, nursing and ambulance services; facilities for the prevention of illness, the diagnosis and treatment of illness, the care and after-care of people suffering from illness; and so on. Whilst the definition of 'all reasonable requirements' is necessarily vague, the section makes it clear that the secretary of state is required by law to know the magnitude of the needs that people have for health care, and to provide services to meet them. The definition of 'need' is contentious, and we endeavour to explore its meaning in more detail in chapter 11, but it seems clear that ill health and infirmity (or the imminent threat of it) must be part of any definition of need.

At once, however, another problem of definition arises. We have talked so far in rather loose terms about 'ill health' and 'infirmity', but what do these mean and how are they to be measured? Commonsense definitions of ill health are notoriously inconsistent and ambiguous when examined too closely. There may be little doubt that, say, a woman with acute appendicitis or a child with bacterial meningitis are ill, but other cases may be less clear-cut. The limbless ex-soldier who has fashioned an active life style within the limitations of his disability; the anxious hypochondriac leading the life of an invalid, but for whom no diagnosis can be found apart from his anxiety; the woman with pre-symptomatic cancer of the cervix that has not yet been detected through screening; the middle-aged man who has recovered from a heart attack and who, with careful diet and exercise, can lead a safe but somewhat restricted life; the alcoholic; the fat boy; the depressed housewife; the unhappy homosexual – all these pose problems of definition. Perhaps they all need some kind of help. But are they *ill*, and do they need the help of the health services?

There is beginning to emerge a language for coping with these ambiguities that offers a tentative framework for classifying different kinds of data about ill health. First, there is the ultimate state of not being well – mortality. There is now a little more uncertainty than there used to be about the moment of death, thanks to the introduction of machines that can artificially ventilate a body in which no brain activity can be detected; but in most cases there remains little doubt about the point at which life ceases. Death is a finite, identifiable event that is legally required to be registered. Whilst everyone must die sooner or later, and a death is not therefore necessarily an event that casts doubt upon the effectiveness of health care, mortality data may be helpful for the purposes of planning and evaluation if they show the rate of 'premature' deaths (especially infant deaths) or variations in death rates between different social classes, occupations or regions of the country, or deaths from causes that ought to be preventable.

Next, the term 'morbidity' is used in an umbrella sense to describe all forms of ill health. Three reasonably distinct categories can be identified. First, the concept of disease is commonly used to describe the presence of clinically diagnosed abnormalities in the structure and functioning of the organs and systems of the human body.[1] As Helman has put it, 'diseases are the named pathological entities that make up the medical model of ill health, such as diabetes and tuberculosis, and which can be specifically identified and described by reference to certain biological, chemical or other evidence.'[2] By this definition, the knowledge of the existence of disease depends upon a diagnosis by a doctor and this, as Kennedy and others have pointed out, gives the medical profession considerable power to define both the standard of normal structure and functioning and also the point at which normal variations around that standard merge into abnormality.[3] In many cases such judgments are quite uncontentious, being based on clear biological criteria; but they may assume significance in such diagnoses as mental disorder, where the standard of normality against which the diagnosis is made may involve social, moral and legal elements as well as purely biological ones. The alleged abuse of psychiatry in the USSR, where political dissidents are claimed to be detained compulsorily under the guise of a psychiatric diagnosis, is an obvious example of the dangers that can arise from the abuse of professional power.[4] Nearer home, an editorial in the *British Medical Journal*, raising the question of where social misdemeanour ends and mental illness begins, has commented that

> there is a growing danger that society will use psychiatry to gloss over its own shortcomings and ills by making its victims 'patients'. Anti-social behaviour must not be confused with mental illness, and psychiatrists must be aware of having forced on them the role of controlling misfits.[5]

A second category of morbidity is that of illness, which is commonly used to denote the subjective feeling by the individual of not being well. In the arresting words of Cassell, 'illness is what the patient feels when he goes to the doctor; disease is what he has on the way home from the doctor's surgery. Disease is something an organ has; illness is something a man has.'[6] There is a large element of overlap between disease and illness, but non-overlapping cases can be imagined. On the one hand, in cases of asymptomatic hypertension or early cancer of the cervix of the womb, patients may be told they have a disease even though they do not (yet) feel ill. On the other hand, hypochondria is an example of a state of illness for which no disease entity can be found (other than the hypochondria itself), and there are many subjective feelings of illness that seem to have a psychological origin, with no detectable disease process present.

The third category of morbidity is that of sickness. The concept of sickness has entered the vocabulary of medical sociology largely through the work of American sociologists of the functionalist school, particularly Talcott Parsons.[7] It is used to denote the special status accorded to those who are socially recognised as being unable, for reasons of ill health, to carry out their usual social roles and obligations. Parsons introduced the concept of the sick role to explain the way in which society may cope with the potentially disruptive effects of illness and disease. In return for the privilege of being permitted to withdraw from their usual social expectations at work, home, etc., those who occupy the sick role are expected to seek competent help and to co-operate with doctors and others in regaining their full functional capacity. People who are 'sick' in this social sense may or may not have a diagnosed disease, and they do not necessarily recognise themselves as being ill. This reply of a woman in a classic survey of the health of an American community illustrates the point extremely well.

> I wish I knew what you meant about being sick. Sometimes I felt so bad I could curl up and die, but had to go on because the kids

> had to be taken care of and besides, we didn't have the money to spend for the doctor. How could I be sick? How do you know when you're sick anyway? Some people can go to bed almost anytime, but most of us can't be sick even when we need to be.[8]

The concepts of disease, illness and sickness are still somewhat imprecisely defined in the literature,[9] but they are useful in distinguishing the clinical, perceptual and social dimensions of ill health. A parallel set of concepts has been developed to distinguish different dimensions of disablement.[10] Impairment is used to denote 'the loss or abnormality of psychological, physiological or anatomical structure or function'. There is a close and obvious overlap between this definition of impairment and the concept of disease. Disability refers to 'any restriction, resulting from an impairment, of ability to perform an activity in the manner or within the range considered normal for a human being'. It might describe, for example, the restriction in mobility resulting from the loss of a leg or the reduction in visual acuity as a result of cataracts. There is a greater objectivity in this concept of disability than in the parallel concept of illness, but the behavioural component is still there. Lastly, the notion of handicap is used to describe the 'disadvantage resulting from an impairment or disability that limits or prevents the fulfillment of a role that is normal for that individual'. The extent of handicap will vary from one person to another, even though their impairments may be comparable, but it will be defined in terms such as the inability to do the same work or to participate in the same leisure activities as the 'average' person of the same age, sex and social experience. The element of social incapacity in this definition of handicap provides an obvious point of conceptual similarity with the sociological idea of sickness.

It will be plain from these brief attempts at definition that much imprecision and ambiguity remains in the language that is available for conceptualising states of ill health, but by maintaining a distinction between disease, illness and sickness on the one hand, and between impairment, disability and handicap on the other, a more sensitive vocabulary is available than either the undifferentiated notion of 'not being well', or the global definition of health offered by the World Health Organisation (WHO) as 'a state of complete physical, mental and social well-being and not merely the absence of disease or infirmity'.[11] (The WHO definition of health, though much derided for its utopian flavour, represents an important philosophical interpretation of health that is much wider than the disease-oriented approach of the medical model; but it does not offer any firm pointers to the measurement of health, and conversely of ill health, in populations.)

Having stumbled over these definitional hurdles, we turn now to the sources of data. What information is available about the amount, nature and distribution of mortality, morbidity and disablement in the United Kingdom? More comprehensive and reliable information is available about mortality than about the different categories of morbidity. Since 1836 all deaths in the UK have been required by law to be notified, and a certificate of the cause of death, signed by a medical practitioner, has been mandatory since 1874. Using death registrations, annual statistics are published by the Office of Population Censuses and Surveys (OPCS) on the number of deaths, by cause, classified according to such characteristics of the deceased as age, sex, place of residence, and so on.[12] From time to time additional mortality statistics are published, the most important of which are contained in the decennial supplement on occupational mortality, showing social class and occupational variations in death rates. The most recent supplement was published in 1978, relating to the years 1970-2.[13]

Because death is usually an unambiguous event, and because all deaths have to be registered, mortality statistics have been regarded for 150 years as one of the best available indicators of the amount of morbidity in the community, and are sometimes used explicitly as substitute measures of morbidity. An example is the formula for the allocation of revenue and capital resources from the Department of Health and Social Security to the health authorities of England and Wales, in which standardised mortality rates are involved specifically as a measure of each authority's need for resources (see chapter 6).[14] There are, however, dangers in assuming that death is an acceptable indicator of morbidity, for many diseases that generate significant demands on the health services are not particularly fatal and do not therefore figure prominently in the mortality statistics. An example is rheumatoid arthritis, which afflicts about 4 per cent of men and about 2 per cent of women over the age of 65 and is a major cause of disability and handicap;[15] but it rarely causes death and is therefore not represented in the mortality statistics to anything like the extent of service use it generates.

There are also certain technical problems surrounding the accuracy of the recording of cause of death, particularly in elderly people.[16] The accuracy of the certified cause of death will vary according to the experience and competence of the doctor completing the certificate. A higher level of accuracy may also be expected if an autopsy is performed, yet the proportion of deaths that are followed by autopsy varies quite markedly between different areas of the country.[17] Moreover, many deaths have multiple, interacting causes, making it difficult for the certifying doctor to select a single underlying cause of death. As Benjamin has put it, 'the recorded causes of death are essentially statements of medical opinion, however well informed and even when based on post-mortem investigation.'[18] In spite of these problems, however, mortality statistics are widely regarded as more reliable than the variety of available morbidity statistics. It is to these sources that we now turn.

The first category of morbidity identified above was that of disease, defined as clinically diagnosed abnormalities in the structure and/or functioning of the organs and systems of the human body. The emphasis in this definition on clinical diagnosis means that statistics about disease in the population can derive only from records of contacts between patients and doctors. Four main sources of data about disease patterns in the United Kingdom are available. First, diagnostic and other clinical and social data are abstracted regularly from the case records of hospital in-patients and are subsequently analysed and published. Since 1957 the Hospital In-Patient Enquiry (HIPE) has collected information about every tenth patient leaving non-psychiatric in-patient care in England and Wales, and summaries of the information are published on an annual basis.[19] A parallel enquiry takes place in Scotland.[20] Annual HIPE reports display such information as the numbers of patients discharged, their average length of stay and their diagnoses, classified by such variables as age, sex, marital status and area of residence. Although the Hospital In-Patient Enquiry does not extend to psychiatric hospitals, a separate survey (the Mental Health Enquiry) supplies similar information about patients treated in these hospitals.[21]

Second, some information is available about the diseases diagnosed in general practice. No national recording system exists in general practice that is comparable to the Hospital In-Patient Enquiry, but partial information about the volume and variety of diseases seen by general medical practitioners (GPs) is available. Between 1970 and 1972 just over one hundred GPs throughout England and Wales collaborated in collecting diagnostic and other data about all patients seen by them during two twelve-month periods. The results were analysed centrally and published jointly by the Royal College of General Practitioners, the Office of Population Censuses and Surveys, and the Department of Health and Social Security.[22,23] They represented the best available data about diagnosed morbidity in general practice at the time, but they were flawed by the small number and unrepresentative nature of the participating GPs. Since then, a vast amount of additional information has come from GPs keeping and publishing records of their own workloads,[24] and from sources such as the Birmingham Research Unit of the Royal College of General Practitioners.[25] Such data, too, are likely to be atypical of the whole country, for they derive from self-selected doctors who happen to enjoy research as well as clinical practice; but there is sufficient information now available about the patterns of disease in general practice to enable the construction of disease profiles for a 'typical' practice.[26]

Third, some infectious diseases are notifiable by law (there are currently twenty-nine notifiable diseases in the United Kingdom), and statistics of such notifications are published annually.[27] In addition, since the introduction of cancer registries in 1945 most new cases of malignant neoplasms have been notified, providing a good national picture of the occurrence and prognosis of this diagnosis. Fourth, limited information is collected and published nationally about pre-symptomatic disease that is detected at screening clinics. The most important diseases for which national data of this kind are published regularly are cancer of the cervix of the womb and tuberculosis of the chest.[28]

Apart from errors arising in the diagnosis of disease and in the recording and processing of the data, the most obvious limitation in the use of the available statistics of disease is that they are, by definition, confined to those that come to the attention of doctors. They do not represent the full volume of clinically diagnosable disease in the community. In some cases this limitation is negligible. Virtually all cases of, for example, fractured femurs are probably referred for hospital care, and therefore the number of people admitted to hospital with this diagnosis is a good indication of the number of cases occurring in the community. But there is good evidence that many clinically diagnosable diseases are not always taken for professional care,[29] and assertions about their incidence in the community based upon the frequency of hospital admissions or general practitioner consultations may be seriously misleading.

The second category of morbidity identified above was that of illness, defined as the subjective feeling by the individual of not being well, whether or not a clinical diagnosis of disease has been made. This definition, by its very nature, means that information about the amount of illness in the community must be culled from interview surveys in which random samples of the population are questioned about their subjective perceptions of their health. Such surveys may be regular or ad hoc. An early example of a regular survey in Great Britain was the Survey of Sickness, begun in 1944.[30] Interviews were held with randomly selected members of the general public in which questions were asked about self-perceived symptoms of illness and the action that was taken about them. The Survey of Sickness ended in 1952, but in 1971 a new government-sponsored survey began in Britain among some 15,000 households each year.[31] Known as the General Household Survey (GHS) it includes questions on a range of topics, but one section is devoted to self-perceived chronic and acute illness, and the use that people make of different health services.

Ad hoc surveys of illness are rarely carried out at the national level. Dunnell and Cartwright's study of the consumption of prescribed and non-prescribed medicines was carried out among a national sample of respondents,[32] but most such studies, like those of Wadsworth[33] and Hannay,[34] have been restricted to local populations.

The definition of sickness, the third category of morbidity identified above, as the social position of those who are accepted as being unwell, raises difficult problems of measurement, for it is concerned as much with the social reactions to people who claim to be ill as with the ill people themselves. One of the most important features of the sick role, however, is the socially sanctioned exemption it gives from normal everyday obligations;[35] and if it is assumed that occupational expectations are prominent among these obligations for many people, then certified absence from work offers one perspective on the amount of sickness in the community. It is only a partial glimpse, however, for certified absence from work may reflect many factors as well as incapacity to work through ill health.[36] Many of those who miss work through illness are not required to produce a certificate, and about half of the married women at work are not included in the published figures because they have opted out of the national insurance system.

The third concept of ill health identified above is that of disablement. Many of the problems and difficulties surrounding the data on morbidity apply also to the available information about impairment, disability and handicap; and there is the added problem that many disabled people have no more than an occasional contact with the health and social services, and may therefore be missed in the compilation of official statistics. Because of the hidden nature of much disablement, the best statistics about the prevalence of disablement come from interview surveys and assessments among randomly selected samples of the population.

The prototype of such a survey in Great Britain was carried out by the Office of Population Censuses and Surveys in 1968-9.[37] About a quarter of a million households were included in the first stage of the survey, and the results revealed a substantially higher proportion of disabled and handicapped people than had hitherto been suspected. In 1970 the Chronically Sick and Disabled Persons Act was passed by parliament, laying a duty on local authorities to inform themselves of the numbers of chronically sick and disabled people living within their boundaries who could benefit from the support of the personal social services. Prompted by the act, surveys were carried out by local authorities up and down the country, and whilst they varied in their technical quality, they provided a better basis than had hitherto existed for identifying and meeting the needs of this group of people.[38]

Having reviewed briefly some of the conceptual problems involved

TABLE 3.1 *Standardised mortality ratios and expectation of life for men and women in selected countries*

Country	Standardised mortality ratios			Expectation of life (years) at age 1 year		
	Year	Males	Females	Year	Males	Females
Australia	1977	96	93	1977	69.9	76.8
Austria	1977	104	104	1977	68.8	75.6
Belgium	1976	106	108	1976	69.1	75.5
Bulgaria	1977	105	123	1977	69.1	74.0
Canada	1977	90	82	1975	69.9	77.3
Czechoslovakia	1975	120	123	1975	67.5	74.4
Denmark	1977	85	85	1977	71.7	77.5
Eire	1977	105	120	1975	69.4	74.4
Finland	1976	118	102	1975	67.2	75.9
France	1976	95	88	1976	69.7	77.7
Germany–East	1977	106	119	1976	69.0	74.4
–Federal Republic	1977	101	102	1977	69.4	76.0
Greece	1977	78	93	1976	73.2	77.4
Hungary	1977	118	127	1977	67.7	73.8
Iceland	1977	71	75	1977	73.2	79.5
Israel	1977	86	114	1977	71.8	75.0
Italy	1977	92	96	1974	70.7	76.6
Japan	1977	78	85	1977	72.6	77.8
Netherlands	1977	83	82	1977	72.0	78.4
New Zealand	1977	104	102	1975	69.2	75.4
Norway	1977	81	83	1977	72.1	78.5
Poland	1977	116	108	1976	67.9	75.4
Portugal	1975	121	125	1975	67.1	74.2
Romania	1977	108	131	1977	68.5	72.7
Spain	1976	90	96	1975	70.7	76.4
Sweden	1977	81	82	1977	72.4	78.8
Switzerland	1977	83	82	1977	71.8	78.7
UK–England and Wales	1978	100	100	1977	70.3	76.3
–Northern Ireland	1977	119	120	1977	67.8	74.3
–Scotland	1977	111	110	1977	68.6	74.8
USA	1977	94	85	1976	69.3	77.0
Yugoslavia	1977	104	114	1976	69.4	74.2

Source: DHSS (1980), *On the State of the Public Health for the Year 1979*, London, HMSO.

in thinking about ill health, and the principle sources of data about the prevalence of ill health in the United Kingdom, the remainder of this chapter introduces some of the published information. The picture presented of the epidemiological environment is necessarily sketchy, and readers who wish to fill it out are referred to the original sources.

Beginning with some of thc information about mortality, table 3.1 shows the position of the United Kingdom in relation to some other developed countries of the world in the late 1970s.[39] The standardised mortality ratios require some explanation. First, they are based upon the mortality *rates* for men and for women in England and Wales, which for convenience are expressed as 100. Thus, for example, the standardised mortality rate among men in Northern Ireland was 19 per cent higher than among men in England and Wales in 1977-8, and among women it was 20 per cent higher. Second, the rates upon which the ratios are based are standardised to take account of the different age structure of the countries' populations, making direct comparisons possible between countries with differing proportions of young, middle-aged and elderly people. The expectation of life at 1 year, shown in the last two columns of the table, is self-explanatory.

Several countries had lower mortality rates and a greater life expectancy at 1 year than England and Wales, including such European countries as Denmark, France, Greece, Italy, Holland, Norway, Spain and Sweden. It appears to be biologically possible to achieve lower death rates in England and Wales, though not necessarily by spending more on the health services. For example, Cochrane and his colleagues have related death rates from selected causes in eighteen developed countries to a variety of 'input' or 'independent' variables, including the provision of health services, dietary patterns and other social and economic indices.[40] The most important variable accounting for the inter-country differences in death rates was the gross national product (GNP) per head of the population: the higher the GNP, the lower the mortality. There was a marked *positive* association between the availability of doctors and deaths among younger people, an anomalous finding that the authors were unable to explain. In a subsequent paper dealing specifically with ischaemic heart disease, Cochrane and his colleagues reported a positive but inconsistent association between deaths from this disease and the intake of saturated and mono-unsaturated fat, and a strong and specific *negative* association with alcohol consumption.[41] This latter (unexpected) finding was apparently attributable to variations in wine consumption.

Another way of breaking down the statistics of total mortality is through the separate recording of infant and maternal deaths. Table 3.2 shows the trend in these two components of mortality in England and Wales from 1906 to 1981.[42] The infant mortality rate (IMR) is the number of deaths under 1 year of age per 1,000 live births, and the maternal mortality rate (MMR) is the number of women dying from causes associated with childbirth per 1,000 total births. The two

TABLE 3.2 *Infant and maternal mortality rates, England and Wales, 1906-81*

Year	No. of deaths in infants under 1 year of age per 1,000 live births	No. of deaths in women due to direct and indirect causes (excluding abortion) per 1,000 birth occurrences
1906-10	117.1	3.74
1911-15	108.7	4.18[a]
1916-20	90.9	4.33[b]
1921-5	74.9	4.08[c]
1926-30	67.1	3.43[d]
1935	57.0	3.41
1940	56.8	2.24
1945	48.0	1.47
1950	26.6	0.72
1955	24.9	0.59
1960	21.8	0.31
1965	19.0	0.24
1970	18.2	0.38
1975	15.7	0.26[e]
1980	12.0	0.10
1981	11.1	0.08

[a] 1915; [b] 1920; [c] 1925; [d] 1930; [e] 1974.

Sources: OPCS, *Mortality Statistics*, Series DH, London, HMSO; DHSS, *On the State of the Public Health*, London, HMSO; Registrar General (1937), *Statistical Review of England and Wales, 1935*, London, HMSO.

rates display a different pattern over time. The IMR has fallen fairly regularly throughout the century, from 117.1 per 1,000 live births in the period 1906-10 to 11.1 in 1981, although there were small increases during the two world wars. The MMR, by contrast, fluctuated irregularly for the first four decades of the century, but has declined sharply since 1940. The basic explanation for these different patterns is that infant and maternal deaths are influenced by different factors. Infant mortality reflects to some extent the living conditions and behaviour patterns of families, and these have changed for the better throughout the century. Maternal mortality, on the other hand, is more reflective of the standards of antenatal and obstetric care, improvements in which came later in the century and were associated with the introduction of sulphonamide drugs. In international compari-

TABLE 3.3 *Infant mortality rates in selected countries, 1948, 1968 and 1978*

Country	1948	1968	1978
Australia	27.8	17.8	12.2
Canada	44.4	20.8	12.4
USA	32.0	21.8	13.6
Denmark	35.3	16.4	8.9
Finland	57.9	14.5	12.0
Iceland	26.2	14.1	11.3
Norway	29.6	13.7	8.6
Sweden	23.2	13.0	7.8
Belgium	59.1	21.7	13.9
England and Wales	34.5	18.3	13.2
France	55.9	17.0	10.6
West Germany	68.1	22.8	14.7
Italy	72.1	32.7	16.0
Netherlands	29.3	13.6	9.6
Switzerland	35.9	16.7	8.6
Japan	61.7	15.3	8.4

Sources: DHSS (1980), *On the State of the Public Health for the Year 1979*, London, HMSO; Doll, R. (1973), 'Monitoring the National Health Service', *Proceedings of the Royal Society of Medicine*, vol. 66, pp. 729-40.

sons, England and Wales fare well in *maternal* mortality, suggesting that standards of obstetric care are relatively good,[43] but the *infant* mortality rate in England and Wales remains high in comparison with many developed countries, and the decline in the IMR since the introduction of the National Health Service in 1948 has not been as great as in many other countries over the same period of time. Table 3.3 shows that, in 1978, the IMR in England and Wales was higher than in all the other countries, except the USA, Belgium, West Germany and Italy, and the rate of improvement since 1948 was bettered by several of them, including Canada, Finland, Belgium, France, West Germany, Italy and, most spectacularly, Japan.[44,45] Such data suggest that the IMR in England and Wales is capable of reduction to single figures, and that policy measures must focus on the elimination of child poverty as well as the improvement in health services.[46]

Table 3.4 presents another perspective on mortality statistics that may carry implications for social policy. It shows regional variations in the standardised mortality ratio (SMR) from all causes of death, and in the infant mortality ratio in England and Wales from 1969 to

TABLE 3.4 *Standardised mortality ratios from all causes of death, and infant mortality ratios, by region, 1969-73 (England and Wales = 100)*

Region	Standardised mortality ratio Males	Standardised mortality ratio Females	Infant mortality ratio
East Anglia	89	93	88
South East	93	95	90
South West	93	96	94
East Midlands	98	100	101
West Midlands	104	102	104
Yorkshire/ Humberside	105	104	112
North West	112	109	113
North	109	108	107
North Wales	103	100	105
South Wales	111	107	101

Source: Chilvers, C. (1978), 'Regional Mortality 1969-73', *Population Trends*, no. 11, pp. 16-20.

1973.[47] The standardised mortality ratio, as noted above, takes account of regional variations in the age structure. The infant mortality ratio is merely the ratio of the regional to the national infant mortality rate. In both cases the figure for England and Wales as a whole is expressed as 100. The first line of the table shows, for example, that the infant mortality rate in East Anglia was 12% lower than in England and Wales.

The table indicates first that a close relationship existed between regional variations in the male and female SMRs. Regions that were low in one tended to be low in the other and vice versa. A close relationship also existed between SMRs and IMRs. Regions with low SMRs tended to have low IMRs, and vice versa. Most importantly, however, the substantial regional variations in mortality experience reflected a marked north-south disparity. The horizontal line in the table between the South West and the East Midlands regions not only divides regions with below-average and above-average rates, it also coincides approximately with a line from the Wash to the Severn. Again, it must be emphasised that such differences are the result of a large number of social, economic, environmental and occupational factors, as well as inequalities in the distribution or quality of medical care in different regions of the country, but they emphasise the failure of the health services system to compensate wholly for regional variations in the forces of death, and they raise the question of whether effective action can be taken within the system to diminish them in the future. As will be seen (chapter 6), the regional differences in mortality have provided the basis of a major revision in recent years in the method by which health service resources are distributed.

A final illustration of the implications that mortality data might hold for health services is shown in Figure 3.1. It is taken from the most recent analysis of occupational mortality in England and Wales (1970-2), and it sets out the SMRs of men aged 15-64, by social class and selected causes of death, and also the SMRs of married women, by their husbands' social class.[48] The figure highlights another dimension of inequality which, whilst not attributable exclusively to inadequacies in the health services system, has persisted for a sufficient length of time to suggest that the National Health Service has failed to achieve the egalitarian hopes that many of its early adherents held for it. For most major causes of death there was a clear and consistent social class gradient for men, with lower death rates than average in the professional, managerial and skilled non-manual classes (classes I, II and III non-manual), and correspondingly higher death rates than average among the manual classes, particularly the unskilled manual class (class V). A similar pattern occurred among married women, but some interesting exceptions are apparent. The class differences were quite small in the case of malignant cancers, and the trend was actually reversed in deaths from mental disorders (although the actual number of cases on which the rates are calculated was quite small). The DHSS working group on inequalities in health concluded, on the basis of a much more extensive analysis of the nature, causes and implications of social class differences in health than has been possible here, that there had been little improvement, and in some respects a deterioration, in the health experience of social classes IV and V relative to class I between the 1960s and the 1970s.[49]

We turn now from mortality to the evidence about morbidity. The first category of morbidity identified above, that of disease, was defined as clinically diagnosed abnormalities in the structure and/or functioning of body systems or organs, and four main sources of data about disease patterns in the United Kingdom were described.

First, the Hospital In-Patient Enquiry provides information about the diseases that are diagnosed among those admitted to in-patient care. Tables 3.5 and 3.6 present two illustrations of the kind of information available.[50] Table 3.5 shows the principle diagnostic groups of patients who were discharged from, or died in, non-psychiatric hospitals in England and Wales in 1978. The total figures are estimated from the 10 per cent of deaths and discharges included in the enquiry, and they exclude patients admitted for obstetric deliveries. They

FIGURE 3.1 Standardised mortality ratios by social class and cause of death for males (solid bars) and married women (hatched bars, based on husband's occupation) aged 15-64, England and Wales, 1970-2.

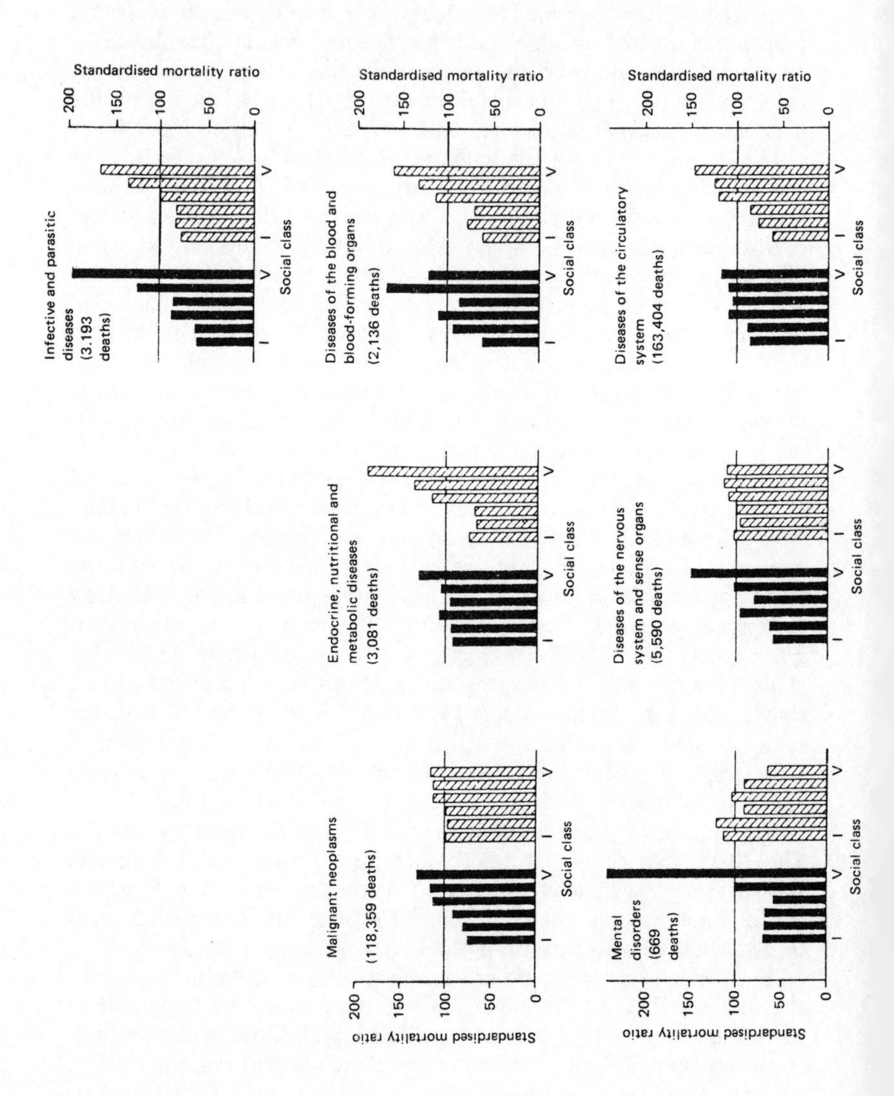

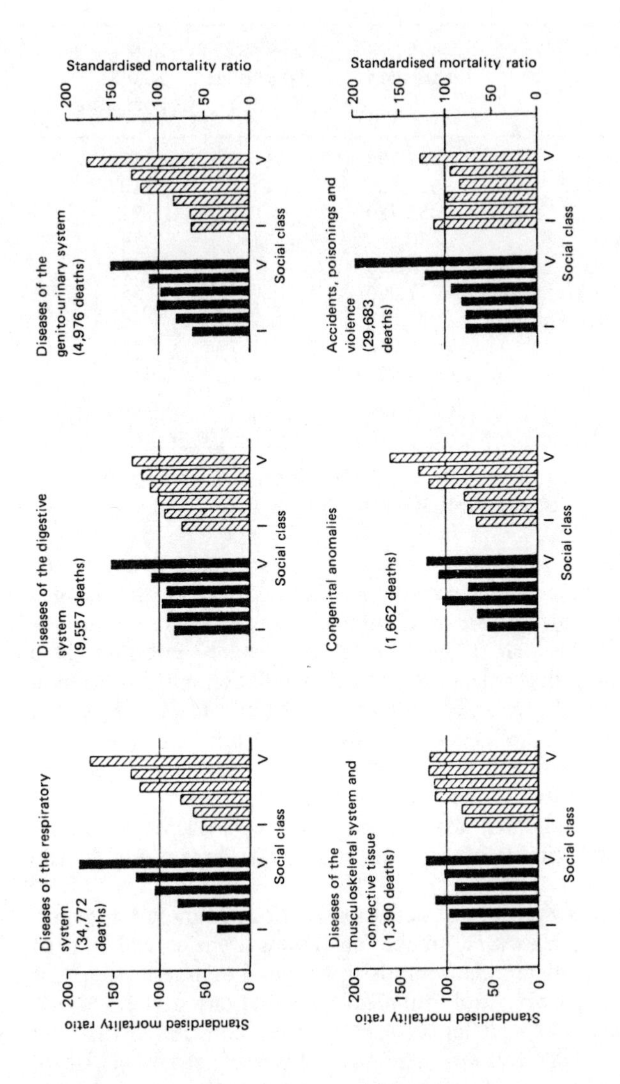

Source: OPCS (1978), *Occupational Mortality 1970-72: Decennial Supplement*, series DS, no. 1, London, HMSO.

TABLE 3.5 *Estimated number of deaths and discharges, by diagnosis, from non-psychiatric hospitals in England and Wales, 1978 (excluding obstetric deliveries)*

Diagnostic group	Number of discharges	Percentage of all discharges	Rate per 10,000 population
Ill-defined symptoms	562,790	13	112
Injuries and fractures	555,300	13	110
Digestive system	453,780	11	91
Respiratory system	370,110	8	74
All malignant cancers	315,350	7	63
Hypertensive and heart disease	277,000	6	55
Peripheral circulatory system	230,540	5	46
Breast and female genital	226,920	5	45
All other diagnoses	1,415,950	32	283
Total	4,407,740	100	879

Source: DHSS, OPCS, Welsh Office (1980), *Hospital In-patient Enquiry: Preliminary Tables*, series MB4, no. 11.

amounted to almost 4½ million deaths and discharges, or about one for every ten people in the population. (Some of the deaths and discharges would be of patients who entered hospital on more than one occasion during the year. It is therefore incorrect to interpret these figures as meaning that one in ten of the population entered hospital during the year.) Thirteen per cent of the deaths and discharges had been admitted for 'ill-defined symptoms', 13 per cent for injuries and fractures, 11 per cent for diseases of the digestive system, 8 per cent for respiratory diseases, 7 per cent for malignant cancers, 6 per cent for hypertensive and heart disease, and 5 per cent each for diseases of the peripheral circulatory system and of the breast and female genital organs.

Table 3.6 shows the surgical operations performed most frequently in 1978. In total, almost 2 million operations were carried out, of which abdominal operations comprised by far the largest group. Of these, hernia, appendix, and gall-bladder operations accounted for almost half. Operations on female genital organs constituted the next largest group, of which more than two-fifths was accounted for by the single procedure of dilatation and curettage of the womb. Orthopaedic operations, particularly the setting of fractures, ranked next in numerical importance, followed by ear, nose and throat operations, with the removal of tonsils and adenoids prominent among them

TABLE 3.6 *Most frequently performed surgical operations in England and Wales, 1978 (excluding obstetric deliveries)*

Operation	Number performed
Abdominal	388,270
Hernia	78,220
Appendix	69,190
Gall bladder	37,690
Female genital organs	286,140
Dilatation and curettage	126,680
Orthopaedics	230,020
Fractures	81,110
Ear, nose and throat	194,350
Tonsils and adenoids	83,380
All other operations	884,330
Total	1,983,110

Source: DHSS, OPCS, Welsh Office (1980), *Hospital In-patient Enquiry: Preliminary Tables*, series MB4, no. 11.

(although it is apparent from earlier HIPE reports that the number of operations for the removal of tonsils and adenoids has been declining markedly in recent years).

The impression created by this information about the volume of hospital-treated morbidity is one of considerable activity, with many comings and goings and a good deal of surgery being performed, but where much of the workload is relatively minor and the treatment given relatively straightforward. The image sometimes projected by the media of the modern general hospital as a hive of dramatic and heroic life-saving activity is not readily recognisable in the HIPE statistics. But what is happening in general practice? Table 3.7 presents information collated from various sources by the Royal College of General Practitioners about the 'typical' practice of 2,500 patients.[51] The information is intended to represent an average picture, based upon the evidence of different surveys about the diseases seen and recorded by general practitioners.

A large part of the GP's workload consists of minor disease that poses no threat to life and no risk of permanent disability. Some two-thirds of the episodes seen in general practice are minor in this sense, the bulk of them consisting of coughs and colds, emotional disorders, stomach upsets and skin complaints. Their classification as 'minor' does not imply that they are regarded by GPs as trivial (though some undoubtedly are), merely that they would usually

TABLE 3.7 *Average number of consultations per year in a 'typical' general practice of 2,500 patients*

Minor conditions	Persons consulting per year
General	
Upper respiratory infections	600
Skin disorders	325
Emotional disorders	300
Gastro-intestinal disorders	200
Specific	
Acute tonsillitis	100
Acute otitis media	75
Cerumen	50
Acute urinary infections	50
'Acute back' syndrome	50
Migraine	25
Hay fever	25

Chronic conditions	Persons consulting per year
Chronic rheumatism	100
Chronic mental illness	60
High blood pressure	50
Obesity	40
Chronic bronchitis	35
Anaemia	
Iron deficiency	25
Pernicious anaemia	4
Chronic heart failure	30
Cancers	30
Asthma	25
Peptic ulcers	20
Coronary artery disease	20
Cerebrovascular disease	15
Epilepsy	10
Diabetes	10
Thyroid disease	7
Parkinsonism	3
Multiple sclerosis	2
Chronic renal failure	less than 1

Acute major conditions	Persons consulting per year
Acute bronchitis	100
Pneumonia	20
Severe depression	10
Suicide attempt	3
Suicide	1 every 4 years
Acute myocardial infarction	8
Acute appendicitis	5
Acute strokes	5
All new cancers	
Lung	2
Breast	1
Large bowel	2 every 3 years
Stomach	1 every 2 years
Prostate	1 every 2 years
Bladder	1 every 3 years
Cervix	1 every 4 years
Ovary	1 every 5 years
Oesophagus	1 every 7 years
Brain	1 every 10 years
Uterine body	1 every 12 years
Lymphadenoma	1 every 15 years
Thyroid	1 every 20 years

Congenital disorders	One new case expected every:
Heart lesion	5 years
Pyloric stenosis	7 years
Spina bifida	7 years
Mongolism	10 years
Cleft palate	20 years
Dislocated hip	20 years
Phenylketonuria	200 years

Source: Royal College of General Practitioners (1979), *Trends in General Practice*, London, British Medical Journal for the Royal College of General Practitioners.

improve spontaneously without medical intervention. The acute life-threatening diseases make up a relatively small part of the 'average' GP's workload – about 15 per cent of all consultations. Of these, acute bronchitis and pneumonia account for the largest share, followed by severe depression (where the threat to life is the risk of suicide), heart attacks, appendicitis and strokes. New cases of cancer are quite rare: the most common (of the lung and of the breast) are seen on average only once or twice a year, and some may be seen only once or twice in the 'average' GP's entire career. Chronic diseases occupy an intermediate position in the GP's workload between the minor and major diseases. About one-fifth of all consultations are for chronic diseases, foremost among them being rheumatism and arthritis, mental illness, high blood pressure, obesity, bronchitis, anaemia and cardiovascular problems. Serious congenital abnormalities are rare, some being unlikely to be seen by most GPs throughout their careers.

TABLE 3.8 *Number of notified cases of diphtheria, whooping cough, measles and poliomyelitis in England and Wales, 1940-81*

Year	Diphtheria	Whooping cough	Measles	Poliomyelitis
1940	45,479	53,545	407,468	1,066
1945	17,595	62,663	445,412	853
1950	962	157,752	367,598	7,760
1955	155	79,101	693,740	6,331
1960	49	58,030	159,315	378
1965	27	12,945	502,066	94
1970	22	16,598	307,408	7
1975	11	8,910	143,024	3
1979	2	30,808	77,386	8
1980	3	21,131	139,486	3
1981	2	19,395	52,974	6

Source: DHSS, *On the State of the Public Health*, London, HMSO.

Information about the incidence or onset of infectious disease is available from various sources. Table 3.8 shows part of the picture: some common or once-common communicable diseases of childhood. Some of these diseases, which were common forty years ago, are now extremely rare, due principally to effective immunisation programmes. Diphtheria and poliomyelitis are examples. Others, such as whooping cough and measles are less common than they used to be, but are by no means rare. The case of whooping cough is a grim illustration of the fact that the classic childhood infections can be kept at bay only through immunisation.[52] Throughout the 1970s the proportion of children in England who were immunised against whooping cough within two years of birth fell from 79 per cent in 1970 to 31 per cent in 1978 with a consequent rise in the number of cases notified. Epidemic outbreaks of the disease occurred in 1974, 1977 and 1982, the latter yielding the highest number of new cases for twenty-five years.

TABLE 3.9 *Sexually transmitted diseases: new patients seen at hospital clinics in the United Kingdom, 1951-80 (thousands)*

Cases (in all stages) dealt with for the first time at any centre		1951	1971	1974	1975	1976	1978	1979	1980
Syphilis	Male	5	2	3	3	3	4	3	3
	Female	4	1	1	1	1	1	1	1
Gonorrhoea	Male	17	43	43	42	42	40	39	38
	Female	3	20	23	24	24	24	22	23
Non-specific genital infection	Male	1	64	76	76	80	86	89	96
	Female	0	14	16	17	20	21	24	29
Other conditions requiring treatment	Male		45	64	66	70	78	77	88
	Female		57	73	79	82	89	92	105
Other conditions not requiring treatment	Male	31	50	58	58	61	69	68	74
	Female	14	28	33	35	36	40	41	43
Total	Male	54	204	244	245	256	277	276	299
	Female	21	120	146	156	163	175	180	201

Source: CSO (1981), *Social Trends, No. 12, 1982 Edition*, London, HMSO.

Other infectious diseases are still common, sometimes with fatal consequences. The Chief Medical Officer of England and Wales reported 156 deaths attributable to influenza and 834 to tuberculosis in 1980; and there were also in that year four cases of cholera, 5,009 of infective jaundice, 178 of legionnaire's disease, 28 of leprosy, 1,670 of malaria, 8,752 of tuberculosis, 208 of typhoid and 14,329 cases of food poisoning.[53] Surgical sepsis may also be on the increase. One category of communicable disease that is unequivocally increasing is that of the sexually transmitted diseases (STDs). Table 3.9 presents the evidence.[54] It shows an increase between 1951 and 1980 of 245,000 cases among men and 180,000 cases among women that were seen for the first time at any treatment centre for STDs. Some of these diseases can lead to serious complications if left untreated, and it is possible that, with rapid changes in sexual attitudes and behaviour, the increasing difficulty in tracing contacts, and the growing resistance of the gonococci bacteria to existing antibiotic drugs, the sexually transmitted diseases will become among the most intractable infectious disease problems of the future.

In contrast to the data about disease, information about the amount of illness in the community can be obtained only from interviews with randomly selected people, for the concept of illness was defined as the subjective feeling by the individual of not being well, whether or not a clinical diagnosis of disease has been made. Two major sources

TABLE 3.10 *Self-reported restricted activity and long-standing illness in the General Household Survey, Great Britain, 1979, by sex, age and socio-economic group*

(a) Percentage who reported restricted activity in the 14 days before interview

Socio-economic group	Males					Females				
	0-15	16-44	45-64	65 and over	Total	0-15	16-44	45-64	65 and over	Total
Professional	10	8	12	3	9	9	10	7	4	9
Employers and managers	12	8	9	15	10	11	12	11	15	12
Intermediate and junior non-manual	9	10	13	10	11	12	12	15	17	14
Skilled manual and own account non-professional	13	10	14	16	12	12	14	14	16	14
Semi-skilled manual and personal service	12	10	18	14	13	10	13	17	22	16
Unskilled manual	10	14	21	10	14	14	12	16	19	16
All persons	11	10	14	12	12	11	13	14	19	14

(b) Percentage who reported long-standing illness

Socio-economic group	Males 0-15	Males 16-44	Males 45-64	Males 65 and over	Males Total	Females 0-15	Females 16-44	Females 45-64	Females 65 and over	Females Total
Professional	9	17	26	27	19	8	16	27	21	18
Employers and managers	12	20	28	50	23	9	18	33	49	22
Intermediate and junior non-manual	12	18	41	50	25	9	19	37	54	27
Skilled manual and own account non-professional	13	20	40	54	27	9	20	37	60	25
Semi-skilled manual and personal service	12	25	46	51	30	10	21	45	57	33
Unskilled manual	15	24	50	49	34	11	24	46	56	39
All persons	13	21	39	51	27	9	20	38	57	28

Source: OPCS (1981) *General Household Survey 1979*, series GHS, no. 9, London, HMSO.

of data about illness in Great Britain are available. First, the General Household Survey has, since its inception in 1971, included questions about people's perceptions of chronic and acute illness. Table 3.10, drawn from the 1979 report of the survey,[55] illustrates the kind of information it produces. Part (a) shows the proportion of people, classified by sex, age and socio-economic status, who reported having to cut down on the things they usually did because of illness or injury in the two weeks prior to the interview. Twelve per cent of men and 14 per cent of women reported some restriction in their normal activity. There was a clear tendency among women (though not among men) for activity restriction to rise with increasing age, and the proportion of people reporting some restriction increased along the socio-economic scale from professional to unskilled manual workers. Part (b) shows the proportion of people in the survey who reported having any long-standing illness, disability or infirmity. Just over a quarter of both the men and women in the survey reported a long-standing health problem, the proportions rising very considerably with increasing age and with diminishing socio-economic status. Among the men, for example, the proportion reporting a long-standing illness increased from 13 per cent of those under 15 to 51 per cent of those aged 65 and over, and from 19 per cent among professional workers to 34 per cent among unskilled manual workers. Similar trends were evident among the women.

FIGURE 3.2 Percentage of physical symptoms reported in a sample of 1,344 people registered at a new health centre in Glasgow

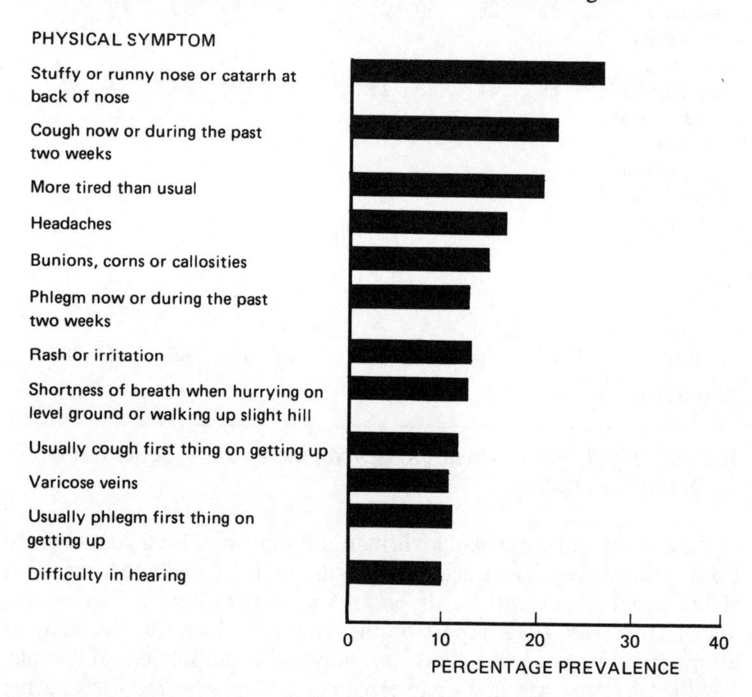

Source: Hannay, D.R. (1979), *The Symptom Iceberg*, London, Routledge & Kegan Paul.

A second source of information about illness was the ad hoc surveys of population samples or groups that have been carried out. In comparison with the General Household Survey, such studies sacrifice generalisability (by concentrating on geographically limited populations) for detail (by asking more searching questions). One of many examples is Hannay's study of 1,344 patients registered at a new health centre in Glasgow.[56] Detailed questions were asked about the symptoms experienced by respondents during the two weeks prior to the interview.

In total, 86 per cent of the respondents said they had physical symptoms of which about one-third were taken to a doctor, and 51 per cent of adults reported mental symptoms, of which 17 per cent were taken to a doctor. The most commonly reported physical symptoms are shown in figure 3.2; they reinforce the impression from other data that many people suffer frequently from minor complaints, most of which are handled without recourse to professional medical care.

TABLE 3.11 *Days of certified incapacity, male workers aged 15-64, by region, 1971/2 – 1978/9 (index: Great Britain = 100)*

Region	1971/2		1978/9	
	Days per man	Index	Days per man	Index
North	20.6	145	25.7	154
Yorkshire/Humberside	18.2	128	20.1	120
East Midlands	13.1	94	15.8	95
East Anglia	10.0	70	9.5	57
South East	9.4	66	10.9	65
South West	12.5	88	12.9	77
West Midlands	12.7	89	16.4	98
North West	18.0	127	21.2	127
England	13.3	94	15.4	92
Wales	25.3	178	31.7	190
Scotland	16.9	119	20.4	122
Great Britain	14.2	100	16.7	100

Source: Office of Health Economics (1981), *Sickness Absence – A Review*, Briefing, no. 16, London, OHE.

Turning from illness to sickness (the third category of morbidity identified above), the problem arises that the definition of sickness as the social response to ill health renders it difficult to measure, for few of the possible varieties of social response are recorded in any systematic way. The most important response about which partial information is available is that of the certification of absence from work. The limitations in the data on sickness absence have already been noted briefly, and they are discussed at length elsewhere.[57,58] They do suggest, however, that sickness absence varies considerably from region to region, and is increasing. Table 3.11 shows the average number of days of certified incapacity among male workers in Great Britain in the early and late 1970s.[59] In 1971/2, the average for the country as a whole was 14.2 days per worker; by 1978/9 it had risen to 16.7 days an increase of 18 per cent. The regional disparities also increased. In 1971/2 the difference between the highest region (Wales) and the lowest (South East) was two-and-a-half fold; by 1978/9 it had increased to almost three-and-a-half fold. Such differences are not easily explained. They are possibly related to the forms of work that are predominant in each region, but it is likely that other social, economic, behavioural and environmental influences are also at work.

TABLE 3.12 *Estimated number of impaired men and women aged 16 and over in private households in Great Britain, by principal causes of impairment*

Principal cause of impairment	Estimated number
Diseases of bone and organs of movement	1,187,000
Unspecified arthritis	595,000
Osteo-arthritis	140,000
Rheumatoid arthritis	135,000
Diseases of circulatory system	492,000
Coronary heart disease	129,000
Hypertension	57,000
Arteriosclerosis	53,000
Diseases of respiratory system	284,000
Bronchitis and emphysema	159,000
Asthma	55,000
Pneumonconiosis	20,000
Diseases of central nervous system	360,000
Cerebral haemorrhage, strokes	130,000
Poliomyelitis	38,000
Multiple sclerosis	24,000
Paralysis agitans (Parkinsonism)	22,000
Injuries and amputations	251,000
Fractures and sprains	124,000
Head injuries	12,000
Other injuries	114,000

Source: OPCS (1971), *Handicapped and Impaired in Great Britain*, pt 1, London, HMSO.

Lastly, we turn to the evidence about disablement. The national survey of handicapped and impaired people in Great Britain, carried out by the Office of Population Censuses and Surveys in 1968-9, produced a large amount of data, part of which is summarised in table 3.12.[60]

The survey estimated that just over 3 million adults living in private households in Great Britain were impaired – that is, they were 'lacking part or all of a limb, or having a defective limb, organ or mechanism of the body which stops or limits getting about, working or self-care'. The five main causes shown in table 3.12 accounted for more than three-quarters of all impairments, with the largest single cause being arthritis. The list of causes suggests that, for most people, disablement is a gradual process resulting from the presence of a chronic disease, not a sudden event caused by accident or injury.

Chapter 4

Spending on health services

In 1950 total expenditure by central and local government on the National Health Service in the United Kingdom was £477 million. Thirty years later, in 1980, the figure was £11,494 million – an increase of twenty-five fold.[1] The key to understanding this large increase in expenditure on the NHS between 1950 and 1980 is the fact that these figures represent the cost of the resources that were used each year in the service. In 1950, £477 million worth of resources was used; in 1980, £11,494 million worth of resources was used; and the cost of these resources, like the cost of all other goods and services, has increased. Inflation affects the health services as well as the housewife, and a large part of the increase in expenditure results from the simple fact that the cost of buying the time of a doctor or nurse, of building a hospital or health centre, of providing meals for patients, and so on, has gone up. It is unlikely, however, that the whole of the difference can be explained in this way, for there has indeed been an increase in many kinds of resources over this period, particularly manpower resources.[2] The effect of inflation can be isolated and controlled by calculating, for each year, the amount that the resources of the NHS would have cost for that year if there had been no inflation – if, that is to say, wages and salaries, building costs, the cost of food and drugs, etc., had remained constant. The calculation is made by selecting one year as the baseline year, and then adjusting the expenditure in all the other years to the actual level of costs prevailing in the baseline year. Any year in the series could be selected as the baseline year, but the results differ according to the year that is selected. The farther back in time the baseline year is located, the greater appears to be the growth in the real resources of the service.

The first column in table 4.1 shows the expenditure on the NHS between 1950 and 1980 at the prices prevailing in 1975. This has been chosen as the baseline year simply because it is the one used in the most

TABLE 4.1 *National Health Service expenditure, 1950-80, United Kingdom*

Year	NHS expenditure at 1975 prices (£m)	Percentage change on previous year	NHS expenditure as % of GDP at market prices	NHS expenditure as % of total government expenditure
1950	2,553		3.7	18.4
1951	2,564	+0.4	3.4	15.0
1952	2,499	–0.3	3.2	13.4
1953	2,542	+1.7	3.1	13.1
1954	2,592	+2.0	3.0	14.0
1955	2,668	+2.9	3.0	14.8
1956	2,730	+2.3	3.1	14.8
1957	2,793	+2.3	3.1	15.4
1958	2,860	+2.4	3.2	16.1
1959	2,961	+3.5	3.3	16.5
1960	3,059	+3.3	3.4	17.1
1961	3,076	+0.6	3.4	17.0
1962	3,134	+1.9	3.4	16.5
1963	3,208	+2.4	3.4	16.6
1964	3,311	+3.2	3.4	16.5
1965	3,460	+4.5	3.6	17.0
1966	3,612	+4.4	3.7	17.0
1967	3,761	+4.1	3.8	16.6
1968	3,875	+3.0	3.8	16.8
1969	3,858	–0.4	3.7	16.9
1970	3,998	+3.6	3.9	17.3
1971	4,092	+2.4	3.9	17.5
1972	4,253	+3.9	4.1	17.9
1973	4,378	+2.9	4.0	17.2
1974	4,574	+4.5	4.6	18.3
1975	4,865	+6.2	4.9	18.3
1976	5,008	+2.9	4.9	18.8
1977	5,081	+1.5	4.7	20.0
1978	5,226	+2.9	4.6	20.3
1979	5,304	+1.5	4.6	20.4
1980	5,432	+2.4	5.1	21.2

Sources: CSO, *Annual Abstract of Statistics*, London, HMSO; CSO, *National Income and Expenditure*, London, HMSO; CSO (1981), *Economic Trends, Annual Supplement, 1982 Edition*, London, HMSO.

recent official statistics.[3,4] The figures include the health services operated by the local authorities until 1974, and they are drawn from the national income and expenditure 'blue books' published each year by the Central Statistical Office.[5] Since the effect of inflation has been removed from these figures, the changes from one year to the next represent changes in the volume of real resources used in the service. The result is quite dramatic: the difference of twenty-five-fold at current prices (that is, at the prices actually prevailing in each year) is reduced to one of little more than two-fold at constant 1975 prices. This is still a considerable 'real' increase in expenditure on the NHS over 30 years, but it puts the figures with which we began this chapter in a more realistic perspective.

Expenditure at constant 1975 prices has increased from one year to the next on all but two occasions between 1950 and 1980 (the exceptions were 1951-2 and 1968-9). In other words, having allowed for inflation, the service has expanded its resource inputs almost continuously since its inception. However, the year-to-year increase (shown in percentage terms in the second column of table 4.1) has been erratic, with no clear pattern. With the exception of certain years, however, the broad trend is one of a rising rate of increase in the first half of the 1950s; a fairly constant rate of increase from the mid-1950s to the mid-1960s; a marked upward turn from the mid-1960s to the mid-1970s; and a substantially lower rate of increase (but an increase nevertheless) in the latter half of the 1970s. Some of the reasons underlying the almost unbroken growth in expenditure on the NHS are examined later, but it may be noted here, in the context of the measurement of expenditure at constant prices, that the effect of inflation has been more marked in the NHS than in the economy generally. The service is a labour-intensive industry, with some three-quarters of total expenditure going on wages and salaries; and when, as has been the case for most of the post-war period, labour costs increase more rapidly than the cost of goods, the labour-intensive industries tend to consume a rising proportion of the national income each year. The difference in the cost of goods and services between different sectors of the economy is known as the relative price effect, and it indicates the tendency of some sectors (especially those that are labour-intensive) to become more expensive over time in relation to the general movement of prices. Evidence given by the Royal Commission on the National Health Service suggested that the relative price effect accounted for about a quarter of the 'real' increase in expenditure on the NHS between 1950 and 1977,[6] and it means that there is, in effect, a built-in tendency for the service to become increasingly expensive, relative to the economy as a whole, over a period of time.

The extent to which the increase in the real resources of the NHS is simply a reflection of the general improvement in the national economy can be gauged by looking at the proportion of the national income that has been spent on the service during the period between 1950 and 1980. There are different ways of measuring and presenting the national income, and although such differences are not inherently important for our present purposes, an understanding of them helps to make sense of the apparently inconsistent figures that are to be found in the literature. One distinction is that between the gross domestic product (GDP) and the gross national product (GNP). GDP is the value of the total output of the whole economy of the United Kingdom: GNP *adds* the interest, profits and dividends earned by UK residents from productive activity abroad, and *subtracts* the profits of foreign-owned enterprises generated in the UK. GNP is slightly larger than GDP, but the difference is less than 0.5 per cent. Another distinction is between the expression of GDP (or GNP) at factor cost and at market prices. 'Factor costs' reflect the amount that employees, suppliers and investors are actually paid for their activities; 'market prices' *add* the taxes that are paid on goods and services, and *subtract* any subsidies that have been given. GNP (or GDP) at market prices is higher than at factor cost, the difference in 1980 being 14 per cent. And, as with expenditure on the NHS, the national income can be expressed in terms either of the level of prices actually prevailing in each year, or in terms of the price levels in a baseline year. The distinction between GDP and GNP, and between factor cost and market prices, is not particularly significant in examining trends over time in the proportion of the national income that is spent on the NHS. Some sources use one definition,[7,8] others use another.[9] It is, however, usual to base the calculation on the current prices prevailing in each year, not on the constant prices of a baseline year, for what is being compared between years is merely the *proportion* of the national income that is spent on the NHS, not the income or expenditure itself.

Whatever definition of national income is used, it is clear that the United Kingdom experienced a sustained economic growth over the thirty years from 1950 to 1980. In terms of the current prices prevailing in each year, the gross domestic product at market prices increased from £12,970 million in 1950 to £225,560 million in 1980 – an increase of seventeen-fold. In terms of constant 1975 prices, GDP at market prices increased from £48,784 million in 1950 to £100,328 million in 1980 – a real increase in the value of the goods and service produced of more than two-fold. It is obvious, then, that even if the NHS had managed to secure a *constant* proportion of the national income each year, the real resources of the service would have increased appreciably. In fact, the service has actually taken up a *rising* proportion of the national income for much of the period under review. The information is set out in the third column of table 4.1, which shows government spending on the National Health Service in the United

Kingdom as a percentage of the gross domestic product at market prices. The data on GDP are drawn from the 1982 annual supplement of *Economic Trends*,[10] and the data on NHS expenditure are drawn from the *Annual Abstract of Statistics* published by the Central Statistical Office.[11] There is a fairly regular pattern in these figures. Spending on the NHS as a proportion of the national income declined in the early years of the service, from 3.7 per cent in 1950 to 3.0 per cent in 1954 and 1955, but thereafter it increased regularly (apart from an odd hiccup in 1969) to a peak of 4.9 per cent in 1975 and 1976. There were signs of another decline in the latter part of the 1970s, but it was interrupted in 1980, when spending reached a record level of 5.1 per cent of GDP. The increase in real resources throughout the lifetime of the NHS is therefore the outcome of two trends: first, a growth in the national income (which would have produced a corresponding growth in the resources of the NHS even if the service had secured a constant proportion of the income from year to year), and, second, a tendency throughout much of that lifetime for the NHS to take up a rising proportion of the national income. About four-fifths of the increase in the real resources of the NHS between 1954 and 1976 was due to the growth in the national income and about one-fifth was due to the increasing share of the national income taken by the NHS.

The association between national income and the proportion of the income that is spent on health services is not unique to the United Kingdom. It is also evident in comparisons between different countries. An illustration is given in figure 4.1, taken from the 1979 Report of the Royal Commission on the National Health Service.[12] The horizontal axis shows the gross domestic product per person in each of twenty-one developed countries in 1974, expressed as a ratio to that of the United States. The GDP is expressed as a per-person ratio in order to allow for the different size of each country, and the data are adjusted to take account of the differences in the purchasing power of different currencies. The US had the highest GDP per person of the twenty-one countries, whilst at the other extreme the GDP per person in Ireland and Greece was little more than 40 per cent of that of the US. The vertical axis in the figure shows the percentage of the gross domestic product that was spent on health services in each country. The US, Sweden and the Netherlands ranked highest on the variable, each spending just over 7 per cent of their GDP on health services in 1974. Greece was the lowest spender (3½ per cent), and the United Kingdom spent a little over 5 per cent. (The slight difference between this percentage and the corresponding figure in table 4.1 is explained partly by the use of factor costs rather than market prices, and partly by the adjustments made to equalise the purchasing power of the different currencies.)

FIGURE 4.1 Per capita gross domestic product and the percentage of gross domestic product spent on health services in 21 developed countries, 1974

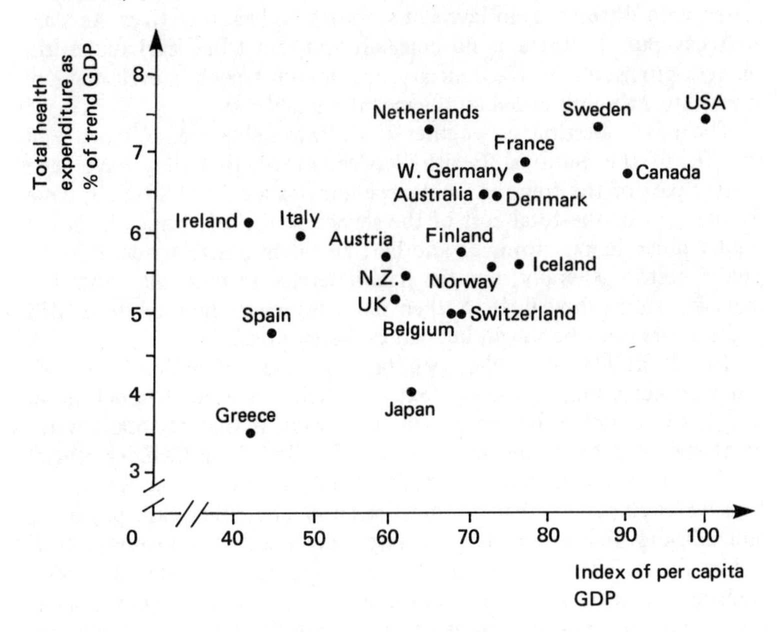

Source: Royal Commission on the National Health Service (1979), *Report*, London, HMSO, Cmnd 7615, p. 333.

The figure shows quite clearly that countries with relatively high incomes tend to spend proportionately more of their GDP on health services than those with lower incomes. The two variables have a high positive correlation (+0.8), and a regression line fitted to the distribution would lie between Sweden and Greece. It is interesting, moreover, that the relationship holds good even among countries that have very different methods of funding their services. In the United States, for example, some 60 per cent of expenditure comes from private sources, whilst in countries such as Sweden, Italy and the UK more than 90 per cent comes from public funds; yet both extremes fit into the general pattern. It is possible, however, that the very close relationship shown in the figure is due in part to the particular countries selected for inclusion, and perhaps even the particular year. An earlier study by Abel-Smith[13] of twenty-five developed *and* developing countries found a positive correlation of only +0.6 between income per head and health expenditure as a percentage of national income; and a later study by Maxwell[14] using only ten developed countries, came up with an even lower correlation (+0.4). Nevertheless, there does seem to be a general agreement that differences in national income are associated with differences in levels of spending on health services. As Maxwell has put it, 'there is no constant and inevitable level of health-services provision. On the contrary, the amount spent in each country is very strongly influenced by the means available.'[15]

The next question is whether these favourable trends have been specific to the National Health Service, or whether they have been merely part of the trend in public spending as a whole. After all, some 97 per cent of the total cost of the service in the UK comes from the public purse in one form or another, and it is possible that it is the public sector generally, not the health service in particular, that has managed to do so well. If so, then the reasons for the growth in NHS expenditure must be sought beyond the service itself.

The definition of public spending, like that of national income, can vary according to the context in which it is used. The definition that is most useful for the present discussion is that of total government spending on goods and services. This definition includes central and local government spending, both capital and current, but it excludes transfer payments – that is, social security and other cash payments and subsidies that are made to private individuals or companies out of public funds. From the point of view of raising the money for them, transfer payments are of very considerable importance: the government must somehow ensure that it has the funds to meet all its commitments, and a pound more on social security payments is either a pound more in taxation or borrowing, or a pound less on other things. From the point of view of expenditure, however, transfer payments do not represent real spending by the government, for all they do (as their name implies) is to transfer spending power from the government's purse to other purses. The real spenders are those who receive the payments. It is for this reason that transfer payments do not form part of the gross domestic product of the United Kingdom, nor do they constitute what is generally regarded as government spending on goods and services. As Walker has put it, 'if we are concerned with the direct use or consumption of resources by the public sector, transfer payments should be excluded.'[16]

Government spending on goods and services in the UK has, like the particular component of NHS expenditure, increased considerably between 1950 and 1980. At current prices (that is, the prices actually prevailing in each year) such spending increased from £2,587 million in 1950 to £54,137 million in 1980 – an increase of twenty-one-fold. As with NHS expenditure, however, comparisons of government spending over time need to be expressed in constant prices to eliminate the effect of inflation; and at constant (1975) prices the figures change to £16,848 million and £27,374 million respectively in 1950 and 1980 – an increase of only one-and-a-half-fold.[17] The fact that this is less than the two-fold increase in spending on the NHS over the same period of time (at 1975 prices) suggests that the NHS may actually have done rather better than public spending as a whole, but we can test this more precisely by looking at the proportion of government spending on goods and services that has gone to the NHS. The relevant figures are set out in the fourth column of table 4.1. They confirm that, for much of the first thirty years of the service, its share of the government's total expenditure on goods and services has been increasing. The early years saw a decline in the proportion, from 18.4 per cent in 1950 to 13.1 per cent in 1953, but thereafter the proportion has increased fairly steadily, reaching a peak of 21.2 per cent in 1980. Indeed, it is precisely the growing share of public expenditure taken up by the NHS that has enabled it to expand so much. About three-quarters of the increase in the real resources of the NHS between 1953 and 1980 was due to the growing share of public expenditure that it consumed and about one-quarter was due to the expansion of general government expenditure on goods and services.

We can now summarise the main trends discussed so far in this chapter. The national income of the United Kingdom has increased steadily for most of the post-war period: at constant 1975 prices, for example, the gross domestic product at market prices more than doubled between 1950 and 1980. Public as well as private spending has benefited from this growth in national income: at constant 1975 prices, total government spending on goods and services increased by about one-and-a-half-fold between 1950 and 1980. About three-quarters of this increase in total government spending was due to the growth in national income, with the remaining quarter coming from an increase in the level of taxation.[18] The National Health Service has benefited from the expansion in public expenditure, and indeed has done increasingly well as the years have gone by, raising its share of government expenditure on goods and services from 13.1 per cent in 1953 to 21.2 per cent in 1980. The favourable position of the NHS was particularly noticeable in the latter half of the 1970s, when it continued to expand its real resources at a time when general government expenditure was cut back. Over the whole period from 1950 to 1980 the real resources of the service more than doubled (compared with an increase of only one-and-a-half-fold in general government spending), and its share of the national income rose from 3.7 per cent in 1950 to 5.1 per cent in 1980. The association between national income and the proportion of the income that is spent on health services is not unique to the United Kingdom, for it has been observed also in a number of cross-national studies.

In summary, then, the National Health Service has done well for resources in relation to the economy as a whole and to government spending in general. Why is this, and what are the prospects for the future? Some of the reasons are implicit in the trends themselves: it is hardly surprising that, as the national income has increased, government spending on goods and services (of which the NHS takes up a sizeable chunk) has also increased. The tendency has been reinforced by such factors as the relative price effect (see above), the increase in the demand for public services in the absence of prices (see chapter 7), the pressure from those working in the services to provide new and more advanced forms of treatment and care, and the continuous generation of new kinds of social needs. All of these play a part, but there are also more substantial theories to explain the general tendency for public spending to increase.[19]

One kind of explanation that has appeared in recent writings on the welfare state is based upon an historical analysis of trends in Western capitalist economies.[20,21] The argument is that, in capitalist societies, the processes of accumulating more and more capital in the private sector require certain kinds of investments, and generate certain consequences, that are increasingly met by the state. For example, as the methods of industrial production become more complex, private manufacturers require more and better transport and communication systems; they need trained and qualified staff; and they need a workforce that is efficient because it has adequate housing, health care, leisure facilities, and so on. The costs of these investments, however, are not (for the most part) borne by the private sector, but are shifted onto the state. Likewise, the accumulation of capital generates certain social consequences that must also be met by state spending. These include an increase in the level of unemployment (resulting, it is argued, largely from the replacement of labour by capital plant and equipment in order to increase efficiency), poverty, and a growing militancy among an assortment of pressure groups that represent neglected or oppressed interests. Hence the state is under increasing pressure to create jobs in the public sector, to provide financial compensation for those who lose their jobs, to subsidise those who cannot earn enough to meet their needs, and to go some way towards meeting the demands of pressure groups. These 'social expenses', as O'Connor has called them, are necessary to promote social harmony, to buy off the potentially disruptive groups in society, and to legitimise, protect and perpetuate the capitalist ethic. They have the effects of exerting a continuous upward pressure on the trend of public expenditure. As O'Connor has put it, 'the state sector expands because state agencies and contractors must supply social capital to the monopoly sector and because monopoly sector growth in turn requires that the state devote even more funds to social expenses.'[22]

A different explanation is to bc found in the literature on public choice.[23] The argument here is that politicians, civil servants and those who work in the public sector services have a natural interest in expanding their territories and building their empires. To some extent this is consistent with the wishes of ordinary people, who also want to see more and better hospitals, schools, roads, pensions, and so on. But the cost of empire-building in the public sector must ultimately be borne by the people themselves in the form of increased taxation, and politicians are hesitant to face the electorate at a general election with a programme of expansion that obviously requires higher levels of taxation. They will therefore try to change people's preferences in favour of spending more on the public services than they might originally have thought appropriate, and this may be done in various ways. One is what Judge and Hampson[24] have called 'political advertising' – that is, 'the dissemination of publicly available information which is intended to influence public policy, as distinct from commercial advertising which is usually intended to encourage consumers to purchase a particular product'. They have identified eight forms of political advertising, including party political broadcasts, reports of official commissions and committees of enquiry, government reports and press conferences, and their conclusion is that 'the public welfare sector is larger than it would otherwise have been in the absence of political advertising.'

These theoretical explanations of the growth of public spending apply to general government spending on goods and services. In addition, factors specific to health care have been suggested that may explain the particularly high rate of growth in spending that has occurred in this sector in all developed countries.[25] First, many more people are surviving into old age, and since the costs of health care are generally higher among older people, expenditure will tend to rise merely to maintain the same level and standard of care. Second, the pattern of disease is changing, with chronic illness, disabilities and mental disorders assuming greater prominence. These problems, however, are not quickly resolved by one-off forms of medical intervention: they require continuing care over a period of time, and for that reason they tend to suck in more resources. Third, there have been spectacular advances in medical technology, particularly in the area of acute hospital care, that have proved to be very costly. Many countries have been caught up in what Fuchs has called the 'technological imperative' – that is, the urge to do everything in medicine that is technically possible, irrespective of the benefit it produces in relation to its cost.[26] Fourth, the expectations of both the public and the health care professions have risen, not only in the technical matters of care but also in ideas about an acceptable standard of care for the elderly, the disabled and the mentally disordered (see chapter 12). The increased reliance on the health services as the vehicle for improving these standards has tended to raise the level of expenditure on this aspect of care quite apart from any increase resulting from larger numbers of potential patients.

It would be reasonable to conclude from the material presented in this chapter that, with one important reservation, the future prospects for the funding of the National Health Service are reasonably good. There has been an upward trend since the war in general government spending on goods and services, and there are various arguments to support the view that the trend will continue. Within this overall trend the NHS has done particularly well, increasing its share both of the national income and of total government spending on goods and services, and again there are reasons to believe that this will continue. The reservation in the material presented in the chapter arises from the association between national productivity and health service expenditure. Productivity appears to be one of the best single predictors of the amount spent on health services, and a growth in productivity therefore seems to be the key to further expansion in the real resources of the NHS. In fact, however, the gross domestic product of the United Kingdom at constant prices has increased much more slowly in recent years than for most of the post-war period, and until productivity picks up again the service is likely to experience lower rates of growth than it has enjoyed in the past.

However reasonable this conclusion might be in the long term, there are signs that it may be over-optimistic in the short term. The latter part of the 1970s witnessed a reduction in government spending on goods and services for the first time since the 1950s. Between 1975 and 1980, for example, expenditure at constant 1975 prices fell by 2 per cent, compared with an increase of 15 per cent over the previous five years from 1970 to 1975.[27] The National Health Service managed to escape relatively unscathed, but ministers have made it clear that the service has no absolute right of immunity from the overall trend. For example, the secretary of state for social services reiterated in his introduction to the 1981 NHS policy document *Care in Action* that the government's principal priority was to 'get the economy right', and that for that reason 'it cannot be assumed that more money will always be available to be spent on health care.'[28] The accuracy of that prediction was borne out in the following year when the government announced that there would be no planned increase at all in the real resources of the NHS in either of the financial years 1983/4 or 1984/5.[29]

It is difficult to judge whether the experience of recent years is a temporary phase or the beginning of a more permanent restructuring of the public sector services. The explanations given by politicians claim that it is merely temporary, reflecting the response of both Labour and Conservative governments to the domestic difficulties arising from the world economic recession, particularly following the sharp increase in oil prices in 1973.[30] The relationship between the level of public expenditure and the achievement of broader economic objectives (such as growth, full employment and price stability) is a matter of debate, but governments of both political parties have tended to regard a reduction in public expenditure as a necessary measure in meeting these objectives.[31] The argument has been that a high level of public expenditure requires a high level of taxation and/or a large deficit on the budget that must be made up by increased government borrowing; and both measures are detrimental to the health of the economy. High taxation, it is argued, reduces people's incentives to work harder, and high levels of government borrowing tend to increase interest rates, making investment more difficult. The argument has been bolstered by influential analyses, such as that of Bacon and Eltis,[32] who have attributed Britain's economic problems to an excess number of workers (most of them in the public sector) engaged in the production of non-marketable goods and services (that is, goods and services which are not offered for sale on the world's markets). By reducing the number of workers in non-marketable production (such as doctors, nurses, schoolteachers and social workers) vital resources would be released for use in the production of commodities that *are* sold, thereby adding to the real income of the country.

There are, of course, rejoinders to these arguments. It does not follow that only those who are actually producing marketable goods and services are contributing to the national wealth. The contributions of doctors, nurses, schoolteachers and social workers are vitally important to the wealth-producing capacity of the nation, even though their services are not usually bought and sold on the market. And the broader argument about the need to restrain public expenditure at times of economic difficulty and recession has also been challenged.[33] Such restraint, it is argued, reduces the demand for goods, thereby adding to the number of people out of work and increasing the amount of money that the government has to spend on social security benefits and the other costs of unemployment. But whatever the intrinsic merits of the different arguments about public expenditure, governments have tended to *believe* that the restraint of public expenditure is necessary at times of economic difficulty and, conversely, have offered the prospect of more public expenditure in future times of economic prosperity.

On the other hand there are grounds for believing that the trend in public spending since the mid-1970s, and the effect it began to have on the National Health Service in the early 1980s, may be more abiding than the argument about economic necessity might suggest. There has been an increasing concern in developed countries about the rising costs of health care, and attention is turning towards ways of controlling them.[34] In part this change of emphasis is a reflection of doubt about the value that has been obtained from past expenditure.[35] Lee has put the matter like this:

> In any society there will come a point at which . . . governments will become reluctant to allocate more money to health services. Seemingly, this point has been reached rather sooner in the UK, where the opportunity cost of increased public expenditure on the NHS has been judged . . . to be greater than its value.[36]

Such a judgment is unlikely to be reversed in the short term.

Chapter 5

Financing health services

The previous chapter described the pattern of expenditure on the National Health Service in the United Kingdom since 1948, and discussed some of the factors influencing the levels of expenditure. But where has the money come from, and are there alternative ways of raising it?

In 1980, about 88 per cent of the £11,494 million spent on the NHS came from a treasury allocation – that is, out of the government's general income from tax revenues and borrowings. The proportion of NHS expenditure from this source has varied from year to year, but has never been less than 70 per cent. The NHS component of national insurance contributions accounted for a further 9 per cent of expenditure and 3 per cent came from direct charges to patients for prescriptions, dental and ophthalmic services, and other services for which a charge is made.[1]

These sources of funds are not just accidental; rather, they reflect explicit policy decisions about the social as well as the medical objectives of the service, and they embody political aspirations about equality of access to health and medical care irrespective of people's ability to pay the economic cost of the services. In particular, three features of the financial organisation of the NHS endow it with a distinctive ideological bias, distinguishing it from most other health services systems. First, the greater part of the money spent on the service is raised through taxes levied on the whole population, not through fees charged to those who receive care or through insurance contributions. Second, most of the important services offered by the NHS are free to recipients at the time of use, including even the most complicated and costly forms of care. Charges are made for certain services to those who use them, but they are usually lower than the economic cost of providing the services, and patients with high needs or low incomes may be exempt from paying them. Third, because the service is financed largely from central government income and is generally free at the time of use, eligibility to use it is not dependent on the financial resources of the user or on his record of contributions to an insurance fund. As will be seen later (chapter 7), methods must exist for determining who will get access to different services when the demand for care exceeds the supply, and such methods may produce a pattern of access that is skewed in favour of the better-off in society;[2] but it is nevertheless true that the financial organisation of the NHS does not *intentionally* discriminate against the poorer members of the community. Indeed, the NHS reflects a much more explicit recognition than is seen in most other health service systems that a just and compassionate society should not allow the costs of health care to lie where they fall, whatever their economic and social consequences may be, but should redistribute them through the whole community in an equitable way.

Because about nine-tenths of expenditure on the National Health Service comes from central government income, the service is in competition with other services and programmes for its share of the national income. It was seen in the previous chapter that the NHS has actually fared rather better than most other publicly financed services in recent years, and that for much of the post-war period, when the economy was doing relatively well, it benefited from its close dependence upon the treasury. But since the mid-1970s, when public spending has been under severe restraint and the NHS has received fewer resources for growth than the health services in many other countries, arguments about alternative ways of financing health care have been resurrected and rehearsed with renewed vigour. Paradoxically, their impetus has sprung from two opposing considerations. From the point of view of government, whose dominant concern has been the control of public spending, the question is whether it is possible to limit (and even reduce) the treasury's contribution to the NHS by tapping other sources of finance. From the point of view of those who work in the service, however, the problem is that of under-funding, not over-funding, and the question is whether the treasury's contribution can be increased and supplemented with funds from other sources. Both viewpoints generate similar questions. Is a treasury-funded service, largely free at the point of use, the best way of providing health care? What alternatives exist, and what are the arguments for and against them? Such fundamental questions assumed a new urgency in the early 1980s when the government began seriously to explore the possibility of dismantling the National Health Service. In 1981 a report was commissioned by the secretary of state for social services on the possibility of changing from a tax-funded to an insurance-based health service,[3] and although the report was allegedly rejected,[4] it was quickly followed by a suggestion from the government's Central Policy Review Staff that about a third of the health services should be denationalised and transferred to the private sector.[5] In the remainder of this chapter we discuss three possible changes to the existing method of financing the health services in the United Kingdom, and we examine their implications not just in financial terms, but also in terms of their social impact. The three changes are supplementary finance, private practice, and insurance funding.

Supplementary finance is probably the least contentious of the three, for it seeks not to disturb the established financial basis of the NHS, but merely to augment it with money from other sources. Three sources are commonly suggested. The first is that of charges to patients at the time they use particular services. Charges are already levied on some services (with exemptions for certain categories of patients), and they amounted in 1980 to 2.7 per cent of total expenditure on the NHS. The question is whether an increase or an extension of these charges would yield sufficient revenue to produce worthwhile savings to the treasury or additional resources for the service. The calculation is tricky, for it must allow not only for the increase in the number of people who might be exempt from the higher charges and the additional cost of administering the exemptions, but also for the reduction in the demand for different services resulting from an increase in existing charges or the introduction of new ones. An illustrative calculation was, however, made by the Royal Commission on the National Health Service, whilst being appropriately cautious about its accuracy.[6]

The Commission calculated the net effect, at 1975-6 prices, of raising prescription charges to 50p, charging £20 per week to hospital patients for board and lodging, charging £5 for each visit to a hospital accident and emergency department, and £2 for each visit to a general practitioner. Dental and ophthalmic charges remained unchanged in the calculation. The estimated net sum was £423 million, or about 8 per cent of total expenditure on the NHS in that year. This proportion is sufficiently large to have caused politicians to think seriously about extending charges in the service, particularly since, according to the Commission's calculations, the majority of the sum saved would be due to the increase in revenue rather than the reduction in demand. There would be some reduction in demand, however, concentrated most heavily among those who could least afford to concede it, and the charges would place the greatest financial strains on those members of the community who would just fail to qualify for exemption on the grounds of low income. In fact the Commission declared itself to be unenthusiastic about *any* charges in the National Health Service.

If we could see that the charges which exist now made for better

> doctoring or discouraged frivolous use of the NHS by the public, then we should applaud them. But we do not see them in that light. (p. 342)

The second possible source of supplementary finance is hypothecation – that is, the earmarking of particular taxes or contributions specifically for use in the NHS. The essential feature of an hypothecated tax is that it is not available to the government for spending in any other way. The existing NHS national insurance contribution is an example of hypothecation: it provided 8.8 per cent of total expenditure on the service in 1980, and there may be a case for raising it. The case has also been made from time to time for introducing hypothecated taxes on the sale of goods (such as alcohol and tobacco products) that are harmful to health. It is a two-pronged case: such taxes might diminish the consumption of potentially harmful products, and they would be a source of income exclusively for the NHS that could not be appropriated by the government for other purposes. It is, however, precisely here that the weakness of hypothecation lies, for governments are not likely readily to surrender control over the disposition of taxes they impose. Moreover, a flat-rate health tax on harmful goods would be regressive, hitting hardest at the poorer consumers in the community.

The third possible source of supplementary finance is the pot-pourri of lotteries, bazaars, appeals, jumble sales and the like. Lotteries and sweepstakes are used in several countries to bolster the funds available to the health services; why should they not also be used in the United Kingdom? The case against them is partly one of practicality and partly one of principle. At the practical level, lotteries and sweepstakes are uncertain in their yield, expensive to administer, and unlikely to contribute significantly to the total resource requirements of the NHS. The Royal Commission on Gambling, which reported in 1978, advocated a national lottery for good causes, but estimated that it would yield only about £37.5 million in the first year at 1976 prices.[7] Even if all the yield was allocated to the NHS, it would amount to no more than 0.5 per cent of total expenditure on the service in that year. The argument of principle is simply that the health service is too important to be left to the gambling instincts of the nation, but should be funded in a planned way as part of the basic responsibilities of government. The possibility of supplementing NHS funds with the proceeds of bazaars, appeals and jumble sales was enhanced with the passage of the 1980 Health Services Act, section 5 of which gave health authorities power to 'engage in activities intended to stimulate the giving of money . . . to assist the authority in providing any services or facilities'. The section caused concern among voluntary organisations, worried that they would not be able to compete successfully with the health authorities for the charitable giving of the nation; but there has been little evidence to support these fears, and in any case such sources are never likely to produce more than a minute fraction of the requirements of the NHS.

The second change that might be made to the financial basis of health care in the United Kingdom is a shift away from the public towards the private provision of care. We deal later in this chapter with one of the main methods of funding private practice (insurance), and concentrate here on the principles involved in such a shift. The first point to note about private practice in the UK is that it covers a number of different activities, falling broadly into two groups within and outside the NHS. Within the service, a small number of beds in NHS hospitals (fewer than 1 per cent) are designated as private (or pay) beds, and patients treated in them pay a fixed charge to the hospital for their stay as well as the fees of the consultant and other staff. Patients may also have private outpatient consultations with consultants in NHS premises, and again a charge is made by the hospital. Outside the NHS, private practice includes not only the care given in privately built and owned hospitals and nursing homes, but also treatment given by practitioners who are not normally employed in the NHS (such as osteopaths and chiropractors), and care given privately by GPs, dentists, physiotherapists and other professionals who may also have NHS patients.

The implications of each type of private practice are different. Practice outside the NHS is clearly an *alternative* to the service, and any significant increase in this type of practice would threaten the very existence of the NHS. By using resources (particularly of highly trained manpower) that might otherwise be used in the NHS, and allocating them on principles that differ fundamentally from those on which the service is based, the private sector represents a challenging alternative to the NHS as a vehicle for providing health care to the nation. It is for this reason that the growth of the private sector is viewed with concern by those who wish to preserve the principles of the NHS. According to the Royal Commission, there were some 35,000 beds in registered private nursing homes and hospitals in the UK in 1977, catering for most kinds of medical, surgical and psychiatric care, but concerned overwhelmingly with abortions and the nursing care of the elderly.[8] Since then, a considerable expansion has taken place in the private provision of acute medical and surgical care, the number of beds used for this purpose increasing by about 75 per cent between 1977 and 1982.[9] The number of people insured for private medical care has also increased substantially in recent years, from about 800,000 in 1966 to over 3½ million by 1980.[10] It has been estimated that by 1985 one in five of the population may have some form of private health insurance.[11]

The arguments about private practice as an alternative to the National Health Service are dealt with in more detail in chapter 7, where we examine the use of the market as a mechanism for bringing supply and demand into balance. Suffice it to note here that the widespread substitution of private for public health care might increase the total amount of resources available nationally (for people may be prepared to pay more privately than they are willing to pay in taxes if they can see a closer relationship between what they pay in and the value of the care they receive); and it would also release the government from many of the problems involved in the public funding of health services.

The treatment of patients privately within the NHS has also been a source of controversy,[12] but it poses less of a threat to the service than independent practice outside the service. Indeed, there are fears that the decline of private practice within the NHS resulting from the recent expansion of the private sector outside may actually be detrimental to the NHS through the loss of revenue. In this sense, pay beds and private consultations can be seen as a form of supplementary finance. Pay beds have, however, been regarded with suspicion by some politicians and trades unions and the 1976 Health Services Act created a Health Services Board, charged with the task of reducing the numbers of pay beds in NHS hospitals. Between 1976 and 1981 the number of such beds fell from about 4½ thousand to about 2½ thousand.[13] The 1980 Health Services Act abolished the Board, but the major initiative in developing private hospital care since then has been outside the NHS, not within it.

The arguments about pay beds are varied. The opponents of pay beds claim that the charges levied on them do not cover the full cost to the hospital, particularly the element of capital depreciation; that they enable the better-off sections of the population to receive preferential treatment; and that they require non-medical staff to provide services outside their normal range of duties without extra remuneration. The counter-arguments of those in favour of pay beds are that, in providing consultants with a limited opportunity for private practice, they help to prevent the exodus of doctors from the NHS entirely; that it is better for consultants to treat their private patients in NHS hospitals, where they can also be close to their NHS patients, than to spend valuable time travelling to a private hospital on a separate site; and that the freedom of people to sell and buy services should be upheld in a democratic society.

The conclusions of the Royal Commission about private practice were low-keyed.[14] The Commission felt that at the time of its enquiries the private sector was too small to make much impact on the NHS except in certain localities and specialities where private practice flourished. Expenditure in the private sector amounted to only about 2 per cent of NHS expenditure. The principal advantage of the private sector, in the Commission's view, was that it probably responded more directly to patients' demands than the NHS, and was therefore a useful indicator of the defects of the NHS. The demand for private abortions was cited as an example. Only about half of all abortions carried out since the passage of the 1967 Abortion Act on women living in the United Kingdom had been done through the NHS, and the Commission recommended that health authorities should aim to increase this proportion to about three-quarters. In general, however, the Commission took the view that the main importance of private practice lay in the controversy it aroused and the dislocation of work it engendered. Whether the Commission would take a similar view in 1984 is a matter of conjecture.

The third change that might be made to the financial basis of health care in the United Kingdom is the switch from taxation to insurance funding. There are obvious links between the arguments about insurance and about private practice; but they are conceptually distinct. Insurance is basically a mechanism for raising money, and whilst it is commonly used as a means of enabling people to pay for privately provided services, it could also be used to fund a state-organised health service. Conversely, whilst private practice is usually linked to an insurance system, it is not a necessary requirement, and in fact only about half of patients treated in NHS pay beds or receiving acute treatment in private hospitals are covered by insurance.[15]

The basic principles of insurance are straightforward. The aim of the insured person is to cover himself against all or part of the cost of an unpredictable event (in this case the cost of medical care) and he does this by paying a regular sum (premium) to the insurer who in turn bears all or part of the cost of the event when it occurs. Insurance therefore differs from the financial principles of the NHS in a number of important respects: people can choose, either individually or through a group, the amount of health care to which they will be entitled; they pay, either directly from their own income or indirectly through their employers' contributions, the sums required to secure the chosen degree of cover; and their entitlement to care is dependent principally upon their contribution record, not upon notions of need or social entitlement.

But although the basic principles of insurance are straightforward, they can be applied in many different ways. There is no one single model of health insurance, and variations may be introduced that carry significant social implications. First, a health insurance scheme may be profit-making or non profit-making. Where the insurer is in business to make a profit, the premiums may be higher and the risks that are covered may be more limited than in schemes that exist principally for the benefit of the insured. The elderly, the poor, the handicapped and the chronically ill are bad insurance risks in commercial terms, and they may therefore have greater difficulty in getting access to needed services than other groups in the population.

Second, the role of government in health insurance might vary, influencing the impact of any scheme on different groups in the population. At one extreme the government might withdraw completely from the funding arena, leaving it entirely to commercial or non-profit organisations to control the insurance funds. At the other extreme the state might actually become the insurer, with responsibility for determining and collecting premiums, deciding questions of eligibility, and so on. Between these extremes the government may take various intermediate positions, for example by subsidising the premiums paid by certain groups of people to existing insurance schemes, or by requiring people to have a minimum amount of insurance upon which they could build voluntarily if they wished. The greater the involvement of government in health insurance the more likely such a scheme is to satisfy criteria of social equity, for governments are better able, and may be more highly motivated, to protect the interests of those least able to cope with their own needs.

Third, insurance may be linked to different ways of remunerating the providers of services. At one extreme the entire provision of health services could be transferred to the private sector and run on an entrepreneurial basis. The arguments surrounding such a course of action have been rehearsed above and are examined again in chapter 7. At the other extreme it would be possible (though perhaps improbable) for the existing methods of employing providers in the NHS to be retained, with insurance forming an alternative method by which the government raises the revenue and access to care is determined. Between these extremes lie the intermediate positions in which some services could be transferred to the private sector and funded through insurance schemes with others remaining within the National Health Service and continuing to be funded by the treasury.

Advocates of a switch to insurance funding argue their case on two main grounds. The first is that insurance would increase the total amount of money available for spending on health services. It is argued that, although people are resistant to providing more resources to the NHS through increased taxation, they would be willing to spend more of their disposable income on health care if they could see a closer link between the amount they paid in and the value of the benefits they received. In order to be different from a tax-funded service, people must have a choice about the amount of insurance they took out, and by tailoring the premiums to the anticipated needs of different groups of insured people, the link becomes more visible than it is in the NHS. Against this it may be argued that, since a proportion of many people's premiums might be borne by employers in one form or another, the link between payments and benefits may not be as visible to the individual as the argument assumes: and in any case a higher level of payments through an insurance system would not necessarily be desirable if much of the increase was spent on higher administrative costs and unnecessary (but financially rewarding) forms of care.

The second argument commonly advanced in favour of a switch to insurance funding is that, by making the link between payments and benefits more visible, people have a direct financial incentive to maintain good health and to curb their demand for care for minor complaints. Insurance, in other words, promotes healthy living and a responsible use of services. The counter-argument is that of 'moral hazard'[16] – that having paid their premiums (or having had them paid by employers or third parties), people will naturally want to receive care up to the limits of their entitlement. Far from curbing the demand for services, insurance may actually increase it in comparison with the NHS. Moreover, much of the demand for care actually originates with doctors in deciding what treatments to use, not with patients themselves, and insurance offers no incentives to doctors to control their demands and minimise costs. Indeed, if insurance is used to pay for the services of doctors through the private market, doctors have a direct financial incentive to encourage the demand for their services.

In addition to these counter-arguments, experience in the United States suggests that several consequences might be expected to flow from any major expansion of insurance funding in the United Kingdom.[17] First, there would be consequences not only for the financing but also for the planning and management of health services. Services might, under certain insurance schemes, consist of an uncoordinated set of commercial undertakings, and the notion of a *national* service with centrally agreed objectives, minimum standards of service between different part of the country, and a method of allocating resources that tries to achieve a measure of equality between different services and areas, would probably have to be abandoned.

Second, an insurance-based scheme would unfairly penalise those groups of the population who are both bad health risks and least able to pay the high premiums that would be required of them. All health insurance is to some extent regressive, and it requires those with a high risk of using services to pay high premiums. Groups such as children, old people, the mentally disordered, and the physically and mentally handicapped currently use about two-thirds of the resources of the NHS, and they would be bound to suffer in any scheme that linked benefits to premiums. Many would be under-insured or non-insured. The gap between the needs and the resources of such people might be bridged either through some form of state subsidy to enable them to pay the necessary premiums or through residual voluntary or state services providing free care to those who cannot or will not buy adequate insurance. The experience in the US is that the residual state service tends to be severely under-funded, it has difficulty in attracting good staff, it consists mainly of hospital care, and it offers little co-ordinated provision for services such as antenatal care. It creates dual standards: a higher standard for those who can afford to pay, and a lower standard for those dependent on the residual service. The alternative approach, of offering vouchers or subsidies to those below certain income levels to enable them to purchase adequate insurance, has likewise met with patchy success in the US. It is massively expensive ('Medicaid' and 'Medicare' together provide more than 50 per cent of hospital revenue from patients[18]), and there still remains an element of discrimination. Doctors are increasingly unwilling to accept 'Medicaid' vouchers because of delays in payment and, more recently, attempts by state governments to set limits on the amount of reimbursement of particular medical and hospital costs. Mindful perhaps of these experiences in the United States, the Royal Commission felt that

> the introduction of insurance systems would incorporate into the NHS a new principle, namely that a different standard of health care . . . would be available to those who chose to pay for it. Some may feel such a change to be desirable but at least it should be recognised for what it is.[19]

Third, insurance funding carries with it the danger of excessive use of services. It has been the experience in the United States that service provision has expanded to fill the insurance coverage available to pay for it, generating inflationary effects on the total cost of care that have proved difficult to control. The medical profession has responded merely by advocating self-restraint among doctors. Roe has observed that

> many physicians are aware of the flaws in the economics of health care delivery, but rather than directly addressing the problem they have tended to assume a helpless posture, in part by accepting the philosophy that human life and comfort are without price.[20]

The consumers themselves have little real control over the costs of medical care, and the third parties (the insurance companies) have little incentive to apply controls, seeing themselves as having 'a mainly passive role in the delivery process . . . acting largely as an accounting system and a conduit for patients' dollars'.[21] It has been left largely to the government to take initiatives in the control of costs.

Fourth, insurance funding tends to encourage the piecemeal development of technological aspects of acute patient care at the expense of integrated and balanced programmes involving preventive, rehabilitative and long-term care as well as acute services. To some extent a similar trend has occurred also in the NHS, but the allocation of budgets to the health authorities (see chapter 6) has required them to think in terms of comprehensive planning across the whole range of services. In an insurance scheme, by contrast, comprehensive planning is much more difficult, and the growth and duplication of expensive and exciting equipment takes precedence over less obviously beneficial expenditure on health prevention and promotion. There is, for example, considerable experience in the United States of preventive schemes, including screening, immunisation and the control of hypertension; but such schemes are almost invariably fragmented in their administration and patchy in their coverage precisely because of the different routes through which people obtain their health care.

One manifestation of this fragmentation of care in the US is the rapid recent growth of minor emergency medical clinics. Sometimes known as 'convenience clinics', they offer an explicit alternative to hospital emergency rooms and general practice. Typically such clinics are open twelve hours a day for the rapid and anonymous treatment of minor emergencies, from abrasions to wasp stings and accidents to venereal disease. Prices are competitive, the atmosphere is pleasantly non-institutional, and the lack of continuity of care is a positive virtue. The clinics are reputedly as profitable as hamburger bars. Greenberg has estimated that 'with about 2,000 square feet they can gross roughly $600,000 a year which is average for a fast food outlet.'[22]

Another form of health care provision, widely tested in the United States, is the Health Maintenance Organisation (HMO).[23] Schemes of this sort have slowly been gaining ground for over thirty years, although no more than about 12 per cent of the population is covered by one or other of the plans. Each HMO is a non-profit organisation providing a full range of services using its own hospital and staff. Doctors and hospitals receive a pre-set sum for each person enrolled, whether or not the service is used. There are no fee-for-service payments. Doctors and hospitals share the financial risk by agreeing to a total budget in advance. The premiums paid by individual subscribers reflect the experience of the community as a whole, not that of the individuals – a form of risk sharing known as 'community rating'. HMOs typically average about 45,000 members, but the range in membership is wide, from about 13,000 to some 800,000.[24]

The HMO system looks much like a cash-limited National Health

Service (see chapter 6), but it contains several potential advantages. There are incentives for preventive care and for the efficient provision of care, partly because of the workable size of the HMOs and partly because of the sharing of financial risks among the doctors. The size of HMOs also encourages experimentation with different methods of delivering care, and since some 5 to 10 per cent of members are government-sponsored through 'Medicare', sanctions exist not only to ensure the attainment of minimum standards but also to pursue equitable and positive health care policies.

A fifth consequence of insurance funding would be the probable increase in the administrative costs of providing health care. If introduced into the UK, it would mean the setting up of insurance companies; the creation of mechanisms for deciding premium levels, collecting them, settling claims and distributing benefits; and the creation of whatever machinery is decided upon for helping the poor and those with heavy needs. It is impossible to predict the additional costs of these activities without knowing the details of any particular scheme, but administrative costs in the United States range from 8-12 per cent for large group programmes to 20-30 per cent for programmes enrolling individual members.[25] Against this, administrative costs in the NHS were about 5 per cent in 1980[26] (although a lot of administrative tasks were carried out by members of the caring professions and not included in this figure). A major reason for the relatively low administrative costs in the NHS is that revenue is raised largely through existing mechanisms (the national insurance contribution and the inland revenue), not through one created specially to cope with the health service.

In summary, the extension of the private market in health care in the United Kingdom, coupled with a demise in the tax-funded basis of the NHS and a growth in insurance funding, might shift the emphasis away from comprehensive family care towards an entrepreneurial pattern of care with a disproportionate emphasis on items of high-cost technology, higher costs and less overt commitment to principles of equity. On balance, the Royal Commission was not convinced by arguments in favour of such a shift, and concluded simply that 'we do not think that the NHS should be funded in this way.'[27]

Chapter 6

The allocation of financial resources

In 1968, Hardin drew attention to a problem that, in his view, had no technical solution.[1] It is the problem of regulating the use of shared resources. Consider, for example, the use of common pasture land by a group of herdsmen for grazing their cattle. As long as the number of herdsmen and cattle remains relatively small, each herdsman is able to increase the number of cattle using the common pasture without detriment to the others. Indeed, it is only sensible for him to do so. But the pasture land, being limited in area, can only accommodate a certain number of cattle; and once that number has been reached, each additional head of cattle that is put out to graze will be detrimental to the wellbeing of the others. It is possible that all the herdsmen will realise when the saturation point is reached, and will refrain from putting extra cattle out to graze; but human nature being what it is, it is also possible that most herdsmen might argue that the addition of a mere one or two extra cattle will have a negligible effect on the others. If all (or most) of the herdsmen behave in that way, the common pasture land will wilt, and all will suffer. 'Ruin', concluded Hardin, 'is the destination towards which all men rush, each pursuing his own best interests in a society that believes in the freedom of the commons. Freedom in a commons brings ruin to all.'

The regulation of the commons has been suggested by some writers to be one of the central dilemmas of the health services.[2,3] In this case, the commons represents the resources available for use in the health services, the cattle represent the patients who actually use the resources, and the herdsmen represent the doctors who control the rate at which patients use the resources. Unless ways can be found of regulating their behaviour, order breaks down and all suffer. A number of solutions might, in principle, be sought. One solution would simply be to enlarge the commons, thus postponing the point at which chaos threatens. As we saw in chapter 4, this has happened to some extent throughout the lifetime of the National Health Service in the United Kingdom; real resources have increased in most years since 1950. But that solution is no longer available, at least in the short term. Another solution might be to limit the number of those who seek access to the medical commons. In reality, however, the number both of people in need and of those who provide care has tended to increase rather than to diminish. A further solution might involve some form of voluntary agreement among the users that limits the claims that each of them can make. The elaborate machinery in the NHS for involving members of the caring professions in decisions about the use of resources is intended partly to facilitate this kind of agreement.[4,5] And a fourth solution might be to encourage self-discipline in the use of resources by increasing users' awareness of the costs to other potential users of their own behaviour. Attempts to inform doctors of the costs of their prescribing, in the hope that fewer and/or cheaper prescriptions will be written in the future, are illustrative of this approach.

In addition to these various ploys, there has been a growing tendency to regulate the use of the medical commons through mechanisms that aim explicitly to allocate packages of resources for use by particular people and sometimes for particular purposes. It is as though the herdsmen, instead of having to arrive at an acceptable solution by haggling amongst themselves, are each allocated a particular piece of the common pasture land by a superior authority. Of course, they may resent the way in which the land has been divided among them, and each herdsman may still be faced with the problem of how to use his particular piece of land to the best effect; but at least a degree of regulatory control is thereby achieved. In this chapter we look at three forms of allocation in the medical commons that take place at central government level, and in the next chapter we focus down to the local level.

The first allocatory mechanism is actually located outside the health services system, for it determines how much of the nation's resources will be available to form the medical commons each year. Following the recommendation of the Plowden Committee on the Control of Public Expenditure[6] in 1961 that public spending should be brought under proper control, a cycle has been established for drawing up government projections and priorities across the range of public expenditure. The cycle typically begins in the autumn, when the treasury issues instructions to spending departments about the assumptions they should follow in drawing up their plans for future spending. Each department (including, of course, the DHSS) then prepares its programmes, costed at prevailing prices, for up to five years ahead, and these are discussed between departmental and treasury officials. A report is then prepared by the treasury, covering all the programmes for all the departments, and sent to the Public Expenditure Survey Committee (PESC). This Committee, which comprises senior officials of both the treasury and the spending departments, has the job of co-ordinating and reconciling the programmes of the different departments as far as this can be done at officer level, and of identifying choices and decisions that remain to be made by ministers. The final report produced by the Committee (the PESC report) is submitted to the chancellor of the exchequer early the following summer, and the cabinet then decides, in the light of the economic forecasts that are available and the welter of political factors that require consideration, the volume of resources that is to be available for public spending in future years. Further discussions then take place between the treasury and the spending departments about the allocation of the total sum of money between the different programmes, and the final package is put to the cabinet for approval in the autumn or early winter (that is, about a year after the initiation of the cycle). The way in which the cabinet arrives at its decisions about the total level of spending and the allocation of money between programmes is not public knowledge, but some insights are to be found in the memoirs of former cabinet ministers. In his diaries, for example, Mr Richard Crossman gave an account of some of the cabinet discussions on the 1965 PESC report, showing quite clearly the role of political negotiation and bartering in the production of the final package.[7]

The outcome of the cycle is the publication of the public expenditure white paper, usually in the first three months of the following year. There is normally only one white paper each year, but unusual circumstances, such as the change of government in 1979, may generate two papers. The white paper sets out the actual pattern of expenditure on each programme in recent years and also the proposed spending for periods of up to five years ahead. Until 1982, the proposed expenditure was expressed in 'survey prices' – that is, the prices prevailing at the beginning of the survey cycle – and it was subsequently updated to take account of increases in prices occurring between the beginning of the cycle and the start of each financial year. The actual figures in the white paper were therefore no more than a rough indication of the amount of money likely to be available for spending in the NHS in the next financial year, for much depended upon the allowance made for price increases. In 1982, however, the system was changed, and the proposed expenditure figures in that year's public expenditure white paper were expressed not in survey prices, but in terms of the actual amount of money that would be available in the next financial year for spending on each of the main expenditure programmes, including the NHS.[8] The white paper made it clear that these figures would not normally be revised during the year: they therefore contained an allowance for price increases (including, of course, increases in wages and salaries) that were expected to occur during the course of the next financial year, but no extra money was to be forthcoming if prices actually rose above their expected levels. By building in a parsimonious allowance for price increases, and insisting that no additional money would be available, the new system may have given the government tighter control over the process of public expenditure, but at present it is too early to judge how it will work.

The value of the annual public expenditure white papers is mixed. On the one hand the Commons' Select Committee on the Social Services has been critical of certain aspects of the content and presentation of the white paper, claiming that it is difficult not only to understand the trends in expenditure from one year to the next, but also that the information presented in the white paper is frequently insufficient for parliament to judge the extent to which policy goals are being achieved.[9] It may also be noted that the frequent economic crises of recent years have made the white papers much less reliable than they used to be as guides to future spending. Some items of expenditure have actually turned out to be considerably above the level planned for them, whilst others have subsequently been cut to below the planned level as part of a wider set of economic measures. In brief, the assumptions about the feasibility of planning public expenditure that worked quite well until the mid-1970s appear to be increasingly questionable in a period of economic recession and uncertainty.[10]

On the other hand, the public expenditure white papers do require the government to specify its policies in very broad terms, and to make judgments about their costs. They also reveal the government's intentions for allocating public money between different departments and programmes. In the case of health care, for example, the papers indicate the priority that the government intends to give to the health services in relation to other areas of expenditure, and within the health services they indicate the relative priority intended for different parts of the services. Most white papers in recent years have emphasised the priority in the allocation of resources that should be given to primary care and to the care of the mentally ill, the handicapped and the elderly, and they have also indicated the intended distribution of resources between capital and current expenditure on hospitals, community health services, family practitioner services, and other services. The specification of objectives even in such broad terms as these provides some basis for parliament and other critics to monitor the effects of policies against their stated objectives, and to call the government to account for policy changes or failures.

The final phase of the cycle comes when the proposals in the public expenditure white paper are translated into annual allocations to the spending departments through estimates approved by parliament. Prior to 1976-7, the estimates were approved in 'volume' terms – that is, they represented an authorisation to each department to purchase a particular volume of resources. The actual amount of money required to do so depended on the rate of inflation during the year, and if necessary supplementary estimates were approved during the course of the year to offset an unexpectedly high rate of inflation. In this way, departments were, in effect, protected from inflation once their initial allocations had been approved; but from the early 1970s onwards, when others were increasingly feeling the effects of inflation, the allegation was often made that public expenditure was out of control and that something should be done.[11] Consequently in 1976 a new control (known as 'cash limits') was introduced. Under this system the estimates approved by parliament contained an allowance for the forecasted rate of inflation during the next financial year, but no topping-up was usually made during the year if the actual rate of inflation was higher than the forecast. The excess simply had to be found by cutting back elsewhere in the budget. The system of cash limits has been applied to the whole of NHS expenditure, with the exception so far of the family practitioner services, and it has enabled the treasury to exercise a firmer control over the amount of money that is actually spent in the NHS. The new method of presenting future expenditure figures in the public expenditure white papers that was introduced in 1982 is likely to increase the treasury's control still further, for the actual amount of cash available (irrespective of subsequent changes in the rate of inflation) is determined even earlier in the cycle.

The public expenditure survey cycle produces a sum of money for spending each year on the health services. In the language of the analogy with which we began this chapter, it specifies the size of the medical commons for that year. The second allocatory mechanism divides the commons among the regional and district health authorities. The problem of allocating financial resources to the health authorities has been particularly prominent since the 1974 reorganisation of the NHS but in fact it has been present since the inception of the service in 1948. The 1946 National Health Service Act created a regional administrative structure for the hospital service, placing responsibility for the hospitals in the hands of ad hoc regional hospital boards (RHBs) and generating the need for some method of transferring finances from the centre to the periphery. The 1974 reorganisation transformed the RHBs into regional health authorities (RHAs) and extended their functions, but the need remained for finances to be allocated to them. In the early years of the NHS the allocations to the RHBs were based mainly on the number of hospital beds they had, the assumption being that the availability of beds was an indicator of need. In time, however, the frailty of this assumption was exposed. It was realised that the regions had inherited very different numbers of beds in 1948 (the Metropolitan and Liverpool regions having high ratios of beds to population and the other northern regions having low ratios), and that such variations could not be justified in terms of the conventional indicators of medical and social need.[12] Indeed, it was well known that the northern regions had higher standardised mortality ratios than other parts of the country, and the claims of equity might therefore have argued for more rather than fewer hospital beds there.

The 1962 Hospital Plan for England and Wales[13] envisaged a move towards a more equal distribution of hospital beds between the regions; but insufficient resources were made available to cope with the transition, and by 1970 the regional inequalities remained almost as large as ever. In that year, for example, the average revenue expenditure per person in the Trent region was £23, compared with £30, £33 and £34 respectively in the South-east, North-east and South-west Metropolitan regions.[14] A new initiative in seeking a fairer allocation of financial resources was made by Mr Richard Crossman during his period of office as secretary of state for social services, and in 1971-2 the regional allocations were based upon a new formula that took account of the total populations of each region and the numbers of patients treated as well as the number of hospital beds. By reflecting the argument that population size and hospital caseload is a better indicator of the needs of each region than the number of hospital beds, the formula represented a more equitable basis for allocation than hitherto; but inadequacies remained. The formula was intended to apply only to the additional real resources available each year, not to the total allocations, and there was still a strong feeling that the allocatory mechanism had not really come to grips with the fundamental problem of measuring the needs of the regions for health care.[15]

A new initiative came in 1975 with the appointment of a working party appointed by the DHSS to 'review the arrangements for distributing NHS capital and revenue . . . with a view to establishing . . . a pattern of distribution responsive to relative need'.[16] In 1976 and 1977 working parties were also set up in Scotland, Wales and Northern Ireland with similar terms of reference. In its final report in 1976 the English Resource Allocation Working Party (RAWP) produced a formula that has been used as the basis for revenue and capital allocations from 1977-8 onwards and that has been the model for allocations from regions to districts. The thoroughly innovative aspect of the RAWP formula was its attempt to measure the relative needs of regional populations for health service resources, and, particularly in the revenue allocation, to ignore historical legacies or traditional variations in bed supply in distributing them.

The basic criterion of relative need in the formula for allocating *revenue* resources is the total population size, using mid-year estimates from the Office of Population Censuses and Surveys. The population is then weighted to take account of a range of other factors, particularly the age and sex structure and the standardised mortality ratios for specific conditions, and also fertility rates (as an indicator of the need for hospital maternity services) and marital status (as an indicator of the need for hospital mental illness services). Adjustments are made to the weighted populations for the movement of hospital in-patients across regional boundaries, for agency arrangements, and for the cost of London weighting allowances. The entire calculation produces a 'notional' population for each region, and the revenue resources available nationally are divided among the regions in proportion to their notional populations to yield a target allocation for each region. The target allocations are then compared with the previous year's actual allocations, and each region's distance from its target is calculated. Redistribution is achieved by giving the largest increases to the regions that are furthest below their targets and the smallest increases to those that are highest above their targets, subject to a decision about the maximum and minimum changes that can be made in any one year. The speed at which regions move towards their targets is known as the 'pace of change'.

The RAWP report also recommended a formula for the distribution of *capital* resources among the regions that had a close resemblance to the revenue formula. Regional populations are weighted in a similar way to that used for revenue, and the capital target for each region is calculated by distributing the value of existing capital stock and the new resources available for capital development in proportion to the notional populations. Again, judgments are required about the speed at which regions can move towards their target allocations.

The immediate acceptance of the RAWP proposals and their subsequent implementation by the government has effected a radical change in the method of allocating resources to the regions (and through the regions to the districts). No longer are allocations based upon the time-hallowed principle of 'last year's budget plus a little more for those who can shout the loudest'. No longer are historical legacies the principal determinant of current fortunes. Instead, the RAWP formulae have tried in a totally new way to follow the principle of equal resources for equal need, and in the first few years of operation they have effected a significant shift in distributional patterns. Between 1977-8 and 1979-80, for example, the average distance of the regions from their revenue targets fell from 8.3 per cent to 6.3 per cent.[17] But whether the new formulae have necessarily achieved a more equitable distribution is a matter of debate, for they have attracted a good deal of critical comment, some of it focusing on arguments about equity.[18,19] There has been extensive criticism, for example, of the RAWP's explicit assumption that standardised mortality rates are acceptable substitute indicators of morbidity, and of the further implied assumption that they reveal the relative needs of different populations for health services. The failure to take any account at all of social and environmental factors in the aetiology of morbidity is cited as further evidence of the abstract nature of the working party's conception of the need for health care. The handling of the undergraduate teaching hospitals has also aroused strong criticism, though issues of self-interest as well as of equity appear to intrude. Prior to 1974 the teaching hospitals stood outside the regional hospital board structure, being administered by independent boards of governors and receiving public funds directly from central government. The 1973 National Health Service Reorganisation Act abolished the independent status of most of these hospitals and brought them within the new regional administrative and financial structures. This has meant that, apart from an additional allowance for the teaching hospitals to cover their extra service commitments connected with their teaching functions, these hospitals are now required to compete with all the other services in their districts for the funds available under the RAWP formula. Some commentators have welcomed this innovation as a way of reducing the privileged status and financial advantages of the teaching hospitals; but in London (where the problem is obviously most acute) it has required the health authorities to make decisions about the balance between teaching hospitals and other services that should probably be taken nationally.

Many other detailed criticisms of the RAWP formulae have been made, some of them of a highly technical nature. In response, the secretary of state appointed an advisory group in 1978 to consider possible changes in the methods by which resources are allocated. The group was disbanded in 1980, but not before issuing a report containing a number of recommendations for change, mostly concerned with the calculation of the service increment for teaching hospitals.[20] It seems clear that the principles of the RAWP formula are here to stay, although the cut-back of resources in the early 1980s has highlighted the contentious nature of its redistributive aims. At times of growth, some redistribution can be achieved among the regions and districts without any suffering an absolute loss of resources, but at a time of standstill, redistribution means that some regions and districts must inevitably lose if others are to gain. Politically, the climate in the early 1980s was rather different from that in which RAWP was born.

One of the fundamental principles underlying the RAWP report was the distinction between the distribution and the use of financial resources. The working party made it clear that it was concerned only with the sharing of resources, not with the uses to which they are put: 'that', said the report, 'must be a matter for the administering authorities and is essentially part of their policy-making, planning and decision-making functions'[21]. Yet it is clear that, as well as its crucial role in the allocation of resources, central government cannot be indifferent to the priorities followed by the regional and district health authorities in using their resources. The National Health Service is capable of generating a good deal of political capital, and the political parties are well aware of this in preparing their election manifestos. Promises are made about the priorities that will be accorded to particular services or programmes, and the public are led to believe that the power to enforce these priorities is available to the government. In fact, as the quotation from the RAWP report suggests, the balance of power between the central government department (the DHSS) and the regional and district authorities of the NHS is far from clear, and the need for centrally defined priorities coexists uneasily with the desirability of decentralised planning that is responsive to local conditions and circumstances.

The problem of central government control over the allocation of resources to service programmes (the third allocatory mechanism discussed in this chapter) can be illustrated through recent government documents on priorities in the health and personal social services. The 1976 public expenditure white paper, published in February of that year, forecast an annual average increase in current expenditure on the health and personal social services of 2.1 per cent at constant prices between 1975-6 and 1979-80.[22] In the following month the Department of Health and Social Security published a consultative document on priorities for health and personal social services in England that attempted for the first time to specify how the additional resources proposed in the white paper should be allocated among different programmes.[23] Within the overall projected annual increase in current expenditure of 2.1 per cent from 1975-6 to 1979-80, the consultative document suggested that some programmes should grow by a larger proportion (for example, primary care by 3.8 per cent, services for the elderly and physically handicapped by 3.2 per cent, services for the mentally handicapped by 2.8 per cent and services for children by 2.2 per cent); others should grow by a small proportion (for example, services for the mentally ill by 1.8 per cent and general and acute hospital services by 1.2 per cent); and others (such as maternity services) should actually be reduced.

The 1976 consultative document therefore represented an explicit attempt by central government to control not only the total volume of resources available for the health services and their distribution to the regional authorities, but also the broad priorities that the authorities were to follow in preparing their strategic (ten to fifteen-year) and operational (three-year) plans. The document was hailed by *The Times* as 'a work of some optimism'[24] and by the British Medical Journal as 'a coherent one in a period of economic recession'.[25] But in spite of widespread support both for the principle of government involvement in the setting of priorities in resource terms and for the particular priorities specified in the document (with the exception of some vigorous pleading for the acute hospitals and maternity services), doubts were raised about the feasibility of central control over local policy-making. *The Times* observed that

> in spite of all the talk that there has been in recent years about the need to concentrate resources on general practice and mental health, it is striking that their share has even in some respects declined in recent years,[26]

and in a follow-up document issued the next year (1977) the Department itself raised the question: 'Can it all be done?'[27]

The doubts appeared to be well founded, for studies of local decision-making in the NHS seem to show quite clearly that central policies can be circumvented by those who control the provision of services at the periphery.[28] We examine some of these studies more closely in chapter 9, but it is scarcely surprising, in the light of their conclusions, to find that the government's proposals in the 1976 priorities document for the allocation of resources to particular programmes have not materialised. Snaith has shown that, between 1975-6 and 1979-80, acute hospital and maternity services grew more rapidly than the priorities document proposed, whilst services for the elderly, the physically and mentally handicapped, and the mentally ill grew more slowly than intended.[29] Some of the reasons for the failure of central priorities to be reflected in local practice have been described by Butts and his colleagues, based upon an analysis of regional health authorities' plans between 1976 and 1979.

> For acute services, the problems of pursuing plans for self-sufficiency were evident. On primary care services and prevention, the national policies seemed to have been accepted but actual progress was absent . . . because the responsibility for these services is diffuse, and a co-ordinated policy is difficult to implement. Policy for the elderly had been questioned . . . . Progress for the younger physically handicapped, the mentally ill and the mentally handicapped seemed to be slow or non-existent . . . . Little coverage on children's services was included in the plans. The over-provision of resources in the maternity sector seemed to have been accepted,

> but regions were cautious in attempting reductions [because of] uncertainties about future birth rates . . . and the fact that no plans to cut services could fly in the face of the inevitable claim that 'babies will die.'[30]

In the light of these experiences the revised priorities of the incoming Conservative government in 1979 were awaited with interest. They appeared in 1981 in the form of a handbook addressed to the chairmen and members of the new district health authorities (see chapter 8), and they represented a considerable departure from the innovatory stance of the 1976 and 1977 consultative documents.[31] Gone were the central government attempts to specify norms of provision for different programmes and sectors; gone were the target allocations necessary to sustain the norms. Instead, the handbook merely specified the groups and services to which 'the Secretary of State expects authorities to give priority'. No indications were given about *relative* priorities, or about those groups and services that were to be restrained in order to allow growth in the priority sectors. The priority groups identified in the handbook were the elderly, the mentally ill, the mentally handicapped, and the physically and sensorily handicapped; the priority services were those for maternity and neonatal care, primary care, and the care of young children at risk. With the exception of maternity and neonatal services these priorities have been echoed in most public expenditure white papers and government pronouncements for more than a decade, and the failure during this period to achieve any significant reallocation of resources is evidence of the problems faced by central government in ensuring that its own priorities are reflected in local spending decisions.

The 1976 and 1981 priorities documents represented differing attempts by central government to influence the allocation of resources to particular services or programmes. The former attempted to secure quite a high degree of control, but did not altogether succeed; the latter devolved much more responsibility from central government to the health authorities. Klein has suggested that the 1981 document had an intrinsic rationality of its own, reflecting a deliberate judgment on the part of the government about the most sensible course of action in a situation of uncertainty.[32] When major planning is rendered very difficult by the unpredictable state of the economy, it is sensible for central government to pass off the responsibility for unpopular choices to the regional and district health authorities. Indeed, even the 1976 document contained an element of this approach, for although it set out what appeared to be clearly defined changes in target levels of spending on particular programmes, these targets were said to be merely 'illustrative', and it was never entirely clear whether they were intended to be followed to the letter or merely taken as guidelines.

More recently the pendulum seems to have swung back towards renewed attempts to make central government priorities stick. In two aggressive reports on the government's spending plans for health and social services, published in 1980 and 1981, the Commons Select Committee on Social Services criticised the Department of Health and Social Security for its inability to formulate and evaluate strategic policies across the range of services for which it is responsible. In its 1981 report, the Committee illustrated its criticism by considering the possible effects of changes in the level of spending on particular services, programmes or client groups. An increase in spending might lead to an improvement in the quality of a service, but it might equally result in an increase in the volume of the service or in its coverage or cost. The Committee felt that these effects were very different in their social impact, and that the Department should be clear about its aims when deciding to increase or reduce expenditure, and should subsequently be able to assess the extent to which such aims had been fulfilled. A similar point was made later in the same year (1981) by the Commons Public Accounts Committee in relation to the staffing in the NHS.

> We recognise the difficulty of attempting overall staff planning for the NHS, but . . . we doubt whether the present largely devolved system of control in England has ensured that the numbers of staff employed have been limited to those strictly necessary to meet the objectives of the NHS.[35]

In response to such criticisms the secretary of state for social services announced early in 1982 a new system for making the health authorities accountable to parliament, through the DHSS, for their implementation of national priorities.[36] Henceforth, the chairmen of the regional health authorities will be required to report annually to the secretary of state on their progress in implementing central government policies, and the district chairmen will be similarly accountable to their regional counterparts. It is too early to assess the impact of this innovation, but the analysis in this chapter suggests that it will bristle with difficulties. Control over the allocation of resources weakens as one moves from the centre to the periphery. Clear mechanisms exist for allocating resources to the NHS, and then to the regional and district health authorities, but the process of turning resources into services is more shadowy and inaccessible. It is to this problem of allocation that we must turn next.

Chapter 7

The allocation of care

The mechanisms described in the previous chapter result in allocations of financial resources to the regional and district health authorities, and (at least in broad intent) to particular service programmes or client groups. In the analogy of the common pasture land, it is as though particular bits of the common land had been allocated for use by individual herdsmen. The problem of allocation may, however, still not be fully resolved, for if each herdsman has more cattle than can be accommodated on the particular piece of land he has been allocated, he must somehow decide upon the best way of using his piece. Various options may, in principle, be open to him. He may have to choose whether it is better to graze a smaller number of cattle well or a larger number of cattle less well. If he chooses the former, he must decide which cattle to graze (the old or the young, the fit or the weak, or simply those that happen to be at the head of the queue), and he must take account of the welfare of those who are denied access to the pasture. If he chooses the latter, he must weigh the benefit of having more cattle against the cost in terms of scrawnier animals, more disease, and the like.

As with any analogy, this cannot be pushed too far, for the point will quickly be reached at which it becomes not merely unhelpful but positively misleading. But the analogy of the common pasture land does produce useful insights for the health services. As we saw in chapter 1, resources are the raw materials of health care, and in order to be productive they must be used to provide care of different kinds for individuals or groups of people. If the resources that are allocated through the various mechanisms are insufficient to provide all the care that people would like to have, then choices must somehow be made about the amount and quality of care that will be given to different people. In the language of economics, when the 'potential demand' or 'want' for care exceeds the capacity of the system to meet it, ways must exist for determining who will have how much of their potential demands or wants satisfied, and in what ways. This is the problem of the allocation of care, and it is distinct from that of the allocation of financial resources. As Judge has expressed it in relation to the personal social services,

> it seems reasonably sensible when talking about the allocation of social services to make a distinction between what one can call financial and service rationing . . . . Financial rationing is concerned with those procedures by which sums of money are allocated between competing claims . . . . On the other hand, the availability to clients of directly consumable services is conditioned by other rationing decisions in political and organizational systems which are largely removed from the consumer.[1]

The premise that insufficient resources exist to enable social workers or doctors to give everyone the kind of care they would wish them to have is part of the conventional wisdom of the social services and is a fundamental assumption that economists make about the world. As the American economist Fuchs has put it,

> it is hardly news that we cannot all have everything that we would like to have, but it is worth emphasizing that this basic human condition is not to be attributed to 'the system' or to some conspiracy, but to the parsimony of nature in not providing mankind with the resources needed to satisfy human wants.[2]

The truth of this assertion in relation to personal material wants is part of the everyday experience of most people. Its truth in relation to health care may be less self-evident, but the clues are plain to see. It is a common observation that an increase in the use of a service usually results from an expansion in its availability (implying that, before the expansion, there had been a reservoir of wants that had gone unsatisfied), and there is no lack of complaint about the shortages that are thought to exist in many areas of the National Health Service. Shortages may even result in the loss of lives that could otherwise have been extended. It was reported in 1981 that ninety-seven children had died waiting for bone marrow transplants at the Westminster Hospital in London, and the director of the transplant programme was quoted as seeking an additional £114,000 to his departmental allocation of £180,000 in order to raise the annual number of transplants from twenty-five to forty.[3] Moreover, much of the initiative in demanding services originates with the providers of care, not the consumers, and they are always likely to be seeking an expansion of their activities – what Fuchs has called the 'technological imperative'.[4] The large growth in recent years in the use of diagnostic technology, some of it of uncertain benefit in improving diagnostic accuracy, is another example of the way in which providers and consumers can conspire together in expanding the horizons of what they want.[5]

It seems clear, then, that the total potential demand for the outputs produced by the health service system is unlikely ever to be fully satisfied. Some commentators imply that the potential demand for care (particularly in a system such as the NHS where services are provided free at the point of use) is actually limitless, but there are common-sense grounds for assuming that certain natural limits exist to the amount of care that people would like to have. The consumption of many forms of medical care is either impossible, dangerous or pointless. Equally important is the fact that the process of receiving care is rarely wholly beneficial: there are usually costs involved that will, for some people in some circumstances, outweigh the benefits. Being a patient involves the commitment of time; it may entail the suffering of pain, discomfort and anxiety; and even in the NHS it may create financial costs through charges, lost earnings, extra travelling expenses, and the purchase of special foods or equipment.[6] Such costs may, in the matrix of personal choice, make the difference between wanting and not wanting care.

The size of the gap between the potential demand for care and the resources that are, or are likely to be, available to meet it is plainly a matter of guesswork. In contrast to the 5.1 per cent of gross domestic product (at market prices) that was spent on the NHS in 1980, it has been suggested that the proportion could easily be a quarter,[7] and the Royal Commission on the National Health Service actually observed that 'we can easily spend the whole of the gross national product on the NHS.'[8] The four-fold variation between these two 'guesstimates' is much less important than their common assertion that the NHS (and indeed the health services system in any country) is still far from the point at which all wants can be met, and that ways must therefore exist for allocating (or, as some commentators describe it, rationing[9]) available services among those who want them.

The need to allocate a limited quantity of goods and services when they are in insufficient supply to satisfy all those who want them is familiar in everyday experience. People understand that there are not enough cars, clothes, cameras, carpets, chocolates and most other commodities to meet everyone's wants for them and that some kind of distribution system is therefore inevitable. It seems, however, that the truth of this assertion has been perceived less readily in relation to health services than to cars, cameras and carpets. The NHS was launched in 1948 in the belief that it could and would satisfy all the nation's wants for health care, and that belief was still widely held until the 1960s. It appeared to come as a shock to many in the 1970s to learn that there always had been the need to allocate care and always would be. In 1975, for example, a speech by the then minister of health (Dr David Owen) was reported in a popular medical newspaper under the headline: 'Now rationing is official'.[10] The article explained that the minister's speech was significant 'because it is the first open admission by a government spokesman of the abandonment of a comprehensive, free service'. It is rather surprising that, as late as 1975, the inescapability of rationing in the NHS appeared to be such hot news.

One reason for the reluctance to understand and accept the inevitability of the allocation of care may lie in the means by which it is done, for the mechanism is much more visible and familiar in the case of cars, cameras and carpets than it is for health services. In the United Kingdom, most goods and services for personal consumption are allocated through the market, which provides a forum for suppliers to sell their goods and consumers to buy what they want. The nub of the mechanism is price: goods and services that are offered for sale carry a price, and this represents the cost (in terms of all the other things that cannot be acquired) that the buyer has to bear in order to secure the things he wants. Buyers are thus faced with a choice: they do not have enough money to satisfy all their wants, and they must therefore decide which things they want sufficiently strongly to be willing to forego other things in order to obtain them. Price therefore acts as an allocatory mechanism by keeping *effective* demand (that is, demand which can actually be satisfied) in line with supply. If the market is working freely, the effective demand for goods and services is inversely related to their prices: the higher the price the lower the demand, and conversely, the lower the price the higher the demand. The price of any commodity at any particular moment in time is, in a free market, that which will 'clear the market'; it is the price at which the quantity of the commodity that is offered for sale by the suppliers matches the quantity that is demanded by the purchasers. If, at any given price, more of the commodity is wanted for purchase than is available, the resulting imbalance between supply and demand is corrected by increasing its price, for demand will fall off at the higher price whilst supply will increase. The higher price thus marks the new point at which supply and demand are held in equilibrium.

This is, of course, a highly simplified account of the function of the market as an allocatory mechanism. In the real world, markets have various imperfections, and a variety of controls, subsidies and restrictive practices distort the free working of market forces. Moreover, suppliers and consumers do not always behave in the rational, calculating way that the theory of supply and demand implies. But it does largely account for the common-sense experience that it is principally the willingness of consumers to pay the market price of goods and services that determines the way in which those goods and services are allocated among those who would like to have them.

The use of the market as an allocatory mechanism has various advantages. A major advantage claimed for it is that it is efficient in the sense that it gives people the maximum benefit for the costs they pay. In the case of health care, le Grand and Robinson have put it like this.[11]

> Since people would be free to pick and choose, doctors and hospitals who provided inferior treatment at expensive prices would lose custom to those who provided better and/or cheaper services. For instance, a doctor who acquired a reputation . . . for getting his diagnoses wrong, for cutting short his consultations and for having an over-crowded waiting room would lose patients to one who was known for his medical successes and ease of access . . . . Thus medical practitioners of all kinds would have a strong incentive to improve their standards and/or reduce their costs.

A related advantage that is claimed for the market is that it offers a greater freedom of choice to patients and a greater incentive to the providers of care to be more attentive to patients' preferences and to the courtesy and civility with which they are treated. Indeed, the Royal Commission on the NHS identified this as the market's supreme advantage.[12] And a third advantage is that the market avoids any moral or paternalistic connotations about people's needs: it is merely in business to meet their demands, not to make judgments about what they should have or what would be good for them. The whole difficult process of determining the relative needs of different groups of patients for the limited care available from the health service system (see chapter 11) is neatly side-stepped.

Yet in spite of the ubiquitous nature of the market as a means of allocating goods and services, extending even to the allocation of commodities such as food and housing that are important in maintaining good health, it has explicitly been rejected in the United Kingdom as the main mechanism of allocating health care. Many of the services provided through the NHS are free at the time of use, and although some services involve a charge to patients, few are charged at the full economic rate. A distinctive feature of the NHS in the United Kingdom is therefore that it has largely abolished the market for health care: within the domain of state provision, which accounts for more than 90 per cent of health care expenditure, services carry no price and they are neither bought nor sold.

The decision to remove health care in the United Kingdom from the influence of market forces was initially a political one, although arguments and insights of an economic nature have subsequently been used to justify it. The NHS came into existence as part of a broad programme of welfare legislation that seemed to reflect the mood of the nation in the later war years. Titmuss has argued that the experiences of war created a national awareness of the unpredictability of disaster, and hence of the need to redistribute the costs of disaster (via the social services) throughout the whole community.[13] Health care was a natural focus for the expression of these sentiments, for ill health, more than other kinds of social misfortune, can be unpredictable and indiscriminate in its incidence, and may be financially crippling in its consequences if necessary care has to be bought. The unhappy consequences of buying care in pre-NHS days have been recorded vividly by Mrs (now Lady) Lena Jeger in describing her childhood memories of visits to the doctor.

> I can remember nothing less dignified than when my mother used to sit in a misery of embarrassment on the edge of a chair in the consulting room on the rare and desperate days when one of us had to be taken to the doctor – opening and shutting her purse, waiting for the right moment to extract the careful, unspareable half-crown. She never knew whether to just slide it across the desk, which she said might make the doctor feel like a waiter, or to actually put it in his hand and make him feel as if he worked in a shop. Sometimes he would shout at my mother for not having come before, like the time we had to wait for my sister's sore throat to turn unmistakably into diphtheria before she was pushed off in a pram to his surgery. 'Good God woman, why didn't you bring this child days ago?' And then even he read the silence as the half-crown came out. 'Damn the money', he said, slipping it into his pocket.[14]

After the war the climate of public opinion was right for the introduction of the welfare state, with the National Health Service as one of the central jewels in the crown. In retrospect, some of the assumptions of the founding fathers of the welfare state about the finite nature of need and the capacity of the social services to meet all reasonable demands seem incredibly optimistic, but the central argument about risk-sharing in health care and the necessity for state intervention in it has been sustained by subsequent experience. The fantastic growth in medical technology has elevated the costs of many forms of care above anything that could have been envisaged thirty-five years ago, and governments in all countries have needed to become increasingly involved in the arrangements for financing them.

Support for the political decision to remove health care in the UK from the influence of market forces has come from some economists who have argued that certain distinctive features of health care make it unsuited as a market commodity. Two such features are commonly cited. First, some kinds of health care have 'external' benefits – that is, they confer a general benefit on the community as well as a personal benefit on the recipients of care. Immunisation is a good example: it not only benefits the individuals who have it, it also benefits the community as a whole by increasing the proportion of immune people and reducing the risk of the spread of infectious disease. But in a health care market, where people are concerned only with weighing their *personal* benefits against their personal costs, the external benefits are forgotten. Thus an individual who decides that the personal benefit of immunisation does not outweigh the personal cost will refuse to be immunised, although by adding the external benefit to his personal one, the balance may shift in favour of immunisation.

Second, it is argued that health care differs from other commodities in that the consumers (the patients) are often unaware of what they need and may be ill-equipped to judge the quality of the care they receive. Moreover, illness is frequently accompanied by some degree of emotional distress, distorting the judgment of patients and making them susceptible to the persuasion of their doctors. Under such circumstances, the buying and selling of medical care places the doctor in a dual role both as adviser to the patient about his needs and as provider of the services to satisfy them, and this duality may conflict with the doctor's traditional obligation to put the patient's interests above his own. Taylor, for example, has indicated some of the ways in which the market encourages doctors to over-investigate patients' symptoms, to perform unnecessary (and sometimes harmful) surgical operations, to specialise in increasingly narrow areas of medical practice at the expense of the whole person, to induce the deliveries of normal babies, to avoid controlled trials of the efficacy of their work, to offer indiscriminate screening services, and to neglect the more mundane but nevertheless important aspects of medical practice.[15] By insulating the doctor-patient relationship from the pressures of the market, the patient is more likely to be protected from exploitation of his ignorance and weakness.

At this point, the argument that we have pursued in this chapter comes up against a question. We have argued that people's wants or potential demands for care exceed the resources that are available to satisfy them, and that, although the balance between supply and demand could theoretically be struck by subjecting the health services to the effects of market forces, such a solution has explicitly been rejected in the United Kingdom. The question then is: what other mechanisms exist for allocating care? Mechanic has suggested that such mechanisms can be described by their position along a spectrum of explicitness.[16] At one end of the spectrum are the explicit means by which government attempts to channel services to particular groups of users. As Mechanic pointed out, the difficulties of imposing the explicit rationing of care are more political than scientific, for by their very nature they limit the freedom of the providers of care (particularly the doctors) to do whatever they judge to be in the best interests of their patients. It is perhaps for this reason that examples of explicit allocatory mechanisms are hard to find in Western European countries, although they appear to be more prevalent in Eastern Europe.[17] An example in the United States are the Professional Standards Review Organisations (PSROs), set up under statute in 1972 and charged with the responsibility of producing explicit specifications of the care to be given to patients treated in hospital under the 'Medicare' and 'Medicaid' programmes (see chapter 12).[18] Until the PSROs began to be phased out in 1981, doctors could be held individually accountable to hospital review committees for any departures from the prescribed procedures. Such stringent procedures have not yet appeared in the United Kingdom, although guidelines, encouragements and sanctions may be used as ways of influencing the allocation of care. General practitioners, for example, are paid for carrying out cervical screening only among women over the age of 35 or those with three or more pregnancies. Forms of negative control may also be used. In 1980 the Chief Medical Officer notified the regional and area medical officers that heart transplant programmes should not be carried out unless certain conditions were met: units must already be centres of advanced cardiac surgery; sufficient medical, surgical, nursing and technical staff and equipment must be available; adequate support services must be readily available at all times; and centres must be carrying out experimental work on immunology, circulatory support, and organ preservation systems.[19]

The principal criticism that is levelled against the explicit allocation of care is that it produces rigid and bureaucratic ways of working, and minimises clinical freedom and local initiative and innovation. Against this, the main advantage of the explicit allocation of care is that it enables coherent and rational decisions to be made about the best use of limited resources. Fair and efficient ways of coping with the potential demand for care are more likely to result from considered judgments, centrally made and universally enforced, about the ways in which limited services should be shared out than by leaving the allocatory decisions to a myriad of local, autonomous professionals. That, however, is precisely what happens at the other (implicit) end of the spectrum. Here, the freedom of doctors to provide whatever care they wish (within the limits of the resources at their command) is accepted without question, and the actual pattern of the allocation of care that emerges at the end of the day is the sum total of all the decisions made by all the individual autonomous doctors up and down the land. Mechanic has pointed out that implicit rationing is more acceptable politically than explicit forms, for it poses no threat to the clinical autonomy of the medical profession. Doctors are free to construct whatever packages of care they desire out of the resources available to them. But implicit rationing may produce outcomes that are less fair and efficient. As Mr Enoch Powell has put it, 'the worst kind of rationing is that which is unacknowledged'.[20] Doctors are likely to differ considerably in their judgments about the relative needs of patients, and the treatments they use may be variable in their effectiveness. Articulate patients may obtain more attention than timid ones, even though their needs may be judged to be less great: there is evidence, for example, that middle-class patients have longer consultation times with their GPs than working-class patients.[21]

In the absence of market forces, the allocation of care in the National Health Service seems to rely much more heavily on implicit than on explicit methods. Relatively little is known about the way such methods actually work, but some general principles have been suggested. Parker has identified four such principles in the social services: deterrence, deflection, dilution and delay.[22] Deterrence refers to the various devices that are employed to discourage prospective patients or clients from making their potential demands effective. In the case of general practice, for example, Foster has observed that

> these devices include the use of telephone answering and deputising services, the use of ancillary staff, including receptionists, to filter and regulate patients' demands, and the use of a full appointment system to impose a delay on patients' access to the doctor.[23]

Deflection occurs when patients are referred to other workers or agencies; the effect is to reduce demand on the original agency and perhaps also to discourage patients from pursuing their demands. Dilution refers to the tendency to reduce standards as a way of coping with excess demand. Services are spread more thinly, and the standard of care given to each patient is lower than would ideally be wished. An explicit acknowledgment of dilution in the health services was made by a former secretary of the British Medical Association in 1978 in observing that an insufficiency of resources was preventing doctors from 'providing for their patients the standard of service they would wish and for which they have been trained'.[24] Delay is all too familiar in the health services, particularly when it takes the form of waiting lists for non-urgent hospital care. But queues are inevitable when services carry no direct price to the user, and when the explicit allocation of care has been eschewed. Queues are necessary rationing devices, and it is no accident that the waiting list for hospital care in the NHS has remained remarkably constant since 1948, in spite of changes in the number of beds available and in the number of patients treated in them. They work in a number of different ways, including the deterrent effect they have on potential new patients and the opportunity that the waiting time gives to patients to withdraw from the queue.

These allocatory devices may seem distasteful and offensive, but they are unavoidable in some form or another. The question cannot be avoided of whether it is preferable to allocate care through the market or through other means, and if the market solution is rejected, whether it is preferable to resort to explicit or implicit means.

Chapter 8

The structure of the National Health Service

There are many points in the health services system at which decisions must be taken about the way resources are to be used. How are such decisions reached? The question is complex, and several authors have addressed themselves to it.[1,2,3,4] In this chapter and the next we outline an answer first by describing the formal decision-making structure of the National Health Service and then by considering the actual process of decision-making. One preliminary note of caution must be sounded. It is by no means easy to identify the points of power and decision-making in a complex institution such as the NHS. The structure can be described straightforwardly, but people in formal positions of power may actually have a limited capacity to influence decisions, whilst those in seemingly humble positions may wield considerable power. Public knowledge of how the system *actually* works is often limited. Moreover, the exercise of power is sometimes far from obvious. It consists not only of the capacity to influence decisions and their implementation, but also the capacity to prevent issues from being discussed and decided upon, and (perhaps the most important form of power) the capacity to influence the way in which others think about their own self-interests.[5]

The legal framework of the National Health Service is decided by parliament and enshrined in its acts. Separate acts are usually passed for England and Wales and for Scotland. The principal acts of parliament affecting the service are the 1946 National Health Service Act, the 1968 Health Services and Public Health Act, the 1973 National Health Service Reorganisation Act and the 1977 and 1980 National Health Service Acts. These are all important acts, although a large number of their sections deal with relatively minor details. Of the fifty-eight sections in the 1973 Act, for example, ten dealt with various aspects of trusts and endowments and nineteen with miscellaneous matters, whilst only nine sections related directly to the organisational structure through which decisions were to be taken and implemented. This paucity of legislative meat is partly a reflection of the fact that many important decisions are taken without direct reference to parliament, and partly a result of the tendency to delegate a lot of detailed decision-making power to the principal minister, the secretary of state for social services.

As the political head of the biggest spending department (the Department of Health and Social Security), the secretary of state for social services has power and responsibility. He has power delegated to him by parliament to make a wide range of policy decisions (affecting the personal social services and social security as well as the NHS), and he is responsible to parliament for the use of that power. Each year some 5,000 parliamentary questions are asked by members of parliament about some aspect of health, and the Commons Public Accounts Committee and Social Services Committee can question the secretary of state (and also his junior ministers, the minister of state (health) and the minister of state (social security), and senior civil servants) about departmental policies and practices. But in spite of his formal power, the secretary of state has only a limited opportunity for influencing the development of services. The tenure of the office is often quite short (only two years, on average, since the first minister of health was appointed in 1919[6]), and the range and complexity of policy issues are so great that one individual can do little to influence the broad progression of events in his department. As Kellner and Crowther-Hunt have expressed it,

> when minister and civil servants disagree it is not an equal contest between two temporary incumbents, but an unequal match between a temporary minister and the permanence of the accumulated experience and policy of the department itself.[7]

At best, secretaries of state can provide leadership to their civil servants, evaluate major initiatives in the light of their political judgment and knowledge, fight effectively in the cabinet for resources, exercise control over the appointment of health authority chairmen, and take an influential interest in a small number of issues dear to their hearts.

One reason for the limited personal effectiveness of ministers, suggested by Kellner and Crowther-Hunt and confirmed by the published memoirs of former ministers, is the capacity of the civil service machinery to limit the effectiveness of the political heads of departments, particularly in issues that seem likely to be decided in ways contrary to established departmental ways of thinking. Mr Richard Crossman has commented in his diaries on

> the tremendous effort it requires not to be taken over by the civil

> service . . . . There is a constant preoccupation to ensure that the minister does what is correct. The private secretary's job is to make sure that when the minister comes into Whitehall he doesn't let the side or himself down and behaves in accordance with the requirements of the institution.[8]

Another reason for the limited personal effectiveness of ministers, to which Ham has drawn attention,[9] is the variety of different jobs they are expected to do. In addition to his departmental duties, the secretary of state for social services is a member of the cabinet, a constituency MP, and probably the incumbent of one or more offices in his political party. Simply in order to fulfil his accountability to parliament for the affairs of the NHS, therefore, he must have about him the paraphernalia of a large government department. The Department of Health and Social Security employs some 5,000 people at its headquarters in London at a current cost of about £60 million each year. The Department, which was formed in 1968 with the merger of the former ministry of health and ministry of social security, is organised in six main groups, each headed by a deputy secretary, and subdivided into divisions, branches and sections. The six groups are concerned with the development of national policies for health and personal social services; co-ordination with the regional health authorities (RHAs); personnel functions, including matters of remuneration; financial planning, management and accountability; central administration; and the development of policy in the field of social security. Each deputy secretary is responsible to one of the two permanent secretaries in the Department, and through them to the secretary of state. The chief medical officer has direct access to the secretary of state. The permanent secretaries, the chief medical officer and other senior professional officers constitute an informal 'cabinet' within the Department that is known as the Top of the Office. The essential functions of the Department in the health field were listed by the Royal Commission on the National Health Service as: obtaining, allocating and distributing funds for the NHS; setting objectives, formulating policies and identifying priorities; monitoring the performance of health authorities; undertaking national manpower planning; dealing with national issues affecting the pay and conditions of NHS staff; advising on legislation; liaising with other government departments on matters relating to health; taking a lead in the promotion of policies to improve health; and promoting the dissemination of ideas on health questions.[10]

In 1975 the chairmen of the regional health authorities were invited to set up a small team to examine the functions of the DHSS, particularly in its relationship to the RHAs, and to make recommendations for change. The team worked quickly, producing its report in little more than four months.[11] It was an unusual exercise in open government. The team concluded that the structure and the functions of the DHSS had become increasingly complex over the years, resulting in an unnecessary growth in size and duplication of effort between the Department and the regions 'to the detriment of the Department's effectiveness, ability to take decisions, and capacity to manage the service as it should'. The team made a series of detailed recommendations to enable the Department to carry out its essential management functions efficiently, whilst shedding, devolving or separating off other advisory and executive tasks. The underlying message of the chairmen's report was that of the need to strengthen and increase the autonomy of the regional health authorities, and to reduce the extent of Departmental meddling in regional affairs; but the chairmen later expressed their disappointment to the Royal Commission on the National Health Service that their comments and criticisms had largely been ignored. A similar view has also been expressed by a former minister of state at the Department, Dr David Owen. In his experience,

> the Department has become bogged down in detailed administration covering day-to-day management that has been sucked in by the parliamentary process. The answerability of Ministers to Parliament may have given the semblance of control, but on some major aspects of health care there has been little central direction or control.[12]

The Royal Commission was 'uneasy' about the size and structure of the DHSS and about the way it controlled the NHS. 'In our view the DHSS has tended to give too much guidance to the NHS both on strategic issues and matters of detail.'[13] The Commission discussed a number of suggestions for reform including the transfer of the NHS to local government, the establishment of a health commission, and the strengthening of arrangements for monitoring the quality of services. Eventually, however, it decided that the detailed accountability for the NHS which parliament required could best be provided by the health authorities themselves. Accordingly, the Commission recommended that the regional health authorities should be directly responsible to parliament (through their chairmen or senior officers) for most of the activities of the NHS, excluding only those (such as the allocation of resources among regions) that must be done centrally. The result of this transfer of responsibility would, in the Commission's view, be a smaller range of functions for the DHSS, a reduction in time-consuming parliamentary business, and less duplication of effort between the Department and the regions. The recommendation was, however, explicitly rejected by the government, and apart from some recent changes in the lower echelons of the Department, most notably the upgrading of the policy planning unit within the regional group, the suggestions for change within the Department that have emanated from various sources have gone largely unheeded.

The regional health authorities represent the top tier of the National Health Service in England (there are no regions in Wales, Scotland or Northern Ireland). It is to them that the secretary of state delegates many of the duties that parliament lays upon him for providing a comprehensive health service, and it is still to him that they are accountable. Regionalism was strong in the original structure of the NHS from 1948, with fourteen regional hospital boards in England having an important part to play in planning the hospital service, and, through the local hospital management committees, in its management. Yet in the first green paper on NHS reorganisation published by the then ministry of health in 1968 the regional tier was missing,[14] and the next green paper, published by the DHSS two years later, envisaged the regional function as being limited to that of an advisory and planning role.[15] It was not until 1971, with the publication of the recently elected Conservative government's consultative document on the reorganisation of the NHS, that the regional tier was firmly established in the future structure of the service.[16] The document's proposals for the regions were carried forward into the 1972 white paper[17] and enacted in the 1973 National Health Service Reorganisation Act. The regional health authorities came into being on 1 April 1974.

The RHAs, of which there are fourteen in England, are the middle link in a hierarchy of authority that runs from the secretary of state down to the district health authorities. The regional authorities themselves comprise between eighteen and twenty-four members, two-thirds of whom are appointed by the secretary of state and one-third by the local authorities in the regions. In December 1980, the membership of the RHAs was made up of sixty-six health and allied workers, fifty-three retired workers, thirty-eight 'other professionals', thirty-five businessmen, fifteen academics, ten managers, nine manual workers, eight trade union officials, seven farmers and six others.[18] The authorities are responsible for a range of functions, including the formulation of strategic plans and policies for their region in the light of DHSS guidelines; the allocation of resources to the district health authorities (DHAs); the monitoring of the performance of the DHAs; manpower planning; computing; research and statistical services; management training; and the direct provision of certain services that can best be done at the regional level.

These responsibilities cannot be discharged by the RHA members unaided, and each region has an extensive staff organisation to support the authority in its work. At the heart of the staff structure is the regional team of officers (RTO), comprising five senior officers: a medical officer, a nursing officer, a works officer, an administrator, and a treasurer. Each officer is individually accountable to the authority for the specialist services that he or she manages (so that the regional administrator, for example, is accountable for the provision of adequate administrative, personnel, management and supply services), and together the officers are jointly accountable to the authority for carrying out the tasks of planning, management and service delivery that have been delegated to the regions. The relationship between the authority members and their professional officers is interesting: in principle it is the members who are in the hierarchy of line management and who are responsible for taking strategic decisions about regional policies, and the officers and their staffs who are the managers, advisers and administrators. In practice, things are not always as clear-cut. Brown has noted in his study of the reorganised service on Humberside that a good deal of overlap occurred between the roles of members and officers, and a degree of interchangeability between the decisions taken by each group.[19] And Klein, reflecting on his experiences as a member of an area health authority, has observed that

> it would be difficult to conclude . . . that authority members played a large part in either formulating or executing policies. With some exceptions . . . their role tended to be reactive and concerned with the small print of local implementation rather than grand strategy . . . . Even if authority members are confident enough to assert their own views about what ought to be done – to reject, perhaps, the priorities of the managers and professionals – they are in no position to show how their policies can actually be carried out.[20]

The bottom tier in the hierarchy of authority in England comprises the district health authorities. (In Wales, there are no districts, the service being managed through nine area health authorities; in Scotland, likewise, there are no districts, there being one one management level comprising fifteen health boards; and in Northern Ireland, where the health and personal social services are unified administratively, management is exercised through four health and social services boards, again with no district level). The English DHAs came into being on 1 April 1982. The earlier reorganisation of the NHS in 1974, which had created the RHAs, had also created a membership authority at area level. There were ninety area health authorities (AHAs) in England, their boundaries coinciding with those of the local government metropolitan districts and the non-metropolitan counties. Each area had its own membership authority and team of officers, paralleling those in the regions, and together they were responsible for carrying out the planning and management functions delegated to them by the RHAs. Fifty-two of the ninety areas were considered too large to be directly responsible for the provision of health services, and they were further divided into districts. The number of districts in the multi-district areas varied from two to six. The districts were not membership authorities in the way that the regions and areas were; they were merely a convenient method of enabling the larger AHAs to carry out their responsibilities effectively in all parts of their areas by delegating responsibility to district teams of officers.

Although there appeared to be sound reasons at the time for including an area tier in the 1974 reorganisation in England, concern was expressed from the outset about the unnecessary duplication of functions between regions, areas and districts. The Royal Commission on the National Health Service came to the conclusion that one tier too many existed in most parts of the country, and recommended that there should be only one management level below the regions in England.[21] Later that year the DHSS issued a consultative paper, entitled *Patients First*, in which it expressed agreement with the Commission's views and concluded that a further structural reorganisation was necessary to eliminate the existing areas and districts and replace them with a new set of districts that would constitute the only principal management level below the regions.[22] The legislative authority for the reorganisation was contained in the 1980 Health Services Act, which gave the secretary of state the power to 'establish authorities for districts in English regions', the authorities having the same functions in relation to their districts as the AHAs had in relation to their areas. The area health authorities formally ceased to exist on 31 March 1982.

There are 192 districts in England, each with a population of between about 100 and 800 thousand people. Many of the districts remained unchanged from the 1974 reorganisation, and several others suffered only minor boundary changes. The crucial change in the districts, however, was their elevation to authority status with the appointment of new district health authorities. Each authority normally contains sixteen members, four of whom are nominated by the local government authorities within the district's boundaries and the remainder by the regional health authority. The RHA nominees include one hospital consultant, one GP, one nurse, midwife or health visitor, and one representative of the appropriate university with a medical school in the region. The DHAs are responsible to the RHAs for the planning, development and management of the health services in their districts, within the guidelines that are set nationally and regionally.

Just as the RHA members need a team of officers and staff to enable them to carry out their functions, so at district level the DHA also requires its officers and staff. The team of officers is known as the district management team (DMT), and comprises four officers employed by the DHA (an administrator, a nursing officer, a medical officer and a treasurer) and two practising clinicians (one GP and one hospital consultant). All decisions of the team must be acceptable to each member (which means that each member effectively has the power to veto any decision), and the team as a whole is jointly accountable to the DHA for what it does. Additionally, each of the four officers is individually accountable to the authority for the specialist services for which he or she is managerially responsible. In this sense, there is a close parallel between the officers of the regional team of officers and those of the district management team. The addition of two practising doctors to the membership of the DMT is, however, a distinctive difference, and it reflects the realistic assumption that team decisions are unlikely to be implemented unless they have the consent of the doctors in the district. The GP and consultant members of the DMT are therefore to be seen as representatives of their colleagues in the district, with the implicit authority to assent to the decisions of the team on their behalf.

The structural arrangements for the planning and management of services within districts vary from one district to another. With regard to management, services are organised into units, each of which is managed by an administrator and a director of nursing services who are directly accountable to the district administrator and the district nursing officer respectively. The units, which also have a medical input in their management, have a good deal of autonomy, and may control their own administrative and nursing budgets. However, the definition of units varies from district to district: they may consist of single large hospitals, the community services of the district, services organised for particular groups of clients, individual hospitals or groups of hospitals and their surrounding community services, or any feasible combinations of these. The choice of units is not simply a matter of managerial efficiency: it also reflects fundamental ideas about the nature of an integrated health service, and about the proper balance between hospital and other services. A positive approach to a balanced pattern of care is more likely to be fostered if hospital and other services are seen as a whole system, to be planned and managed as co-ordinated units, than if they are allocated to separate units for management purposes. The units will, however, never be the vehicles for a fully integrated and co-ordinated service as long as the family practitioner services (general medical and dental, ophthalmic and pharmaceutical services) remain outside the management framework of the NHS. The 1974 reorganisation of the service failed to integrate these services with the hospital and other community services, and general medical and dental practitioners have little involvement with the new units.

It was the intention of the 1974 reorganisation that the focus of planning at the district level should be the Health Care Planning Teams (HCPTs). These teams, which may either have a permanent remit for planning for particular groups of people or may be set up to tackle ad hoc problems, bring together a variety of people (who may or may not be employed in the health service) with a professional or voluntary interest and expertise in the appropriate field. The teams were set up originally by the area health authorities, their task being to provide expert advice to the district management team about the development of services within their districts. They are essentially advisory bodies, not part of the formal management structure of the service. Teams have typically been created in the areas of care for the elderly, children, the mentally ill and handicapped, expectant mothers and the physically handicapped. Where they exist, they often make an important contribution to 'grass roots' planning. But many districts do not have a full set of active health care planning teams, or have teams that function sporadically and inefficiently, and it remains to be seen whether the creation of the new district health authorities will inject new life into the planning teams.

It was an important principle of the 1974 reorganisation that the health care professions, particularly the medical profession, should be involved in the administration of the NHS, and this principle was endorsed by the Royal Commission. Various mechanisms exist: doctors, for example, are involved as members of the regional and district health authorities and the district management teams, and a complicated network of medical advisory committees operates at all the levels in the service. Doctors in the speciality of community medicine are involved professionally in the planning, management and evaluation of health services through their appointments as regional or district medical officers, or as specialists in areas of specific responsibility. Professional advisory machinery also exists for nursing, dentistry and pharmacy, but it is less cumbersome than in the case of medicine. The operation of the advisory machinery (particularly the medical advisory machinery) has created a number of problems in addition to its sheer complexity. Doctors have found it difficult to spend sufficient time away from their clinical practice to make a worthwhile contribution to management, and where they have done so, they have sometimes found it difficult to reconcile their traditional professional obligation to providing the best possible care to individual patients with the managerial perspective of allocating and using resources in the care of whole communities. There is a risk that those who do adapt to a managerial perspective may cease to represent the particular individualistic views of their clinical colleagues.

The policy-making structure of the NHS described so far has indicated the points at which influence can be exerted by politicians, civil servants, members of health authorities, administrators, managers and members of the caring professions. The distribution of power between these groups may not be equal, but all have some point of access to the policy-making process. One group is conspicuous so far by its absence: the users of the NHS. Of course, there is a real sense in which all these other groups are acting on behalf of, and in the interests of, the users, since they are concerned with providing what they consider to be the best pattern of services with the available resources; and the ultimate beneficiaries of a good service are its users. Yet there are limits, for reasons of professional self-interest and poverty of empathy, to the capacity of professionals and managers to understand and identify themselves with the needs of ordinary patients, and tension and even conflict may erupt between providers and consumers. The 1974 reorganisation, particularly in the latter stages of its planning following the election of the Conservative government in 1970, was intended to remove this ambiguity by separating out the twin functions of management and participation.[23] The structure of the service was designed to facilitate the delegation of authority from the central department down to the districts, matched by the accountability of each tier to the one above. It was a classical structure of line management, but its failure to allow for legitimate calls for public participation posed a political problem that the secretary of state could not ignore. The problem, as Klein and Lewis have put it, 'was how to best square the circle of elitism and populism: how to reconcile the emphasis on central planning with the currently fashionable rhetoric of local participation'.[24] The answer was found in the creation of an entirely new mechanism, located outside the management structure, for enabling the opinions of consumers to be heard. The mechanism was the community health councils (CHCs).

From the outset in 1974, the CHCs were never intended to be the means by which consumers or their representatives could participate in the actual management of the NHS. They are not management bodies. They operate, rather, on the different principle that the correct role of the consumer is that of *reacting* to the decisions of management. The CHCs can therefore try to influence policy decisions within their districts and they can publicise their views about the adequacy of the services provided, but they are not part of the management structure itself. It is for this reason that the councils have been described as toothless watchdogs, and their formal powers are certainly limited. They have a right to be consulted by the district health authorities about proposed closures of hospitals, they have a right to ask for information and to visit premises controlled by the DHAs, and they have a right to send observers to DHA meetings. These rights scarcely amount to much in relation to the formal power enjoyed by, say, the medical profession, but imaginative councils have found ingenious ways of publicising important issues within their districts, of educating people about them, and of mobilising public opinion. They have enabled more people to gain access to the political forum of debate in the NHS and, through the entry that CHC members have to the health care planning teams, to participate in the planning process; and for this reason they are a valuable innovation in public life.

The dynamic aspect of the policy-making structure of the NHS lies in the planning system. There has, of course, always been a strong element of planning in the service, but until the 1974 reorganisation it was concerned largely with capital developments in the hopsital sector, and failed to look in a comprehensive way at the total pattern of services required to meet different kinds of needs within the limits of available resources. It was a fundamental aim of the 1974 reorganisation to create a structure that could accommodate a comprehensive planning system, with an emphasis on the integration of planning with the central allocation of resources and the local assessments of needs. The planning system was first described in a manual, issued by the DHSS in 1976, which discussed some of the principles as well as the mechanics of planning.

> Health care planning is concerned with the provision of a complex range of services to meet a wide variety of needs. It has also to respond to changes in health needs and treatment patterns brought about by advances in medical science. Whilst planning needs to be flexible enough to accommodate these changing patterns of need, it must also be directed towards removing the existing substantial inequalities of care and provision between regions, areas and districts. The pace of development of new medical techniques and services needs to be balanced against the absence or inadequacy of many basic well-established techniques or services in some parts of the NHS.[25]

The system described in the manual is exceedingly complex and bureaucratic in detail, but essentially simple in conception. The starting-point is the issuing by the Department of Health and Social Security of guidelines about national policies and priorities and about the likely availability of resources in the future. The guidelines are transmitted to the regional health authorities, which use them as the basis for the development of regional policies, priorities and projections about the availability of resources. The regional guidelines are in turn transmitted to the district health authorities, which decide their own policies in the light of the national and regional considerations, and prepare their plans for implementing them. The district plans are then submitted to the RHAs, where they are melded into the regional plans, and these in turn are submitted to the DHSS where they are used to review national strategies and priorities and to revise the national guidelines before the entire cycle starts again. Planning takes place at three levels: the strategic level, where plans are drawn up on a ten-year basis and reviewed every five years; the operational level, where shorter-term plans are reviewed annually; and at the level of the annual planning review meetings between the DHSS and the RHAs, and between the RHAs and the DHAs (see chapter 6).

However elegant and rational the planning system may be in principle, in practice it has not been an unqualified success.[26] The permanent secretary of the DHSS acknowledged in 1981 that 'the planning system . . . has produced more paper than effective results so far.'[27] The system has been complex to operate within the time allowed for each part of the cycle, and it has made unrealistic assumptions about the speed with which the necessary consultations could be carried out. Planning has been hampered by inconsistent resource assumptions and by delays in announcing them. Information that has been needed has not always been available, and the role of the health care planning teams in preparing the district plans has been confused. Nevertheless, the DHSS reaffirmed its belief in the discipline of planning in its consultative paper, *Patients First*, published in 1979. 'Planning provides the opportunity for the Government's policies and priorities to be reconciled with available resources, and enables health authorities to appraise systematically their own services and to influence the Government.'[28] The Department did acknowledge, however, that the current arrangements were over-complicated and bureaucratic, and simplifications were proposed in 1982.[29] But in spite of subsequent modifications to the 1974 structure, the NHS remains a rigidly hierarchical organisation with a planning system that emphasises a rational approach to choice and decision. In the next chapter we explore some of the tensions between the structure of the service and the realities of the policy-making process.

Chapter 9

The policy-making process

The previous chapter described some of the main features of the structure of the National Health Service, particularly those introduced in the major reorganisations of the service in 1974 and 1982. The reorganisations aimed to create a management structure that would enable more efficient and more rational decisions to be taken and implemented. As Brown has put it

> decisions accumulating over a quarter of a century had resulted in an imbalanced health service in which too much priority had been given to high-technology medicine while prevention and whole areas of socio-medical care had been neglected, and there was also great geographic inequality. Pressure on resources was emphasising the need for rational choice . . . so new structures and processes were introduced to encourage rationality . . . . That, in a nutshell, is what the NHS reorganisation was about.[1]

But what is a rational choice, and how rational are the policy choices that are made in the health service?

The concept of 'rationality' has been employed extensively in analysing the ways in which people take policy decisions.[2] It is often used as an ideal standard: that is, it describes the ways in which decisions *would* be taken in the best of all possible worlds, thereby forming a benchmark against which the quality of decisions in the real world can be assessed. The closer they come to the rational ideal, the better they are assumed to be. In general terms, a rational decision is regarded as one that gives the best possible pay-off between costs and benefits in any particular situation. Policy decisions should lead to courses of action that change things for the better. They should produce benefits. But they may also be costly in the sense that they may use up resources that cannot then be used for other purposes. A rational policy-maker is assumed to want the maximum benefit that he can get from a given amount of resources, and to that end he will find out as much as possible about the different options facing him in any situation of choice, the likely costs of each option, the benefits that could be expected, and the extent to which he could revise his plan of action as he went along. In short, the rational man will aim to be unaffected by prejudice, political pressure or expediency, making his decisions objectively in the light of the best available information about the likely costs and consequences of different choices.

As an illustration of the rational approach to decision-making, we will take the case of the management of advanced renal (kidney) failure. Various options may be open to the policy-maker who is responsible for providing a service to those suffering from the disease: how does he make a rational choice? Once the size of the problem is known, the first step is to identify the techniques that are available for coping with the disease. In the case of advanced renal failure there are five basic techniques: dialysis in a hospital renal unit, minimum-care dialysis in hospital, home dialysis, continuous ambulatory peritoneal dialysis, and kidney transplantation. The second step is to identify and measure the anticipated costs and benefits of each option. It is here that things start to become extremely difficult. Invariably the information that is available is flawed in some way, and the decision-maker has to allow for incomplete, and possibly inaccurate, data. For the purposes of illustrating the measurement of the costs and benefits of different techniques for coping with advanced renal failure, we will use the analysis carried out by Stange and Sumner in the United States.[3] The inherent quality of their data is less important for the present purposes than their methods of deriving and using the information.

A basic objective of Stange and Sumner's analysis was the prediction of future costs (defined as medical-care costs) and future benefits (defined as additional years of life) of cohorts of patients receiving three different forms of treatment: 'facility' (that is, hospital or clinic) dialysis, home dialysis and transplantation. Each cohort contained 1,000 patients, and the analysis covered a ten-year period. The predicted costs and survival rates were based upon the most recent available evidence in the literature, and on discussion with managers of different programmes. The data represented neither the best nor the worst experiences of treatment centres but aimed to offer a reasonable estimate of the future experience in the United States. A number of complexities were built in to the analysis, including an allowance for patients reverting to dialysis after the failure of a transplant, and an annual 7 per cent discounting of both costs and benefits to allow for the fact that costs and benefits are valued more highly in the present than in the future.

The total predicted medical-care costs and life-years saved for each cohort of patients in each type of treatment over the ten-year period are shown in Table 9.1. Two separate predictions were made for transplantation: a pessimistic prediction based upon the assumption of a low survival rate, and an optimistic prediction based upon the assumption that survival rates were likely to improve over the ten-year period. A high-cost and a low-cost prediction was also made for transplantation, depending upon whether patients requiring post-rejection dialysis would be treated in a facility or at home. The life-years saved represent the cumulative totals for the 1,000 patients in each cohort. For example, if all the patients in any one cohort survived the first year, the total saving would be 1,000 life-years after that year. If 950 patients survived the second year, the total saving at the end of that year would be 1,950 life-years, and so on. The maximum possible number of life-years saved in any cohort would be 10,000.

TABLE 9.1

Treatment method	Total costs ($m)	Total life-years saved
Facility dialysis	126	4,700
Home dialysis	83	4,900
Transplantation (pessimistic assumption)	51-9	3,907
Transplantation (optimistic assumption)	57-69	4,435

The data in table 9.1 show that dialysis (whether in a facility or at home) was predicted to save more life-years than transplantation (whether optimistic or pessimistic assumptions were made about its success). Home dialysis yielded marginally more beneficial results than facility dialysis, and it cost only two-thirds as much. Transplantation was less costly than either form of dialysis. On the pessimistic assumption of success, the cost of transplantation was less than half that of facility dialysis and only about two-thirds that of home dialysis. The optimistic assumption raised these proportions to about one-half and three-quarters.

The third step in the process of rational choice, having identified and measured the predicted costs and benefits of each option, is to select the option that yields the most favourable ratio of benefits to costs. Ideally, one out of the range of options would stand out as the 'best buy' by virtue of promising greater benefits at a lower anticipated cost than any of the others. In reality, as in this case, the world is rarely as neatly ordered as that, and personal judgments enter into the choice. From the data presented by Stange and Sumner, some conclusions might readily be drawn by the decision maker who is striving to act in a rational way, whilst others might be more problematic. For example, if it is possible to choose between facility and home dialysis, the data clearly favour the latter; home dialysis has a slightly better outcome than facility dialysis in terms of life-years saved, and is considerably cheaper. Policies to promote home dialysis among patients who are able and willing to accept this method of treatment could therefore be regarded as rational. However, the choice between dialysis and transplantation is trickier. Transplantation is cheaper, whatever assumptions are made about survival rates, but it yields a smaller predicted number of life-years saved than either type of dialysis. Much might depend upon the decision-maker's preference for the pessimistic or the optimistic assumption. If he favours the pessimistic assumption, he might conclude that the lower costs do not compensate for the reduced benefits, and might accordingly prefer a policy of home dialysis. If, on the other hand, he favours the most optimistic survival rates, he might select transplantation as the rational policy to pursue, for its predicted benefits are only about 10 per cent lower than those promised by home dialysis, whilst the cost is some 25 per cent lower.

The final step in the process of rational choice is to review the policy as it unwinds and to build into it the flexibility for change if the anticipated benefits are not being achieved or if the projected costs are being exceeded. Again, the data presented by Stange and Sumner suggest ways in which this might be done. Faced with this information, the rational decision-maker might decide that facility dialysis should not be encouraged (since it has no advantage over home dialysis); that home dialysis is preferable to transplantation if the pessimistic assumptions turn out to be correct; and that transplantation is preferable to home dialysis if the optimistic assumptions prove to be valid. His course of action in implementing this decision might then be: to discourage (by whatever means are appropriate in his particular context) the use of facility dialysis; to encourage home dialysis; to initiate an experimental programme of transplantation with an in-built evaluation of its outcome; and to be prepared to switch the emphasis from home dialysis to transplantation programmes if the experimental programme sustains the optimistic assumptions.

These elements or stages in the process of rational choice are not necessarily an account of how decisions are *actually* taken in the real world; rather, they describe the way in which it is thought a decision-maker *would* proceed *if* he was intent on making the most rational choice. Nevertheless, there is an obvious element of common sense about the rational approach to decision-making, and many people would probably accept it as a reasonable ideal to be striven for, even if its attainment is not always possible. Moreover, at an institutional level, governments and public corporations have espoused a similar goal for twenty years or more. Jenkins has observed that

> any account of government and administrative behaviour in the 1960s and 1970s, particularly one that focuses on activities in the US and Europe, must grapple with the fact that a major drive in these systems has been towards rationality and objectivity in the policy sphere.[4]

In the United States, a number of influential publications by economists in the early 1960s pointed the way towards more rational decision-making by public agencies, and in 1965 President Johnson instructed all federal agencies to introduce methods and techniques (such as Planning Programming Budgeting (PPB) and Management by Objectives (MBO)) that would enhance the rationality of their policy decisions.[5] Glennerster has described the basic elements of such an approach as:

> the clarification of objectives, without which no analysis is feasible; the costing of each alternative approach; the creation of input-output models which would show how much resources had to be expanded in order to achieve given outcomes; and the choice of some criterion with which to judge between the alternatives.[6]

In the United Kingdom, a good deal of effort has been spent in the construction of administrative systems to foster a more rational approach to policy decisions. The introduction of the public expenditure survey cycle in 1963 (see chapter 6), the attempts to co-ordinate social policy developments among different government departments in the 1970s,[7] the reorganisation of local government and the NHS in 1974, and the introduction of the NHS planning system in 1976, are all examples of the desire to create the conditions in which rationality might thrive. There was much talk in the 1970s of comprehensive health planning,[8] and the reorganisation of the NHS in 1974 has been described as 'marking a transition from "muddling through" to the alternative of "rational planning" whereby objectives are established and the best means of achieving them identified'.[9] The formulae for the allocation of capital and revenue resources introduced in 1976,[10] and the government's consultative document on priorities, published in the same year (see chapter 6),[11] were seen as the fruits of the rationalist philosophy.

Yet somehow the promise of rationality has not been fully realised. In relying rather heavily upon idealistic assumptions about the world, it tends to ignore the fact that, as Jenkins has put it, 'in the real world ritual and traditions may be important, nepotism practicable and corruption rife'.[12] The limited impact of rationality has been noted in a number of studies of policy-making in the NHS. In his history of the Leeds Regional Hospital Board, Ham has observed with respect to the development of policies for acute hospital admissions, that

> the policy-making strategy used did not encourage a comprehensive and detailed analysis of the . . . problem. Instead, a strategy of . . . incrementalism was pursued, with small changes to the existing pattern of services occurring – not always in the same direction.[13]

Hunter has concluded from his study of the allocation of development funds in two Scottish health boards that

> there were obvious political reasons, in the form of vested interests and differing value-systems, to account for the development funds being allocated in ways that were non-rational if judged by the criteria adopted to denote a rational process of decision-making . . . While in theory other policy options might have been usefully explored, in practice administrators . . . were predominantly concerned with short-term considerations. The solutions they reached, and the allocation strategies adopted by them in response to particular pressures, reflected this 'crisis management' approach to allocation decisions.[14]

Commenting on the complexity and untidiness of such real-life contexts of choice, Haywood and Alaszewski have remarked that 'the rational-man explanation for behaviour is unlikely to be convincing. The decisions are likely to reflect the bargains struck, or understandings between groups, and do the minimum violence to the status quo'.[15] Kogan and his colleagues, in their study of the working of the National Health Service for the Royal Commission, found that a rational approach to strategic planning was much more evident at regional than at area and district levels, where it was seen as less relevant and more subject to local demands and pressures.[16] And Butts and his colleagues reached a similar conclusion from their analysis of the planning system in the NHS, observing that, in the early years of the system, 'the rational approach was more prominent in the DHSS and at regional level, whereas the district level was more concerned with the political problems of effecting change'.[17]

Why, then, is there apparently such a gulf between the ideal and the reality? The simple answer, implicit in the brief quotations above, is that many decisions, particularly those that involve the commitment of resources, are not taken in an ideal world of enlightened motivations, shared values and the ready access to relevant information. Rather, they are taken in the real world where information is limited, uncertainty abounds, time is in short supply, values conflict, and people are often struggling to maintain their own best interests. The context of decision-making is one of political awareness and conflict, in which people are often more concerned to avoid mistakes than to create possibilitics. As Hunter has put it, 'decision-making is a political activity in the sense that it involves an act of choice, the outcome of which will be to the advantage of some and to the disadvantage of others.'[18] It is scarcely surprising, then, that the actual processes of decision-making are not always consistent with the rational ideal.

These themes can be illustrated by returning to the basic steps in the process of rational choice and identifying some of the probable points of conflict and difficulty. The first step, it is suggested, is the setting out of alternative ways of achieving a particular goal or objective. In the example discussed earlier in this chapter of the management of advanced renal failure, the goal might be described as that of saving the greatest number of life-years for a given outlay of resources. In fact there are profound difficulties even in deciding the volume of resources to be made available for this purpose, for it requires judgments to be made about the value of providing treatment to this particular group of patients in relation to the value to be derived from other ways of using the resources. In 1982 two doctors in Birmingham complained that, because they had overspent their budget for the treatment of patients with renal failure, the Central Birmingham Health Authority had forbidden them to accept further patients into their programme of continuous ambulatory peritoneal dialysis.[19] In reply, a spokesman for the Authority was reported simply as pointing out that there were many other claims on the available set of resources, such as the care of the new-born, the mentally handicapped and the elderly.[20] There is no straightforwardly rational way of making agonising decisions of this kind.

But leaving aside for the moment the profoundly difficult matter of choosing the basic structure of goals to be pursued (though we shall return to it in chapter 11), the different ways of achieving those goals may also be unclear. As it happens, the currently available options for extending the lives of patients with advanced renal failure are clear-cut, but the possible routes to other goals may be more obscure. It was seen in chapter 3, for example, that the infant mortality rate in England and Wales is higher than in many countries at a similar stage of economic development, and the Chief Medical Officer of Health for England and Wales drew the conclusion in his 1977 annual report that 'the clear implication is that infant mortality rates are capable of reduction to single figures'.[21] But how? If this becomes an explicit policy goal, is it to be achieved by increasing the maternity allowance, by providing better obstetric facilities in hospitals, by improving community nursing services, or by more effective educational and support services among single-parent families?

The second step in the process of rational choice is to identify and measure the anticipated costs and benefits of each option. Here the difficulties positively bristle, even in the relatively straightforward case of the different treatment options for advanced renal failure. There are problems surrounding the accuracy of available information. In many situations of choice, adequate information about the anticipated costs and benefits of different courses of action may be lacking and difficult to obtain with the resources of time and money that are available. The rational approach is itself costly, and can be justified only if the benefits outweigh the costs. There are also serious problems surrounding the definition of costs and benefits. On the cost side, is the analysis to be limited (as in the exercise by Stange and Sumner) to the direct costs of treatment, or is it to include other real costs, such as those incurred by the patients and their families as a result of undergoing treatment, and those falling on other services? Had the total costs been taken into account by Stange and Sumner, it is possible that the apparent advantage of home over facility dialysis would have been diminished. On the benefit side, Stange and Sumner limited their analysis to survival, but had they been able to take account also of the *quality* of the lives saved under each treatment method, the implications for choice might have been different. It is possible, for example, that transplantation might become a more attractive option than dialysis, since the quality of the lives of transplant patients might well be regarded as better than that of patients on dialysis. These are, however, deeply contentious issues: there is no objective, value-free way of measuring the quality of life, and the collection of more complete data would be a costly and time-consuming business.

The next step in the process of rational choice requires the optimum choice to be translated into action. One difficulty here is that, if the optimum choice departs significantly from existing ways of doing things, barriers to action will probably arise. Once particular patterns of services are established, those who provide them are committed to maintaining them, and a momentum rapidly develops in which they come to be seen as indispensable. It is rarely possible to wipe the slate clean and start again from scratch, particularly if such a course of action is likely to question the established practices of the doctors. As the University of Warwick team observed in their research report for the Royal Commission, 'clinicians are a highly intelligent and articulate group .... Indeed, they may be so formidable as to dominate decisions about resource use, sometimes using the doctrine of clinical autonomy'.[22] Moreover, the way in which resources have been invested in the past may restrict the scope for change in the short- to medium-term future, even if those who would be affected by such change are agreeable to it. Klein, reflecting on his experience as a member of an area health authority, has put it like this:

> [I]n practice, most decisions about 'policy, planning and resource allocation' have been pre-empted by the past. At any one point in time the scope for taking strategic decisions is constrained . . . . Most developments flow from decisions about the capital investment programme: so, inevitably, given the long lead time, authority members are the prisoners of past planning policies now embodied in concrete.[23]

Other general difficulties may also be noted. The rational approach, particularly in complex areas of choice, makes heroic assumptions about the abilities and motivations of policy-makers. It assumes that they are capable of gathering, analysing and interpreting the large amount of information that may be involved in assessing the costs and benefits of alternative courses of action, and it also assumes that they actually want to do so. Such assumptions are open to question. Cost-benefit exercises in the health field are invariably complex and taxing, often having implications beyond the health services system itself, and there is no reason to suppose that policy-makers will wish to make life unnecessarily difficult for themselves. Higgins has argued that policy-makers tend to operate within restricted time-scales, and they may find that the extra time required to assemble and assimilate a mass of data is too restrictive.[24] Ministers and senior civil servants are often over-supplied with information, and do not feel they require yet more to help them reach decisions. They have to respond quickly in situations of uncertainty, and are more likely to choose the politically feasible option than the technically correct one.

The observation about the political basis of choice is important. Any decision, however rational it may be in an objective sense, is likely to threaten someone's interests, and if those whose interests are threatened possess the political power to resist change or to block new policies, then rationality is suffocated. One of the criticisms of the rational perspective is that it tends to assume an apolitical world in which sectional interests do not exist and people act in enlightened ways in the pursuit of optimum solutions. But the real world is a political place in which people *do* have vested interests to preserve, and are sometimes more willing to use their power in defence of those interests than in securing the most rational disposition of resources. It is a world in which the rational model of policy-making is of limited value in explaining what *actually* happens, laudable though it may be as an exemplar of what *ought* to happen.

An alternative model of the way in which policy-making actually proceeds has been propounded by Lindblom in his celebrated essay *The science of muddling through*.[25] Central to Lindblom's argument is a different (and, he would argue, more realistic) account of the world and its inhabitants than is implied in the rational perspective. According to this view, policy-making in a democratic society is rarely a specific activity that is the sole prerogative of a few individuals or agencies; rather, it is the outcome of a process of bargaining and adjustment that continually takes place among people, groups, organisations and agencies, with different degrees of power, trying to extend their own interests whilst remaining sensitive to the needs and interests of others. In such a society, with power widely (though not necessarily fairly) distributed, a higher value tends to be placed on policies that command widespread agreement than upon those that are, in some rational sense, 'good' policies. Moreover, according to Lindblom's view of the world, policy-makers are rarely the dispassionate and calculating people who inhabit the rational model, coolly identifying options, calculating costs and benefits, and making disinterested judgments about the balance between them. Instead, they are more likely to be ordinary warm-blooded human beings, with assorted strengths and weaknesses, prejudices and ideals, trying to do the best they can in a messy and uncertain environment without driving themselves to an early grave through overwork or nervous exhaustion.

Out of this different account of the world there emerges a different view of the goals and activities of policy-makers. For example, they are usually hesitant to spell out their objectives (an essential ingredient of the rational approach), partly because the more clearly objectives are specified the more likely they will be to arouse the opposition of those who are adversely affected by them, and partly because the specification of objectives sets up hostages to fortune by providing benchmarks against which future performance can be evaluated. Policy-makers also, according to this view, have modest aspirations: knowing the nature of the environment in which they have to operate, they are usually more interested in getting small-scale changes to work than in constructing grand, utopian (but quite unworkable) strategies. Above all, they are concerned with rectifying perceived problems and inadequacies in the existing state of affairs: they are responsive to political pressures about things that are unsatisfactory, and they endeavour to produce the most widely acceptable solutions that will do the minimum violence to the status quo. In Lindblom's delightfully clumsy word, policy-makers are in the business of 'satisficing'. Hence this approach to policy-making is described as 'disjointed', because it deals with small discreet changes rather than comprehensive strategies, and 'incremental' because it involves continuous small adjustments rather than large and sweeping changes.

Both the rational and the incremental models of policy-making are 'ideal' in the sense that they encapsulate two different approaches to decision-making in pure forms that cannot necessarily be replicated in the real world. Even the incremental model (which, unlike the rational model, claims to describe the way in which policy-making actually proceeds) is clearly at best a caricature of what actually happens. It is because of their somewhat theoretical nature that other writers have abandoned these models in favour of more middle-of-the-road accounts. Etzioni[26] and Dror[27] are two such writers who have attempted to circumvent the least defensible features of each model by combining the best features of them. Etzioni, for example, has offered what he calls the 'mixed scanning approach', in which an initial broad sweep of policy options is made in a rational manner, but where policy-making within the selected options proceeds incrementally. Yet at least the analysis of the rational and incremental models offers some important insights into the nature of policy-making in the National Health Service, reminding us of the complex interactions of facts, analysis and politics in producing declarations of intended action.

Chapter 10

Thinking about outputs

In his book *Effectiveness and Efficiency*, Cochrane has recounted how he once asked a worker at a crematorium what he found so absorbing about his work.[1] The worker replied that he was fascinated by the way in which so much went in and so little came out. Cochrane used the story as a kind of parable about the National Health Service, inviting us to be equally fascinated by the way in which so many resources are put into the NHS and so little is produced from them. Yet as Cochrane himself acknowledged, the parable is not altogether fair. The output of a crematorium can readily be classified in various ways. It can be weighed, touched, described and analysed. The problem with the output of the NHS, by contrast, is not so much that it is so sparse as that it cannot as easily be defined and quantified. The NHS *may* not be producing as much as it should for the volume of resources it consumes, but much of the critical writing about the output of the service is really a commentary on the lack of appropriate ways of measuring it, not the paucity of output per se. How, then, can we think about the outputs of the NHS, and why is it important to do so? This chapter and the next address themselves to these questions.

The first point to note is that outputs (what we get out of the service) are not the same as inputs (what we put into it). Obvious though this point may seem, the distinction is often blurred in arguments about the NHS, and opinions are expressed about inputs that seem to assume they are the same things as outputs. It is frequently said, for example, that more money should be spent on the NHS, as though that would be an inherently desirable action. But money, and all the resources that are bought with it, are merely inputs to the health services system, and it is only worth spending more money on the NHS if it enables more or better services to be produced. The outputs are the services themselves and the impact they have on the health and well-being of those who use them; and whilst it is always to be hoped that the injection of more money will produce a commensurate increase in outputs, the link is complex and the hope cannot always be fulfilled in predictable ways. Inputs, then, are the raw materials that go into producing all the different activities of the system. They are means to ends, not ends in themselves. Outputs, on the other hand, are the whole variety of things that result from using the inputs in different ways. They are the products of the system, and to the extent that those products are beneficial and valued, they can be seen as true ends in themselves.

The recent history of medical manpower planning in the United Kingdom is an interesting example of the difficulties that can occur when inputs are regarded as though they were outputs. The time and skills of doctors are resources that have no intrinsic value in themselves. They are inputs to the system, and they become valuable only when they are used to produce outputs that society wants to have. The outputs of doctors can be thought of in at least two different ways. The ultimate or final output is the benefit that patients obtain from the care they receive. There may, of course, be many different ways of measuring these benefits, ranging from the extension of life through the alleviation of pain and functional incapacity to the prevention of future ill health. But in order to produce these benefits, doctors must usually see their patients, and must combine their own time with other resources in providing different items of diagnostic and therapeutic service. The contacts between doctors and patients and the different items of service provided can therefore be seen as a second category of outputs, but they are best thought of as intermediate outputs, for they are no more than the means towards the ultimate goal of improving the well-being of patients. There is, after all, little value in a doctor busily seeing lots of patients and prescribing many treatments if, at the end of the day, the patients are no better off in any way at all.

Because doctors themselves are resources, and are valuable only when they produce intermediate or final outputs that are valued, decisions about the number of doctors the nation needs, and the specialities and localities in which they should be working, cannot be taken satisfactorily without reference to the things they do. Doctors are expensive resources, both to train and employ, and whether it is worth the nation's while to increase their number should depend upon whether the extra output produced by more doctors is worth the additional cost involved. That is obviously not an easy judgment to make, but it is the right way to think about national manpower requirements.[2] There is no *inherent* justification for either increasing or decreasing the current stock of medical manpower. Yet arguments about the number of doctors required in the future have sometimes ignored the distinction between inputs and outputs, and have suggested production targets that seem to regard doctors as an end in themselves.[3] For example, the Royal Commission on Medical Education, which reported in 1968, was concerned amongst other things with the number of doctors that the medical schools should be training in the future.[4] In estimating the nation's future requirements for medical manpower, the Commission relied quite heavily on past trends in the ratio of doctors to population. It found that, between 1911 and 1961, the ratio in Great Britain had increased at a remarkably regular rate (about 1¼ per cent per year), and the Commission assumed that a simple extrapolation of this trend would provide a good indicator of future requirements. 'The needs of the future', the report said, 'will not be met by an annual growth rate of less than 1½% in the doctor-population quotient.' Some analysis was made of the expected future demand for medical care, but the Commission felt that this could not be measured at all accurately, and little attempt was made to identify the possible contributions that doctors might make in meeting it. As a result, there was no rational basis for the Commission's recommendations about the future size of the medical schools other than the opinion that the future should continue to be the same as the past. Yet as the experience from Scotland[5] and elsewhere[6] shows, more doctors do not necessarily mean better health or lower mortality rates.

How, then, can we think about the outputs of the National Health Service? First, there is a range of outputs not directly concerned with the basic functions of prevention, treatment and care, that reflect the social and economic significance of the NHS as a national institution. It is, for example, one of the largest employers of labour in the country, and its policies for the recruitment and payment of staff will inevitably have wide implications. From the government's point of view, the NHS has sometimes been seen as the vehicle for setting standards of pay in the public sector and for helping towards target reductions (or increases) in the number of people employed in the public sector. Similarly, at times when the current level of public expenditure is thought by the government to be too high, the NHS, by virtue simply of the large share of public expenditure that it consumes, may be used explicitly as a means of controlling expenditure. Indeed, the fact that most of the expenditure on the NHS is prebudgeted and controlled through such devices as cash limits has sometimes been seen as a considerable virtue, particularly by politicians and administrators in countries where health care expenditure is open-ended and difficult to control.[7] These wider implications of the NHS may not usually be regarded as part of the output of the service, but it is not unreasonable to do so. The NHS has also been seen as a means of reducing some of the inequalities in society. By creating a service that is funded largely out of government revenues and that provides care on the basis of need rather than ability to pay, the NHS has always had an air of social justice about it, aiming not only to treat disease and maintain health, but also to narrow the gap between the health experiences of different social classes. In fact the evidence suggests that although the health status of people in all social classes has, in general, improved throughout the lifetime of the NHS, wide differences still exist between social classes in the use made of services, in the private costs involved in using services, and in rates of ill health and death.[8,9] In some instances the differences have actually widened over the last 30 years. They may, of course, have been still wider if the NHS had not existed, but it remains true that the service has been unable to eliminate them.

A second way of thinking about the output of the NHS is in terms of its contribution to care in the future. Many activities are concerned more with education, training and the advancement of knowledge than they are with the care of patients. The NHS plays an important part in the training and education of those who work in the service, and it enables a good deal of research and development to take place. These outputs may not directly benefit people in the present (indeed, they may actually be seen as a nuisance by patients who are involved in teaching and research activities) but they are an important form of investment in the future, and as such they are a deferred part of 'what we get out of' the service.

A third way of thinking about the output of the NHS is in terms of the number of people with whom it deals. Data are available about the number of patients who receive in-patient care (or more accurately, the number of episodes of in-patient care), who attend out-patient clinics, who consult their general practitioners, who are immunised or screened, who are examined in school health inspections, and so on. This is one of the most visible forms of output, and there are some useful purposes to which this kind of data can be put. For example, one indicator of the effectiveness of a community screening programme might be the number of people in the target groups who actually come to be screened. But it is for many purposes a limited dimension of output, and can best be seen as an intermediate output, or a necessary step towards a more fundamental objective. In the last analysis, health services are concerned with health, and whilst people's encounters with different parts of the system are often important means to that end, there is no *necessary* connection between the two. At best, some encounters may be neutral in their effect; at worst, if something goes wrong, some may actually be harmful.

A fourth way of thinking about the outputs of the health service is in terms of the things that are actually done to or for patients. This dimension focuses not just upon the number of people who come into contact with the service but also upon the particular items of service (whether of diagnosis, treatment, education, advice, prevention, rehabilitation, and so on) that they receive during those contacts. Included here would be the number of different operations performed, the number of prescriptions written, the number of X-rays taken, the number of immunisations received, the number of teeth filled or extracted, and the like. For many purposes it is a useful dimension of output, particularly if it can incorporate information about the costs of providing each item of service, for it would then be possible to compare the relative costs of different kinds of caring activities. However, it does suffer from the same limitation as the previous dimension: some items of service may be ineffective in enhancing people's health, and some may be positively harmful. It cannot simply be assumed that more services always mean better health. It is possible to do too much as well as too little. For example, McPherson and his colleagues have highlighted the large variations in surgical operating rates both between countries and between regions in England and Wales which cannot be explained entirely in terms of variations in the incidence of disease.[10] Factors in addition to the presence of disease influence operating rates, and the more operations that are carried out the greater is the risk of unnecessary and even damaging surgery. Lichtner and Pflantz have reported a study conducted in Hanover in 1966-7 to investigate the very high death rates from appendicitis in the Federal Republic of Germany, in which it was found that the operating rate for appendicitis was very high, but that only one quarter of the cases actually involved a diseased appendix.[11] The authors concluded that 'the consequences of the high rate of appendectomy are a high mortality from appendicitis, diseases tending to develop later, and considerable additional costs for unnecessary hospitalization.' As Cooper has put it, 'the appendix was healthy but the patient was dead.'[12]

This sobering observation leads directly to a fifth way of thinking about the outputs of health services, namely in terms of the changes they produce in those who use them. There is some inconsistency in the terminology used in the literature to describe this dimension of output. Economists tend to prefer the term 'final outputs'; epidemiologists tend to favour the term 'outcomes'. But the underlying thinking is the same, and it is helpful, whatever terminology is used, to distinguish between outputs as items of service and outputs as the effects produced by the services in those who use them. Because the NHS exists *ultimately* for the benefit of the population (in terms, for example, of the prevention of disease and premature death, the easing of pain and suffering, the promotion of good health, the minimisation of disability, the restoration of normal biological functioning, the enhancement of feelings of satisfaction and wellbeing, the care of the chronically ill, and so on), measures of 'final outputs' or 'outcomes' are widely regarded as a strong basis for evaluating health services. The effectiveness of the NHS should be judged ultimately not in terms of the number of people passing through the service or even in terms of the particular items of service they receive, but rather in terms of whether they are any better as a result of their encounters with the service. Likewise, the efficiency of the NHS should ideally be conceived not in terms of the cost per 100 patients treated or even the cost of any particular type of treatment, but rather in terms of the cost per unit of improvement in health and wellbeing.

However attractive this argument might be in principle, in practice it is exceedingly difficult to derive feasible measures of outcome that can actually be used in evaluating the effectiveness and efficiency of services. First, it is sometimes difficult to identify the precise outcomes that are to be sought from specific interventions. Forms of treatment that aim to extend life, to eliminate symptoms and to reverse pathological processes suggest the kind of outcome measures that might be used in evaluating them, but it is much more difficult to identify the outcome of activities that have no such clear-cut clinical intent, like the advice and reassurance given by a general practitioner or the care provided in an old people's home. Nevertheless, it is essential to persevere with the development of these measures of outcome, for without them informed judgments about the past or plans about the future are difficult to make. And in spite of all the difficulties, progress is being made. In the seemingly unpromising area of the care of the elderly, for example, Challis has identified seven dimensions of outcome that could be used in assessing the effectiveness of care: nurturance, compensation for disability, maintenance of independence, morale, social integration, family relationships and community development.[13] Further work of this kind is of great importance.

A second difficulty in deriving usable measures of outcome is that of establishing the causal links between interventions and outcomes. The fact that a change in the health status of an individual occurs following the administration of some kind of intervention is not itself sufficient evidence that the intervention caused the change. It might have resulted from other events or circumstances that happened to coincide with the timing of the intervention, or it might simply have come about through natural healing processes. The problem of establishing causal connections has been discussed particularly in the case of general practice, where many of the conditions that are treated will eventually improve spontaneously whatever remedial measures are applied. The Royal College of General Practitioners has estimated that some two-thirds of all conditions seen in general practice are self-limiting,[14] and although the intervention of the GP may help patients to recover more quickly and with less distress than would otherwise be the case, it is, as Ginzberg pointed out, difficult to use clinical outcome measures to assess the effectiveness of treatments for self-limiting conditions or conditions where no generally recognised treatment exists.[15] Increasingly, however, scientific evaluations are being made of a number of medical care procedures, and some of the results of these studies are discussed in chapter 11.

A third difficulty in the use of outcome measures is that they are neither cheap nor easy to acquire. For national purposes it would be necessary to follow up samples of patients after their encounters with the service and collect relevant information about the chosen dimensions of outcome. Ideally the information would be analysed in a way that took account of other major factors (in addition to the treatment received) that might have affected the outcome. In view of the difficulty and cost of doing this on a regular basis, it is scarcely surprising that most of the routinely available data about the outputs of the NHS concern either the number of contacts that people have with the service or the items of service they receive. Most of what is known about health outcomes derives from ad hoc studies, and they too are often difficult to set up, costly to carry out, and limited in the conclusions they enable to be drawn.

A final way of thinking about the outputs of the health services is in terms not only of the changes they produce in those who use them, but also of the value that society places on such changes. The distinction between the outcome of care per se and the value that is placed on it is potentially important. Since there are insufficient resources to assure all the beneficial outcomes in health care that are technically possible, it is obviously helpful to know which outcomes are more important, or valued more highly than others. The choice is painfully difficult, and gives rise to deep social questions about the way it is done. Circumstances are important: even the extension of life is not always an overriding value. Jennett, for example, has had this to say about neurosurgery:

> Perhaps the most serious of all misdirections of effort is the vigorous and sometimes prolonged treatment of patients with brain damage so extensive that, although death may be deferred, the postponement brings to the family and society only misery and expense.[16]

From one perspective, such treatment is clinically successful – the lives of patients are extended. But from another perspective, as Jennett clearly emphasises, it is unsuccessful treatment, and may not have value in the eyes of society.

Our ability to think conceptually about the valuation of outcomes outstrips our ability to make consistent and sensible valuations in the real world. There are no generally agreed techniques that can be called into action to determine whether one kind of outcome is valued more highly than another. There are, however, some indications of how, in principle, such judgments might be approached.

The most obvious way of registering values is through the market (see chapter 7). Where services are bought and sold, the value that people place on the outcome of different services is reflected in the price they are willing to pay to secure them. The more that people are willing to pay for a service, the more they value the benefit they expect to get from it. There are, of course, limits to the extent to which this argument can be taken, and it is of no practical use in cases where the market has been spurned as a mechanism for the allocation of care. An alternative approach is to simulate the conditions of the market. People are given a hypothetical budget, a list of all the services that are available and the price for which they can be bought, and perhaps some indication of the chances of each service 'succeeding' in what it is trying to do. They are then invited to 'spend' their budgets on different amounts of different services, knowing that the more they 'spend' on one service the less they will have available to 'spend' on another. The packages of services that are 'bought' in this way are then indicative of the values that the participants place upon the different outcomes of each service. Participants representing different groups in society may arrive at different valuations. Charlton and his colleagues used the technique of simulated budgets in a study of the priorities that professional and lay policy-makers held among six major service categories (general and actue hospitals, mental handicap services, services for the elderly and physically handicapped, and community health services).[17] The total available budget was fixed, so that an increase in spending on one service could be made only at the expense of reductions elsewhere. The results indicated some variability among the participants in the study in the value placed on the outcome of different services: members of community health councils, for example, favoured community aspects of care to a greater extent than officers and members of health authorities.

A different approach to the problem of the valuation of outcomes is through the economic concept of 'human capital'.[18] The argument here is that death, disease and disability reduce the productive potential of people, and that the value of any particular outcome can therefore be measured in terms of the extent to which it minimises those productivity losses by maintaining people's earning capacity. The productive potential of each person is commonly indicated by the amount of money he or she is expected to earn during the remainder of his or her life; hence services that enable people to continue earning large sums of money are seen as more valuable than those that enable them to earn smaller sums. This approach has been adopted in studies of alcoholism, hypertension, smoking, spinal cord injury, cancer, strokes and road traffic accidents.[19] However, the human capital approach has its weaknesses, not only in the assumption it makes about the value of people's health being proportional to their earnings capacity (which, if carried to its logical conclusion, would withhold all medical care from those with no future earnings capacity until the remainder of the population had had all their needs met), but also in the practical problems involved in making sensible estimates of probable future earnings. It also omits from its calculation intangible factors such as pain, suffering and disability.

Recent work by economists has gone some way towards elucidating the principles underlying the valuation of outcomes. An illustration has been set out by Williams,[20] who has suggested that two important dimensions of ill health are pain and the restriction of activities. If reliable ways can be found of measuring the degree of pain that people experience and the extent to which their activities are restricted, it would be possible to construct categories of ill health reflecting these two dimensions, and to allocate people to them at any particular point in time. People's health status could then be measured both before and after their encounters with the health services, thereby yielding an index of the outcome of the service (provided, of course, that a causal link is shown or assumed to exist between the treatment received and the subsequent change in health status). If the relative undesirability of different categories of pain and disability could then be assessed, the relative value of improving the health of different groups of people would emerge. But there are difficulties. Is a person who is rated as, say, 6 out of 10 for pain and 3 out of 10 for activity restriction better or worse off than one who is rated as 3 for pain and 6 for restriction? And how do these two compare with one who is rated as 5 and 5? Williams suggested that, in fact, there would probably be a reasonable measure of agreement among doctors and nurses about the *ordering* of different categories, and that such ordering could then be used as a basis for making social judgments about the *distance* between them. By way of illustration, Williams offered the following scale of intensity of ill-health: 0 = normal; 1 = able to carry out normal activities, but with some pain and discomfort; 2 = restricted to light activities only, but with little pain or discomfort; 3 to 7 = various intermediate categories reflecting various degrees of pain and/or restriction of activity; 8 = conscious, but in great pain and activity severely restricted; 9 = unconscious; 10 = dead. Williams's comment on this scale is important.

> Since it is intended to use these numbers as weights, and not simply as rankings, it must be stressed that society's judgments concerning

> the relative importance of avoiding one state rather than another are represented by the actual numbers attached to them. Thus, state 2 is twice as bad as state 1, and state 10 is ten times as bad. This implication must not be shirked, and it must be regarded as a statement about health policy and not a technical statement about a medical condition.

The same point has been made, and extended in an important way, by Culyer.[21] 'The making of value judgements lies at the heart of medical care, and is crucial in the concept of the NHS . . . . It is a question of major importance as to who should be making these value judgements.' Yet although such judgments are implicit in any statement of the relative needs of different groups of people and in the volume of resources that are allocated to different kinds of activities, they are rarely made explicit, and they are not the agreed responsibility of any particular group in society, whether politicians, doctors, managers or whoever. Williams's argument is therefore important in identifying the steps that must be taken in principle in arriving at a consistent and explicit social valuation of outcomes, but understandably (in view of the complex and emotive nature of the issue) he has left open the question of *who* is to make the ultimate judgments, and *how* they are to be made.

One study that has attempted to grasp this particular nettle is that by Rosser and Watts, who have used the size of compensation awards made by courts of law to victims of injury and disease as a basis for assessing the value of the work done by a district general hospital in South London.[22] They argued that court awards come as close as possible to a 'social' judgement of the undesirability of different states of pain and discomfort, and that such awards therefore offer a reasonable basis for assessing the value of avoiding or eliminating them. Rosser and Watts devised a 'state of health' index, not dissimilar to that proposed by Williams, consisting of two dimensions: disability and distress. Each in-patient in the study was rated by the hospital doctors on a four-point scale of distress and an eight-point scale of disability, giving thirty-two categories in all. Patients were rated both on admission and at discharge, and the change in their state of health between the two points of time was taken as an indicator of the output of the hospital. The relative value of different changes in health status (whether, for example, an improvement from category 28 to category 16 should be regarded as the same as, or better than, an improvement from category 16 to category 4) was assessed through an examination of the compensation awards made to people whose conditions were judged to fit each of the thirty-two categories.

It is, of course, not suggested that the judgments of the courts are necessarily the most appropriate ones on which to base a general social valuation of the outcomes of health care, but the study by Rosser and Watts underlined the important principle that the process of valuation is an exercise in social and political judgment, not in medical judgment. And the auguries for the future are not altogether gloomy, in spite of all the difficulties involved in making further progress. Interest is growing in the use of epidemiological indicators to monitor the output of the NHS,[23] and Williams has opined that, building on such foundations,

> before long we may even reach a stage when some bold politician will have the nerve to put the issue to his constituents in these terms: 'if elected, my policy will be . . . to devote an extra 5% of the community's resources to improve health by one (extra) point. . . . .'[24]

The interplay of the scientific assessment of the effectiveness of services in producing their intended outputs and the further development of ways of valuing those outputs, is the key to further progress in the sensible choice of policy priorities.

Chapter 11

The importance of measuring outputs: effectiveness, efficiency and need

The previous chapter discussed a number of different ways in which we can think about the outputs of the health services, some of which are much more amenable to definition and measurement than others. It is easier to count the number of people who come into contact with the NHS than to measure their consequent changes in health, but the latter is a much more penetrating indicator of the actual achievement of the service. Yet although there is undoubtedly a long way to go in the development of techniques for measuring different dimensions of output, the importance of trying to do so is overwhelming, for without the tools of output measurement there is no firm basis for deciding what the service should be doing or judging how well it is performing. As the Treasury and Civil Service Committee has put it, 'Measures of output are inadequate. Consequently there are no systematic means of guiding and correcting the use of resources.'[1] The previous chapter hinted at the importance of measuring outputs: in this chapter we try to develop the argument under three headings – effectiveness, efficiency and need.

Effectiveness has been one of the fashionable concepts in the literature on health care during the last ten years or so. Yet it is none the less an important concept. If there is no point in doing things that are ineffective, and only a limited point in doing things that are of limited effectiveness, then the effectiveness of different activities must be understood if sensible decisions are to be made about what is and is not worth doing. The definition of effectiveness is not without difficulty, however. Cochrane (who has probably done more than anyone else to emphasise the importance of measuring effectiveness) has defined the effectiveness of a particular medical action in terms of its capacity to 'alter the natural history of a particular disease for the better.'[2] Knox has subsequently suggested that it is helpful to distinguish between medical *procedures* that are carried out at an individual level and *services* that are provided for a population.[3] He has pointed out that it is possible to have a medical procedure that produces good results being used in a way that produces poorer results. For example, rubella (German measles) vaccination is effective in the sense that it prevents the vaccinated person from catching the disease, but the rubella vaccination service has not been wholly effective in preventing the birth of babies with serious impairments (such as defects of the brain and heart and of hearing and sight) caused by the disease: between 1948 and 1977 there was an annual average of forty-seven such cases. Similarly, there is a world of difference between the development of effective drugs in the treatment of infectious disease and the creation of world-wide supply systems to ensure that they reach all those who could benefit from them. It is important, then, to be as clear as possible in distinguishing between the effectiveness of individual procedures and of community-wide services. It is also important to appreciate that statements about effectiveness (whether of procedures or of services) imply the prior existence of objectives. Whether or not a particular activity is judged to be effective will depend upon the assumptions that are held about the purpose of that activity. It is difficult to see how something can be said to be effective unless it substantially achieves what it is intended to achieve, but often in health care the intended achievements or objectives of any procedure or service are not explicitly stated in advance, and are decided only when the outcome is known.

All of this makes it difficult to talk confidently about the effectiveness of things that are done in the health services, but it does not diminish the importance of trying to do so. It also means that any discussion of effectiveness must be located in the context of outputs, for effectiveness is a measure of the relationship between objectives and achievements, and the achievements of the health services are, in a broad sense, its outputs.

A good deal has been written in recent years about the effectiveness of medical care and health services. There are several strands to the literature. One strand is the growing interest in the scientific evaluation of clinical procedures of prevention, treatment and diagnosis. An important tool in this evaluation is the randomised controlled trial (RCT), in which people are *randomly* assigned to either an experimental group (where they receive the particular procedure that is being evaluated), or to a control group (where they receive no treatment, or a placebo (inert) treatment, or an alternative treatment). After an appropriate period of time, the two groups are assessed in order to see whether the experimental group has done any better (in terms of whatever measures of outcome are considered to be appropriate) than the control group. The importance of randomly allocating people to the experimental or control group is that factors *other than* the procedure that might influence the outcome are thereby evened out between the two groups. In order to overcome the possibility that people's *belief* in the effectiveness of a procedure might affect the outcome, it is possible in some trials for the participants to be unaware of whether they are receiving the 'real' or a placebo procedure, and in some trials (particularly trials of the effectiveness of drugs) the doctor might also be unaware. Such trials are known, respectively, as 'single-blind' and 'double-blind' trials.

Although RCTs are sometimes advocated as the solution to all the ills of medical practice, they do have limitations.[4] It can be difficult to enrol sufficient numbers of patients to permit statistically valid conclusions to be drawn; they often have a low rate of enrolment; they are sometimes regarded as unethical; and the outcome measures employed may be inadequate or incomplete. Nevertheless there is a widespread agreement about the importance of continuing to set up good trials, and some striking results have already emerged. As Cochrane has put it, 'recent publications using this technique have given ample warning of how dangerous it is to assume that well-established therapies which have not been tested are always effective.'[5] The same might also be said of certain preventive procedures, particularly screening for the early signs of disease. Among the therapies which, according to Cochrane, have been shown to be less effective than was once thought, are oral therapy in the treatment of mature diabetes and the surgical treatment of some forms of cancer. In the United States, Hiatt has identified a number of procedures that have been shown to be of little value, though some of them are still performed.[6] And Taylor, after reviewing the evidence for the effectiveness of different ways of treating cancer, has concluded that

> the role of modern therapeutic medicine in coping with this disease has been vastly over-emphasised. Except for a few uncommon cancers, medical and surgical treatment produces results which are less than dramatic and in many instances frankly dismal.[7]

An RCT that is widely quoted as an illustration both of the potentiality and the difficulty of such enterprises is a comparison of home and hospital treatment for patients suffering an acute myocardial infarct (heart attack). The trial, conducted by Mather and his colleagues in the South-West of England, randomly allocated 450 patients (all of whom were men under the age of 70) to care either at home by their family doctor or in hospital in an intensive care unit.[8] The two groups of patients were followed up for a year, and their survival rates compared. When the study was first conceived, in 1965, it was generally considered that intensive care treatment in the first forty-eight hours following an acute myocardial infarct would significantly increase the chances of survival, but in fact the trial revealed no significant difference in the survival rates of the two groups, either at 28 or 330 days following the attack. Indeed, patients who had been treated at home by their family doctors did marginally better than those treated in intensive care. After twenty-eight days, 12 per cent of the former had died, compared with 14 per cent of the latter, and the proportion of deaths after 330 days was 20 per cent and 27 per cent respectively.

Mather's study illustrates the importance of measuring the effectiveness of different forms of care rather than relying on the judgments and impressions of those who provide them. The importance is enhanced if, as in this case, an expensive form of care appears to have no advantage over a cheaper form. But it is one thing to provide evidence about effectiveness and quite another thing to change the behaviour of planners or clinicians. The results of Mather's trial, taken at face value, were discomforting to those who had accepted the value of intensive care, and a joint working-party of the Royal College of Physicians and the British Cardiac Society dismissed them on the grounds of defects in the design and conduct of the trial.[9] It was pointed out that only 31 per cent of patients suffering a suspected myocardial infarct had actually entered the study (the remainder being considered unsuitable for various reasons for entry into the trial), and many patients were seen late after the onset of their symptoms.

In an attempt to overcome these criticisms, a new trial was set up in Nottingham by Hill and his colleagues.[10] Sixty general practitioners took part in the study, and of the first 349 cases of suspected myocardial infarction they encountered, 264 (76 per cent) were randomised between home and hospital care. By more than doubling the proportion of cases that entered the trial, Hill's study overcame one of the major criticisms that had been levelled against Mather's trial; and since nearly 60 per cent of the patients had called for medical help within two hours of the onset of their symptoms, the other major criticism was also avoided. Like Mather, Hill found that there was no significant difference after six weeks between the proportion of people dying in the home-care group (17 per cent) and the hospital-care group (14 per cent), and he concluded that

> for patients with *uncomplicated* suspected myocardial infarction who have suitable home circumstances and continuity of general practitioner care, hospital admission does not confer any significant benefit . . . . The results of our present study [are] probably applicable to most patients who develop chest pain in the United Kingdom. (emphasis added)

A second strand in the literature on the effectiveness of medical care and health services is pitched at a higher level of generality and attempts to assess the effectiveness of medical practice in relation to all the other influences on health and disease. In recent centuries people have increasingly been able to enhance the beneficial aspects of their environment and tame its hostilities, with positive consequences for health. But what has been the role of medicine in all of this? What has been the contribution of medical care, relative to environmental change, in improving the lot of mankind? A major attempt to answer the question has been made by McKeown in his book *The Role of Medicine*.[11] A central part of the book is taken up with an account of the decline in the death rate in England and Wales over the past 250 years. Between 1700 and the middle of the twentieth century the standardised death rate fell from approximately thirty per 1,000 of the population to about five per 1,000, and McKeown estimated that 86 per cent of the total reduction in the death rate over this period was due to the decline in infectious diseases. Dealing first with the decline in mortality from the *non*-infectious diseases, McKeown concluded that some of the credit must be given to medical measures, but most of the decline was due to contraception and the improvement in nutrition.

> Indeed [he argued], since the reduction of deaths from infanticide probably made the largest contribution to the decline, the change in reproductive behaviour which resulted in the avoidance of unwanted pregnancies may have been the most important influence on the decrease of deaths from non-infective conditions.[12]

As far as the decline in mortality from the *infectious* diseases is concerned, McKeown offered the following general conclusions about the main influences. First, nutritional improvements were the earliest influences, and, over the whole period since about 1700, the most important. Second, hygienic measures which arrested the spread of water- and food-borne diseases accounted for at least a fifth of the reduction in the death rate from the mid-1800s to the present day. Third, with the exception of smallpox vaccination (which was made compulsory in 1852), medical measures, including immunisation, had little effect on the decline in the death rate until the introduction of sulphonamides in 1935. Since then, medical measures have certainly not been the only influences, and probably not the most important ones. Fourth, the decline in the birth rate has been very significant, since it has meant that the improvements in health resulting from environmental control have not been dissipated by rising numbers of the population.

McKeown summarised the implications of his analysis in clear and simple terms.

> The appraisal of influences on health in the past suggests that we owe the improvement not to what happens when we are ill, but to

> the fact that we do not so often become ill; and we remain well not because of specific measures such as vaccination and immunisation, but because we enjoy a higher standard of nutrition and live in a healthier environment .... In the light of these conclusions the requirements for health can be stated simply. Those fortunate enough to be born free of significant congenital disease or disability will remain well if three basic needs are met; they must be adequately fed, they must be protected from a wide range of hazards in the environment, and they must not depart radically from the pattern of personal behaviour under which man evolved, for example by smoking, overeating or sedentary living.[13]

Conspicuous by its absence from this list of prerequisites of health is medical care.

McKeown's thesis has aroused a good deal of controversy, and many more words have been expended in criticism both of his logic and of his philosophy than were contained in the original book. Among the criticisms that have been levelled against him are: that he has skipped too lightly over the effectiveness of medical care in the alleviation and treatment of non-fatal conditions; that in contrasting the influence of environmental factors at a time when death rates were high with the influence of medical intervention when death rates were much lower, he is not comparing like with like; and that he has belittled the interest of clinicians in trying to understand the environmental influences in disease and to minimise their impact.[14,15]

A third, and yet more radical, strand in the literature on the effectiveness of medical care and health services is represented in arguments that medicine has not only been largely ineffective in improving the lot of mankind, it has actually been harmful to health. The name most readily associated with this perspective is Illich, who began his book *Limits to Medicine* with the uncompromising declaration that 'the medical establishment has become a major threat to health.'[16] He argued that

> the pain, dysfunction, disability and anguish resulting from technical medical intervention now rival the morbidity due to traffic and industrial accidents together, and make the impact of medicine one of the most rapidly spreading epidemics of our time.

The harmful impact of medical practice is brought about by both indirect and direct means. Indirectly, Illich raised the paradox that some of the most widespread successes of medical practice have added substantially to the total amount of ill health in the community. Why is this? One of McKeown's conclusions from his analysis of the influences on the decline in mortality in recent decades was that the introduction of sulphonamides in the 1930s, and of antibiotics in the 1940s, contributed materially to the subsequent improvement in mortality from acute infections. But a large number of those who would formerly have died from these infectious diseases, and who now are kept alive through the successes of drug therapy, have other chronic and disabling conditions that diminish their capacity to cope unaided with the rigours of modern living, and that make substantial demands upon the caring services. The lives that have been saved have been the lives not only of those who are otherwise fit and healthy, but also of those with residual long-term needs. In labelling this paradox 'the failures of success', Gruenberg has identified some of the categories that have been swollen numerically by the life-saving successes of medical care.[17] They include mongolism, senile brain disease, hypertension, schizophrenia, diabetes and spina bifida. 'The net contribution of our successes', Gruenberg concluded, 'has actually been to worsen people's health.'

Directly, Illich argued that medical practice is implicated in the manufacture of illness in a variety of ways. The phenomenon is known as iatrogenesis (from the Greek words 'iatro' and 'gennan', which may be translated as 'resulting from the activity of physicians'), and it is claimed to be the most rapidly growing form of morbidity in industrialised countries. Illich identified three forms of iatrogenesis. The first is clinical iatrogenesis. It occurs through errors in drug prescribing, unnecessary surgery, incorrect treatments, damaging side effects, cross-infections in hospitals, and the human failings of complacency, negligence and incompetence. Illich quoted American sources indicating that 7 per cent of all hospital patients suffer injuries for which they could be compensated, and one in five patients admitted to a university hospital acquires an iatrogenic disease requiring special treatment.[18] In the United Kingdom, it has been claimed that one consultation in every forty in general practice may be the result of iatrogenic disease.[19]

The second form of iatrogenesis is social in origin. It takes the form of what Illich called 'the medicalisation of life', and it arises when health care policies and the medical practices of a society regard more and more areas of human experience as constituting health problems, and therefore suitable for medical intervention. Societies are in the grip of social iatrogenesis when all experiences of pain and suffering and mourning are seen as needing relief through medication; when people expect to consult their doctor for every ache and pain, and, having done so, to receive medical treatment; when the basic human experiences of birth and death are regularly clouded by anaesthetics and analgesics; and when the expenditure of another 1 per cent of gross national product on medical care is hailed as an achievement greatly to be acclaimed.

The third form of iatrogenesis is cultural. It is a consequence of social iatrogenesis, and it describes the way in which the personal challenges and the personal opportunities for growth that are posed through experiences of pain, suffering and bereavement are transformed into impersonal and technical problems of medical management. Cultural iatrogenesis, Illich argued, impairs people's capacity to cope with, and therefore learn from, their frailties and vulnerabilities. It over-protects them and undermines their confidence in caring for themselves and their fellows.

> Medical civilisation [he wrote] is planned and organised to kill pain, to eliminate sickness, and to abolish the need for an art of suffering and of dying. This progressive flattening out of personal, virtuous performance constitutes a new goal which has never before been a guideline for social life.[20]

Illich's thesis is not new. Many of his ideas and arguments have been heard on the stage of public debate for many years. His particular contribution has been in gathering them together and setting them out in a flamboyantly provocative way. And, like McKeown, he has not been without his critics. He has been accused of exaggerating the kernel of truth in an argument, of glamourising human experiences of pain and anguish, and of ignoring the many forms of medical practice that have unarguably enhanced the quality as well as the quantity of countless lives. His solution to the problems of iatrogenesis, to wrest back control from professional hegemonies and to eliminate the controlling and depersonalising features of modern industrial society, would probably not appeal to many people, even if it were feasible. But the general thrust of his argument, that the effectiveness of modern medical practice must continuously be assessed in terms of its total impact on people's welfare, is a powerful one.

If it is true that 'effectiveness' has been among the most fashionable concepts in the recent literature on health care, 'efficiency' cannot have been far behind. It has been a central theme in the writings of economists, and, for the obvious reason that it hints at the saving of money, it has been espoused enthusiastically as a policy goal by governments of both the major political parties in the United Kingdom. Exhortations to greater efficiency in the NHS were made in the Labour government's two priorities' documents in the mid 1970s[21,22] and they were repeated in the corresponding Conservative government's document in 1981 (see chapter 6).[23] The 1982 White Paper on Public Expenditure specifically envisaged a saving of 0.5 per cent in each of the following two years as a result of greater efficiency.[24] But, like effectiveness, efficiency is a difficult concept to pin down. When invited by the Commons Select Committee on Social Services in 1980 to say how he would recognise efficiency in the NHS, the secretary of state for social services was unable to reply to the Committee's satisfaction; and in their report the members of the Committee expressed their disquiet that 'the Department [DHSS], while embracing the rhetoric of greater efficiency, does not appear to be in a position to measure its actual achievement.'[25]

The notion of efficiency has been well established in the vocabulary of engineering for over two centuries. The efficiency of a machine is the relationship between the output of energy that is theoretically possible and the output that is actually achieved. The smaller the gap, the more efficient the engine. Transferring the same way of thinking to non-mechanical systems, Hall and Winsten have suggested that the term 'productivity' might be used to denote the output (of whatever kind) that is achieved from a given unit of input, and that the term 'efficiency' might be used to compare one method of productivity with another.[26] If, for example, two different methods exist for producing the same output, one of which achieves a productivity of x units of output from each unit of input and the other of which produces 2x units of the same output from the same unit of input, the latter method of production would be regarded as twice as efficient as the former.

Far removed though this formulation might appear to be from the real world of psychiatric hospitals, child health clinics and GPs' surgeries, it is in fact very close to the approach to health services that we have adopted throughout this book. Resources, or inputs, are made available to the health service system and are used to produce a range of different kinds of outputs. Some resources are more costly than others; doctors, for example, are more costly than nurses, and the resources required to provide care to a patient in an intensive care unit are usually more costly than those involved in caring for a patient at home. If two different ways exist of producing the same benefit to the patient, one of which requires less costly inputs than the other, then that is the more efficient way of going about things. Efficiency, in this view, is not simply about cutting costs and reducing expenditure: it is about finding the least costly way of achieving the outputs that we want the health service system to produce. The fact that more than one method might exist for producing a particular output is not really surprising. At a basic level, people can be kept free of some diseases either by maintaining them in a healthy state in the first place, or by curing them of their diseases when they do contract them. Prevention and cure are not always equally effective, to be sure, but neither are they always equally costly. In the case of common diseases, prevention (if it can be achieved) may be a less costly alternative to cure, but rare diseases may be more costly to prevent than to treat in the occasional cases that do occur. More generally, however, there is often scope for producing outputs in different ways by interchanging or substituting the resources involved in the production process. This, too, is part of everyday experience. Williams and Anderson have observed that

> any alert and imaginative person . . . will be only too keenly aware of such possibilities through the professional journals or through personal contacts or experience. Those who assert that there is no way other than *their* way of doing things are either of severely limited vision or being obstructive.[27]

What may be interchanged with what in order to do things more efficiently? The skills of different workers may, in some circumstances, be interchangeable. Nurses are increasingly being used in general practice to do things that traditionally have been the exclusive preserve of the doctors, and, since nurses are usually a less costly resource than doctors, it is possible to increase the efficient production of services in general practice by delegating appropriate jobs from the doctor to the nurse. There is evidence that some practices have been able in this way to accept more patients onto the practice list,[28] and if all else remains unchanged, there is a gain in efficiency. The condition 'if all else remains unchanged' is, however, an important one. The introduction of a nurse into general practice might not enhance the efficiency of the practice if she created new work that had not been done before, or if she did not do the delegated jobs as well or as quickly as the doctor, or if the time of the doctor that was freed by delegating certain jobs to the nurse was taken as leisure time. Second, the places where care is given may be interchangeable. Things that traditionally have been done in hospital may be able to be done just as well, and at lower cost, in health centres or even at home. The randomised controlled trials by Mather and Hill of hospital versus home treatment for certain patients suffering acute myocardial infarction are illustrative of the interchangeability of the place of care; but by ignoring the cost of each form of care, these studies had little to say about the efficiency of one method of treatment in comparison to the other. Of course, the reader is tempted to assume that home care is less costly than hospital care, and that, since it is apparently just as effective as hospital care, it must be a more efficient way of ensuring the survival of patients. It is, however, important always to take account of all the costs, wherever they fall, and when this is done, common-sense assumptions about the relative costs of the care given in different places may be shown to be false. For example, in a well-conducted study in Essex of the relative costs of domiciliary and institutional care for the elderly, the average weekly cost of an elderly person living in a medium-sized residential home was lower than in a high-value private house, and only about 10 per cent higher than in a medium-value house. It was only in comparison with elderly people living in lower-value houses that residential care was markedly more costly.[29]

An interesting study illustrating both the potentiality and the difficulty of studies of the efficiency of health care provision has been reported by Piachaud and Weddell.[30] The study involved a comparison of two different ways of treating varicose veins: injection-compression sclerotherapy, which can be done on an out-patient basis, and conventional surgery, which required in-patient care. Patients accepted into the study were randomly allocated to the two forms of treatment, and they were followed up for three years to see if any differences emerged in the success of each treatment. Care was taken to ensure that the outcome measures were applied in the same way to all patients. The authors concluded that 'the clinical results show no significant difference between the two forms of treatment.' Eighty-six per cent of patients treated by surgery required no further treatment during the three-year follow-up period compared with 78 per cent of those treated by injection-compression sclerotherapy, and the proportions who were prescribed support stockings were 11 per cent and 9 per cent respectively.

Given, then, that the two different forms of treatment appeared to be equally *effective* after three years, Piachaud and Weddell turned to the question of whether one was more *efficient* than the other – that is, whether it was less costly. The authors tried to take account of all the financial costs involved, wherever they fell. Four categories of cost were included in the study: the direct costs to the NHS of each type of treatment (including wages and salaries of staff; the materials used in treatment; the heating, lighting, cleaning and maintenance of the buildings; the pathology tests ordered; and the medical records involved); the time patients spent off work; the time they spent undergoing treatment; and, for those in full-time employment, the amount of earnings lost. All the financial costs referred to the period 1967-8 when the study was carried out. The average costs per patient treated are shown in Table 11.1.

TABLE 11.1

	Surgical treatment	Injection-compression therapy
Direct costs of treatment (£)	44.22	9.77
Time off work (days)	31.3	6.4
Time undergoing treatment (hours)	100	30
Loss of earnings (£)	118	29

The results appeared to be clear-cut: for each category of cost, injection-compression sclerotherapy was less costly than surgical treatment, and given the comparable clinical outcome of each form of treatment, it could therefore be regarded as more efficient. But few things in the world of health services are perfect, and this particular story has an interesting sting in the tail. The patients in the study were subsequently followed up for a further two years (that is, five years after the initial treatment), and over 90 per cent of the patients receiving each form of treatment were reassessed.[31] This time, significant differences were noted between the two groups. Seventy-six per cent of those originally treated by surgery had required no further treatment after five years compared with only 60 per cent of those originally treated by injection-compression sclerotherapy. Patients who required further treatment were described by the authors as 'treatment failures'. The situation after five years was therefore as follows: injection-compression sclerotherapy was considerably less costly initially than surgery and, for the first three years, was just as effective. In the longer term, however, it proved to be a less effective form of treatment, and presumably (though the authors do not give the figures) it also became more costly as relatively more patients who were treated initially in this way required further treatment. It was estimated that one in nine of the patients treated initially by injection-compression sclerotherapy might have avoided the need for further treatment if the initial treatment had been surgery, but the *additional* cost to the NHS of doing this would have been £1,500 (at 1977 prices), and the *additional* cost to the community in terms of lost earnings would have been £2,480. The issue, as the authors concluded, 'must then be whether the benefit of avoiding one case needing retreatment justifies these costs'.

The study illustrates a number of points about the measurement of efficiency in health care. First, such measurement requires both costs and outputs to be considered together. Not only is it difficult to think about the efficiency of a procedure or service without having some indicators of output available, it is also difficult without some indicators of cost, for it is only through the use of such indicators that standard units of input can be described. Second, it is extraordinarily difficult to carry out studies of efficiency in health care. Even for the treatment of a relatively straightforward condition like varicose veins, an elaborate study had to be set up involving the long-term follow-up of over 200 people, the careful control of measurements, and the construction of costing categories out of a mass of information collected originally for different purposes. Third, the results of such studies do not necessarily come up with a 'best buy' solution. In this particular study, injection-compression sclerotherapy appeared to be the 'best buy' after three years since it was just as effective as surgery but less costly. After five years, however, it was shown to be somewhat less effective and its cost advantage had been eroded through the greater need of patients for further treatment. Eventually, then, a rational choice between the two forms of treatment requires a judgment to be made: is it worth spending more money initially in order to secure a better outcome later on? And *how much* more is it worth spending in order to secure *how much* better an outcome?

The third concept that requires an understanding of outputs is that of need. It is an important concept in the NHS, for it has long been a guiding principle of the service that if resources and services are in short supply, they should go first to those who are in greatest need of them. The principle was enunciated by Mr Aneurin Bevan at the outset of the NHS ('the service will be available to rich and poor alike in accordance with medical need and by no other criteria'), and it is the guiding principle underlying the current method of allocating revenue and capital resources within the service (see chapter 6). Yet although there may be widespread assent to the *principle* of allocation by need, its application requires a means of defining and measuring the concept of need – a task which, as the Resource Allocation Working Party discovered, is fraught with difficulty.[32] Some writers have even suggested that the word 'need' should be abolished from the language of the social sciences.[33] Yet it seems to be a concept that cannot be easily dismissed, and rather than do so, it may be helpful to tease out some of the implications it contains. We neither aim nor claim to present a comprehensive review of the contemporary literature on need, but merely to identify some of the assumptions that often remain unstated in the use of the concept.

The analysis can start at a simple, common-sense level. When it is said that 'this man needs a doctor,' two separate ideas are being expressed: that the man's condition is unsatisfactory in some way and should be improved, and that the intervention of a doctor is likely to secure the required improvement. If either of these ideas is missing, the concept of need becomes meaningless. It follows, then, that in describing someone as being 'in need' or as 'having a need', two judgments are being made. The first judgment is that something is unsatisfactory and should be changed for the better, and the second judgment is that whatever is needed will be effective in producing the change. The statement that 'this man needs a doctor' implicitly involves both judgments: it implies a need *for* something *in order to* achieve a change that is regarded as beneficial.

Whilst this initial analysis seems to have a common-sense ring about it, it immediately raises two difficulties. The first is that people may differ in their opinions about the desirability of change in the underlying condition. There may be widespread agreement that, say, a man who is badly injured in a road traffic accident is in an unsatisfactory condition that should be improved if at all possible, but other conditions are rather less clear-cut. In July 1979, a girl then aged 13, having been convicted of theft, was placed in the care of a local authority.[34] In November 1980 she gave birth to a son, and in August 1981, whilst still in the care of the local authority, she became pregnant again. The girl herself apparently regarded her condition as undesirable and, supported by the doctors and social workers involved in the case, she sought an abortion. Her parents, on the other hand, were opposed to an abortion on religious grounds: their perception of the situation was different. The local authority responded by making the girl a ward of court, effectively placing the decision of whether or not to abort in the hands of a high court judge. In this and in many other similar cases, the judgment about the change (if any) that should be made in the underlying condition was not universally agreed: it involved the application of moral considerations, and different people held quite different opinions on the matter. The second difficulty is that, even where the desirability of change *is* widely agreed, there may be uncertainty or controversy about the most effective way of bringing it about. Again, this is not an inevitable problem. The intervention required in the case of a man with acute appendicitis may be quite uncontroversial, but some interventions are highly controversial (for example the use of leucotomy in the treatment of mental illness, or the use of long-acting injectable contraceptives), and others may arouse doubts about their use. Such doubts may be of a technical nature, concerning for example the chances of a particular form of treatment producing the desired change in a morbid condition; or they may involve moral issues, for example when the most effective available treatment carries a high risk of serious side effects. Where such doubts exist, different judgments may be made by different people about the kind of intervention required.

The concept of need as the need for something in order to achieve a worthwhile change in the underlying condition is, therefore, not without its difficulties. Being in need is not a technical, objective state of affairs: it may involve moral, social and technical judgments and different people may consequently hold different views about the matter. But leaving these problems on one side, how does this definition assist the problem of selecting priorities on the basis of need? The answer seems to be 'not very much', for the definition that we have advanced so far potentially includes *every* condition where there is *any* prospect of improvement through medical intervention. The basic difficulty remains that there are many more such conditions than can be alleviated through the available resources for intervention. Priorities still have to be selected among different conditions of need.

We can get round the difficulty by accepting that need incorporates a qualitative dimension, and that some needs are more urgent or more pressing than others. Some needs, in other words, are *relatively* more important than others. The proposition might then be advanced that, since it is impossible to intervene in *all* conditions of need, the available resources should be used to alleviate the more urgent or serious needs. The proposition is attractive, not least because it probably accords with most people's intuitive feelings of what is fair and equitable. To take a grossly simplified example: if a doctor is confronted simultaneously with two people, one of whom has a nasty dose of 'flu and the other of whom is bleeding profusely from a wound, most people would probably agree that the doctor should turn his attention first to the wounded person. Both have a need (in the sense in which it has been defined so far), but there would probably be little argument that one has a greater need than the other, and should therefore have the first claim on the limited resource of the doctor's time.

But why? The answer may, for most people, lie in the first element in the concept of need that we discussed earlier, that of the improvement in each person's condition that might be expected to result from the doctor's intervention. Thus, the best that the doctor might be able to do for the 'flu victim is to alleviate his symptoms through the administration of drugs, whilst for the wounded person he might literally be able to remove the threat of imminent death. In other words, people may recognise the latter person as being in greater need of the doctor than the former because they would value the expected outcome of the doctor's intervention more highly in the latter than in the former case. If this is correct, then it follows that a judgment about relative need is a reflection of the value that is placed upon the expected outcome of intervening in different conditions of need. Although both the victim of 'flu and the profusely bleeding person are both in need of medical attention, the latter is in greater need because the possibility of preserving life is valued more highly than the possibility of alleviating the symptoms of 'flu. Relative needs are judged in terms of relative benefits.

This analysis is helpful in unscrambling some of the unspoken assumptions and hidden components of the judgments that people make about relative need, but it does not offer an objective method for making them. The twin difficulties still remain that different views may quite legitimately exist about the desirability of changing the underlying condition and about the best way of producing change. To these is added the further problem (raised in chapter 10) of assigning valuations to different outcomes. This particular problem was minimised in the illustration used above, for the contrast between the two potential outcomes (preserving life and alleviating 'flu symptoms) was sufficiently stark to permit few doubts about their relative value. Many outcomes, however, are much less amenable to the assignation of relative values. What value is put upon an improvement in the condition of long-stay psychiatric patients compared to the value of providing prompt surgery for minor conditions, domiciliary dental care for household people or regular cervical cytology for all women over the age of 20? Such valuations are required if systematic judgments are to be made about the relative needs of different groups of people, but the process of assigning such values is plainly a subjective one, and will result in a variety of judgments. There is not yet a nationally approved formula that rates, say, an improvement in the happiness and self-respect of long-stay psychiatric patients as worth x units of social benefit and the extension of life of a person with advanced renal failure as worth y units.

Casual observation of the working of health services does suggest that a rough-and-ready hierarchy of valuations exists among those who control the use of resources. Conditions of need which threaten life tend to be given top priority, followed by those which threaten functional capacity and then those which merely cause discomfort. But this is not an unvarying hierarchy of valuations – or at least it is not systematically reflected in the priorities that are followed in the NHS. Each year in the UK between one and two thousand people are dying from advanced renal failure whose lives might have been prolonged,[35] whilst some £25m is spent through the NHS on sedatives, tranquillisers and minor analgesics. Moreover, different valuations are placed upon the extension of different lives in different circumstances. Few people probably have their lives extended to the maximum length that medical intervention could make possible, suggesting an implicit limit to the amount of money that it is thought worth spending on life-extending activities. In some cases the implicit limit is quite low. Gould, for example, has calculated that the decision by the minister of health in 1971 not to proceed with the child-proofing of drug containers on grounds of cost implied the value of a child's life as less than £1,000 in that year.[36] In other cases the implicit value is much higher: the net cost of a heart transplant, where a 50 per cent survival after two years is regarded as a good outcome, was estimated in 1980 at between £20,000 and £30,000.[37]

There are complicated reasons underlying these apparent inconsistencies. Policy-makers and clinicians have not usually been accustomed to weighing the value of life or the freedom from major pain and disability in cold economic terms, even though such valuations are implicit in any decision about the disposition of resources. Moreover, established ways of doing things cannot easily be changed, even in the light of persuasive evidence of their inappropriateness. Even if it is agreed that the provision of renal dialysis facilities is more important than the availability of tranquillisers and minor analgesics, it is difficult to envisage a mandatory prohibition on the prescribing of such drugs until all those with advanced renal failure who are suitable for dialysis treatment have gained access to it. At best, the systematic approach to the judgment of relative need is confined to the margins of change: is it worth doing a little more or a little less of *this* particular activity at the expense of a little less or the gain of a little more in *that* particular activity? It is rarely possible, once something has become an accepted activity, to contemplate abolishing it entirely.

Because of the absence of standard, commonly agreed ground rules for translating the benefits of different kinds of outcome into a common currency, judgments about relative need can never be entirely objective and incontestable. They are bound to involve subjective choices, reflecting values and opinions that in the last resort cannot be defended in a totally rational or objective way. Obvious though such a conclusion may be, it is to some extent in conflict with the rational, managerial approach to decision-making that has been a major hallmark of the NHS since 1974 (see chapter 8). There is a tendency to regard planning as a purely technical activity involving the collection of data and the application of such techniques as cost-benefit and cost-effectiveness analyses. There is undoubtedly an important role for the technicians to play in the planning process, but at certain points of choice the application of technology must yield to the exercise of values, judgments and opinions. The assessment of need, and particularly relative need, is never an exclusively technical activity, and cannot therefore be the exclusive property of the technicians.

The argument pursued in this chapter, that judgments about relative need are basically judgments about the value that is placed upon beneficial changes in the underlying conditions, needs one further gloss.

Even if it were possible, using the framework outlined above, to judge the relative needs of different groups of people by forecasting the changes that would result from particular forms of intervention and by placing values upon those changes, sensible decisions about the allocation of care would have to take account also of the costs of producing those changes. Most things that are wanted in life (including the benefits of medical care) carry a cost, and things which may be valued highly for themselves may rank lower in one's order of preference when the cost of obtaining them has to be met. In principle, therefore, the process of selecting priorities in relation to need involves judgments not just about the anticipated benefits of intervening in different conditions of need, but also about the expected costs of doing so. It is the ratio of costs to benefits that is the critical criterion in the formulation of judgments about relative need.[38]

The importance of measuring outputs

Readers who have persevered thus far may be forgiven for experiencing a sense of *déjà vu*, for we have indeed been here before, albeit by somewhat different routes. It was argued in chapter 9 that, when faced with competing claims on resources, the rational decision-maker will try to select the course of action that gives him the best return for his expenditure. A rational choice is one that maximises the ratio of benefits to costs. And it was argued earlier in this chapter that efficiency can be defined in a similar way: efficiency is about finding the least costly way of achieving the outputs that we want the health service system to produce. The unifying focus is that of priorities. Where resources are insufficient to provide all the services that people wish to have, some services will inevitably have priority over others. These priorities might simply emerge in an unplanned and uncontrolled way out of the maze of routes through which resources are allocated, spent and used in the health service, or they may consciously be selected according to a set of agreed principles. In our view, the conscious selection of priorities is preferable to their unplanned emergence, and the principles upon which the selection should be based are the complementary principles of need, rationality and efficiency. They are principles that require us to grapple with the measurement of outputs and their costs.

Chapter 12

The evaluation of health care

A distinctive feature of health care in recent years, not only in the United Kingdom but throughout the western world, has been the growing emphasis on its evaluation. An important influence has been the pressure of economic trends and circumstances. The growth in health service resources in most western countries has failed to keep up with the expanding expectations of their people and the accelerating technical possibilities of medical care, and increasingly insistent questions are being asked about the value that is obtained for the money spent. The conventional wisdom of the 1960s that, since health is priceless, the more that is spent on health services the better, is no longer accepted uncritically. A second reason for the growing interest in evaluation has been the dramatic advance in medical and surgical technology, and the consequent need to assure patients that proper standards and safeguards are being observed. In the face of steadily increasing numbers of legal claims against health authorities and doctors for allegedly inadequate care, the need for 'quality assurance' is strong. A third reason has been the general trend towards more open government, towards the 'demystification' of professional activities, and towards a greater measure of accountability by those employed in public services. The trend has found expression in the NHS in the increasing use of auditing techniques to monitor the activities both of service managers and of professional carers. The term 'audit' is more familiar in the world of finance than of medicine, but the principles are the same. A treasurer's records are audited by someone with the authority to do so, and the treasurer may be called to account for his stewardship if there is a suspicion of incompetence or impropriety. Similarly, a doctor's records may be audited, but, in contrast to a financial audit, the authority of the auditor is often more obscure, the basis for judging incompetence or impropriety is less clear, and the accountability of the doctor is less well defined.

At the same time, the resistance to evaluation is strong. Patients may be suspicious of evaluation by virtue of what Cochrane has called 'the layman's uncritical belief in the ability of the medical profession at least to help if not to cure.'[1] Confidence in the ability of the doctor is often a vital ingredient in a successful therapeutic relationship, and measures that might erode such confidence run the risk of being counter-productive. There is, moreover, an understandable reluctance on the part of the medical profession to have their work exposed too critically to the evaluation of others, particularly those outside the profession. It is not merely the reluctance that any worker might feel at the possibility of being found wanting in his job, it is also the belief that a good deal of medical practice (the psychiatric interview being an obvious example) is still as much an art as a science, and ill-suited to evaluation by scientific means. Indeed, it is arguable that the use of inappropriate techniques of evaluation, involving inadequate criteria or using faulty methods of measurement, is positively dangerous, creating the impression that all is well when it is not, or, just as bad, the reverse.

The basic idea of evaluation is simple, although its application to health services raises difficult questions of definition, measurement and control. The core act of evaluation is an appraisal or assessment of how good something is: literally, it is the act of judging the value of something. Evaluation therefore involves two separate components: first, the setting of objectives or standards that act as indicators of how things *should* be done; and second, the appraisal of how things actually *are* done in the light of the objectives or standards that have been set. Both components are equally important. Without the existence of objectives or standards, however implicit or unspoken they may be, there can be no evaluation, merely description. And without any indicators of performance there is nothing to be evaluated. Standards and performance are two sides of the same coin of evaluation.

Simple though the essence of evaluation may be, it has proved difficult to apply. Several questions arise from the basic formulation set out above. What aspects of health care are to be evaluated? Is it the structural and financial features of the health services, the actual activities of care that are carried on within them or the results produced from them? And who is to set the standards? In order to command the respect of those whose performance is subsequently to be judged in the light of them, standards must presumably be set by those with both knowledge and authority. But who actually possesses such virtues? Is it the politicians, the members of health authorities, the managers of the service, the leaders of the caring professions, the representatives of the general public, or who? And what happens when, as a result of an evaluation, things are found to be unsatisfactory? Can anything actually be done to rectify whatever has been found wanting and to prevent similar lapses from happening in the future, or is evaluation merely a symbolic activity, lacking the power to effect change? In this chapter we concentrate particularly on the first of these questions: what is to be evaluated? In the following chapter we address the other two questions: who does it?, and what can be done when things are found to be unsatisfactory? It will soon be realised, however, that the three questions are interlinked and the division and ordering of material is to a considerable extent arbitrary.

A useful framework for classifying evaluative activities in health care has been developed in the United States by Donabedian, whose writings over many years have tried to develop and refine the definition and measurement of quality in health care. Donabedian has defined the essence of quality as 'the maximisation of patient welfare, after one has taken account of the expected gains and losses that attend the process of care in all its parts',[2] and he has suggested that health care can be broken down into a number of component parts, each of which can be evaluated in terms of the contribution it makes towards the maximisation of people's wellbeing.

The first component part has been termed by Donabedian 'the structure of care', and it corresponds closely with what, in the language of the health services system, we have called resource inputs.

> The evaluation of structure [he wrote] is concerned with such things as the adequacy of facilities and equipment; the number of qualifications of medical staff and their organisation; the administrative structure of institutions providing care; financial organisation; and the like.[3]

Statements about desirable standards in the structure of care can readily be found in the NHS, emanating from professional groups, patients' organisations, and health authorities. Central government has issued countless guidelines or norms about the number of staff, beds, day places and so on that ought to be provided, and that can then be used to evaluate the actual level of provision. Norms of provision have also been set out by professional groups (for example for occupational therapy[4] and for clinical neurophysiology[5]) and by numerous committees and working parties. In 1982 the DHSS produced a set of 'core standards' for staffing and equipment in maternity and neonatal units in the hope of reducing the incidence of perinatal mortality (that is, still births and deaths in the first week of life) and handicap in Britain.[6]

The promulgation of standards, norms or guidelines about the structure of the service was particularly marked in the early years of the NHS, perhaps reflecting the inadequacy and maldistribution of the resources that the new service inherited in 1948. McLachlan has put it in these words: 'In the beginning of the NHS, planning for quality came to be mainly associated with the provision of plant (i.e. buildings, equipment, etc.) and manpower provision, following comparisons with what was available elsewhere.'[7] An example of this approach to evaluation was the ministry of health's 1962 Hospital Plan for England and Wales, which specified the target number of hospital beds per 1,000 population in each of the main specialities that the hospital regions ought to achieve by 1975.[8] The targets were somewhat lower than the existing levels of provision. For acute beds, for example, the standard or target national ratio was 3.3 per 1,000 population (compared with the existing provision of 3.9); for geriatric beds it was 1.4 (1.5); and for mental illness beds 1.8 (3.3). In the following year, 1963, a complementary plan for community care was published which set out similar targets for local authority services.[9] But the precision of the figures implied a degree of authoritative judgment about their quality that could not be justified. Although the ministry attempted to do so, it had to concede the lack hitherto of 'any generally accepted criteria for assessing the number of hospital beds of various kinds which are needed by a given population', and that 'in arriving at these ratios it has not been possible to take full account of the potential development of services outside the hospital or of the scope for increased efficiency in the hospitals themselves.'[10] When the question was posed of why the target ratio for acute beds was 3.3 per 1,000 population rather than, say, 3.2 or 3.4, there was no rational answer.[11]

Another example of the uses and limitations of structural standards is seen in policies for the geographical distribution of general practitioners.[12] At the outset of the NHS in 1948 there was widespread concern about the supposed maldistribution of GPs, and policies were introduced to prevent GPs from setting up practices in areas with small average list sizes and to encourage them to work in areas with large average lists. The definition of a 'large list' for this purpose was approximately 2,500: areas with average lists in excess of this figure were 'designated' as being short of doctors, and financial incentives were introduced into them to encourage GPs to practise there. Implicit in this policy was the assumption that an average list size of about 2,500 patients per doctor represented the upper limit for doctors to provide an acceptable standard of care, and that lists in excess of this figure were unacceptable. The assumption has been endorsed, with small variations, by most commissions and committees of enquiry during the last thirty years.[13] But as with the Hospital Plan's target bed ratios, it is not clear why a list of 2,500 should be seen as the appropriate standard against which to evaluate the supply of GPs, either nationally or in any particular locality. Why not 2,000 or even 3,000? What is the rational basis for the choice of 2,500? At present there does not seem to be a clear answer to this question. In this and many areas of health service provision, evaluative judgments are continuously being made about what Donabedian has called 'the adequacy of staff, facilities and equipment', but the structural standards on which the judgments are based are sometimes difficult to justify.

A further important aspect of Donabedian's category of the structure of care is that of the qualifications and competence of people working in the caring professions. Well-established mechanisms exist in the United Kingdom for setting standards and evaluating this aspect of structure. They are most elaborately developed with respect to the medical profession, and have been summarised in the 1975 Merrison Report on the Regulation of the Medical Profession.[14] The Medical Act of 1886 specified that, in order to be eligible for registration, doctors must have passed qualifying examinations at a 'standard of proficiency . . . sufficient to guarantee the possession of the knowledge and skill requisite for the efficient practice of medicine, surgery and midwifery'. Responsibility for controlling entry to the register was vested by the Medical Act of 1858 in the General Medical Council (GMC), a statutory body that is independent of the universities and the medical corporations, and responsible through the Privy Council to the Crown. The Council exercises its control over the standard of the basic (undergraduate) education of doctors in various ways: it can refuse to recognise the educational qualification of any institution; it can supervise the examinations held by these institutions; and it can make recommendations about the scope and content of the undergraduate curriculum. At the postgraduate (specialist) level the mechanisms for evaluating the qualifications and competence of doctors are less precise. The Merrison Committee likened the state of specialist medical education in the 1970s to the state of undergraduate medical education prior to 1858, and it concluded that 'insofar as any overall control of the standards of specialist education exists, it is by the NHS, through its appointments procedure for hospital specialists.'[15] Following the Merrison Report, the 1978 Medical Act was passed to promote high standards of postgraduate education; and the Education Committee of the General Medical Council, in conjunction with the Royal Colleges, the universities and the Joint Committees on Higher Training (that provide accreditation in particular specialities) began to introduce a more co-ordinated approach to the maintenance of standards of specialist education.

Statutory mechanisms also exist for controlling the educational standards and evaluating the proficiency of people entering other health caring professions. In 1919 the Nurses Act established the General Nursing Council (GNC), which until 1982 had similar functions to those carried out by the GMC in the medical field: maintaining a register of qualified nurses, overseeing the content and form of nurse training, approving nurse training schools and determining the qualifications of nurse tutors. The Central Midwives Board (CMB) had separate responsibility for the education and training of midwives, and the Council for the Training of Health Visitors (CTHV) likewise had statutory control over the training courses for these workers. In 1980, following the passage of the Nurses, Midwives and Health Visitors Act in the previous year, the GNC, the CMB, the CTHV and their counterparts in Scotland and Northern Ireland were abolished and their statutory responsibilities were combined in a new body, the United Kingdom Central Council (UKCC). The professions supplementary to medicine also have their own controlling bodies. In 1960 the Professions Supplementary to Medicine Act established the Council for Professions Supplementary to Medicine and set up seven (now eight) boards covering the main professions involved (chiropodists, dieticians, medical laboratory technicians, occupational therapists, physiotherapists, radiographers, remedial gymnasts and orthoptists). The boards are legally responsible for the maintenance of registers, for specifying the qualifications required for state registration, and for approving training institutions and syllabuses.

The evaluation of entrants to the caring professions is, then, firmly established and represents an important aspect of the assessment and control of quality. The setting of standards and the evaluation of those who are *already* in practice and well-established in their professional fields is a more difficult and delicate matter, and short of gross incompetence or serious professional misconduct, there is often little that can be done to ensure a minimum standard of competence. We touch upon this in more detail in the next chapter.

The second category in Donabedian's framework of evaluation is that of the processes of care. They consist of 'the set of activities that go on . . . between practitioners and patients', and their evaluation is based on such considerations as

> the appropriateness, completeness and redundancy of information obtained through clinical history, physical examination and diagnostic tests; justification of diagnosis and therapy; technical competence in the performance of diagnostic and therapeutic procedures; co-ordination and continuity of care, and so on.[16]

Statements about desirable standards in the processes of care emanate from various sources and are used in various ways as a basis for evaluation.

First, many standards about the processes of care emerge imperceptibly out of the day-to-day routines of practice and are communicated in different ways within the profession or occupational group. In the area of standards of clinical practice, for example, Eddy has observed that

> the overwhelming majority are produced not by a recognisable group but by hundreds of physicians acting individually. These [standards] are not made; they flow. The main stream is the literature – the reports of results, conclusions of articles, editorial comments, and letters to editors. Other tributaries range from comments at meetings and rounds to conversations in X-ray reading rooms and hospital cafeterias. Over a period of years, hundreds of comments can converge to form a policy which, if widely accepted, will become 'standard practice'.[17]

Second, there are explicit statements about 'good practices' in medical, nursing and other care, and in management and administration, emanating from professional groups, voluntary organisations and government departments. Shaw has observed that 'it should be possible to formulate general statements of good organisation that are comprehensible, acceptable and accessible to all staff,' but he concluded that in fact there are few explicit guidelines as to what constitutes good practice.[18] Codes of practice have been published by the Department of Health and Social Security in technical matters such as the control of laboratory infection[19] and ionising radiation,[20] and in certain aspects of hospital administration.[21] In clinical care, the Department has recommended a specific procedure for screening newborn babies for phenylketonuria,[22] and various professional groups have developed statements of good practice in different aspects of obstetric and neonatal care.[23,24,25] Professional and Departmental guidelines have been published for patients in different kinds of long-term hospital care,[26,27] and a study sponsored by the International Hospital Federation has gathered together and published accounts of what are regarded as good local practices in the care of the mentally ill and the promotion of good mental health in the UK and abroad.[28] In an ambitious attempt to devise ways of assessing the quality of care given by established general practitioners, the Royal College of General Practitioners has devised a detailed series of criteria defining good standards of care in general practice.[29]

An interesting example from abroad is the Professional Standards Review Organisation (PSRO) programme in the United States. The programme is interesting because it grew out of two quite separate national concerns, yet reflected many of the elements of Donabedian's concept of the quality of care. One concern was the escalating costs of medical care. The so-called 'Medicare' and 'Medicaid' legislation of the mid-1960s had enabled federal and state funds to be used to assist elderly and poor people in America to receive hospital care that they might otherwise not have had, but by the end of the decade there was growing concern about the abuse of the system by some doctors who were thought to be performing unnecessary services for inflated fees. The other concern, which initially was only secondary to that of escalating costs, was the alleged poor quality of the care that was given to patients supported from public funds. The medical profession came under pressure to justify itself, and in 1970 the American Medical Association proposed a system of peer review as a way of curbing the abuse of the system. The Association's proposals formed the basis of PSRO legislation that was passed by Congress in 1972.

The legislation created a nation-wide network of organisations, run by the doctors themselves, and charged with the responsibility of controlling both the costs and the quality of the care given to 'Medicare' and 'Medicaid' patients. Each PSRO produced profiles of the different elements in the treatment of each condition. The profiles varied in detail from one organisation to another, but they typically included the criteria justifying hospital admission for that condition, the diagnostic tests to be performed, the types of treatment to be given, the typical length of hospital stay for that condition, and so on. The profiles constituted, in effect, explicit statements of 'good practice' in the hospital care of each condition – 'good' being defined in terms of efficiency as well as effectiveness, for it is implicit in Donabedian's definition of quality that an inefficient practice cannot be regarded as a good standard of care. Once the profiles had been produced, they were used as benchmarks against which the performance of individual doctors could be assessed, with financial penalties being levied against those who could not justify significant departures from the standards. By 1980, shortly before the PSROs began to be phased out, largely for reasons of cost, more than 11 million hospital admissions were being reviewed annually.[30]

A third example of the use of standards in evaluating the processes of care is the growth of different foms of medical audit. The notion of audit has recently been imported into the language of medicine from the more familiar domain of finance, but it has the similar function of checking the performance of people against a notional standard of 'good' or 'proper' behaviour. In a well-conducted audit these standards will be stated explicitly before the audit begins, but in many reported audits they are only implicit or intuitive, reflecting the personal feelings of the auditor about the appropriate ways of doing things. Audits may be carried out by colleagues in the profession (when they are sometimes described as peer reviews) or by practitioners themselves (self-audit).

Peer reviews are an important means towards the maintenance of a good quality of care. Sometimes they are set up as formal exercises in audit. An example of a formal audit is the study by Pippard and Ellam of the use of electroconvulsive treatment (ECT) in Great Britain,[31] described by the *Lancet* as 'the most complete and thorough medical audit of a particular form of treatment that has ever been undertaken'.[32] The audit consisted of four parts: a survey of all the members of the Royal College of Psychiatrists, a detailed record of the use of ECT over a three-month period, a survey of GPs about the effects of ECT on recently treated patients, and visits to over a hundred ECT clinics. The audit showed that fewer than half the clinics met the minimum criteria set out by the Royal College of Psychiatrists.[33] In 30 per cent of clinics the standards were unsatisfactory and in 27 per cent there were serious deficiencies. Only a third of psychiatrists were thought to be doing their job in a satisfactory way. The *Lancet* commented that

> the picture painted is one of ECT being given in many clinics in a degrading and frightening way with little consideration for patients' feelings, by bored and uninterested staff, with obsolete machines operated by ignorant or uncaring psychiatrists.[34]

In contrast to a formal audit of the kind conducted by Pippard and Ellam, most peer reviews take place in informal settings and may not even be recognised for what they are – an audit by colleagues of one's processes of care. An example of informal peer review is the supervisory relationship between consultant and junior hospital doctor within the 'firm', where the consultant is evaluating the work of his juniors in the light of his own standards of good practice. Another example is the case conference, where different workers who are involved in the care of the same patient come together to review (and perhaps to try to change) the care that each is giving. Self-audit occurs when individual workers attempt to evaluate the care they are providing in the light of either explicit or intuitive standards of good practice. An example from general practice is Doney's self-audit of the control of known diabetics.[35] Doney examined the information recorded in the case notes of 119 such patients, and found that it was inadequate to enable him to provide what he regarded as a proper standard of care. For example, body weight was recorded in only 14 per cent of cases, random blood sugar levels taken in the previous year in only 63 per cent of cases, and the results of urine tests in the previous year were recorded in only 37 per cent of cases. Doney concluded, with commendable honesty, that 'the strict recording of the criteria of diabetic control and the regular follow-up of diabetic patients were poor in this practice.'

A fourth mechanism through which the processes of care may be evaluated is that of visitations and enquiries. The recent history of such activities goes back to 1965, with the publication in *The Times* of a letter alleging the use of degrading practices in long-stay hospitals. The letter invited readers who knew of similar occurrences to pool their knowledge, and in 1967 a book was published, containing a collection of distressing case histories.[36] The minister of health responded by asking the Regional Hospital Boards to investigate, but their reports claimed that most of the allegations were unfounded, and the minister subsequently told parliament that they had been authoritatively discredited. The matter did not end there, however, and in the following years further allegations of malpractice and cruelty were made in hospitals for the mentally ill and the mentally handicapped, many of which were later upheld by investigating committees.[37]

One effect of the scandals of the 1960s was the creation in 1969 of the Hospital Advisory Service (HAS), renamed in 1976 the Health Advisory Service.[38] The service operates independently of the DHSS, and its objective is to help to maintain and improve the standards of management and patient care (but excluding matters of clinical judgment) in the hospital and community health services in England and Wales. It does this in two ways: by encouraging and disseminating ideas about good practices and constructive attitudes and relationships, and by acting as a catalyst to stimulate local solutions to local problems. The HAS was limited initially in its remit to mental illness, mental handicap and geriatric services, but this was extended in 1976 to include the long-term care of children in hospitals. Teams consisting of five or six experts in different fields are assembled, and they visit the chosen hospitals and community health services either on their own initiative or by invitation. The visits usually last for several days during which meetings are held with all the different groups of people who work in, or are interested in, that particular institution. Following the visits, reports are prepared and sent to the secretary of state and the health authorities concerned. Summaries of any recommendations are forwarded to the local community health councils. Follow-up visits may be carried out to discuss progress in implementing the advice given in the initial reports, but the HAS has no power to enforce its implementation. Ultimately, therefore, the Health Advisory Service cannot itself ensure the maintenance and improvement of standards in the processes of care, but it can help to formulate and disseminate good standards, and draw attention to deviations from them.

An interesting example of the fate that can befall an HAS report is given in the report of the Committee of Enquiry at St Augustine's Hospital, near Canterbury.[39] The Committee had been set up in 1975 following allegations of cruelty and maltreatment of long-stay psychiatric patients, and in its report in the following year the Committee dwelt at some length upon the visit made to the hospital a few years earlier by the Hospital Advisory Service (as it then was). Following the visit, extensive advice was offered to the hospital by the HAS, ranging from such matters as the internal management structure of the hospital and the organisation of multidisciplinary teams to the use of surgical facilities in the hospital for non-psychiatric patients. According to the Committee of Enquiry, however, the report of the HAS team (which was circulated widely within the hospital) was 'on the whole tolerated rather than welcomed, and some parts were resented'.[40] Many of the observations and recommendations in the report were ignored or rejected, and the Committee of Enquiry concluded that, had they been fully discussed and implemented, the subsequent allegations of cruelty and maltreatment would probably not have arisen. Instead, however, the Committee found that 'the report was treated with something approaching a patronising disdain,' and it recommended that

> all future follow-up visits to Hospital Advisory Service reports should result in reports which detail the progress made on each recommendation . . . . If an HAS report comments, for example, that care in certain wards is largely custodial and that there is an absence of multidisciplinary working, the follow-up report, no matter who it is produced by, should state whether that is still the position and, if so, what is being done about it.[41]

The third category in Donabedian's framework of evaluation is the outcome of care, and it is a concept that we have already considered in some detail (see chapters 10 and 11). Outcome, in Donabedian's terms, is 'a change in a patient's current and future health status that can be attributed to antecedent care', and whilst outcomes remain 'the ultimate validators of the effectiveness and quality of care, a number of considerations limit their use'.[42] These include the difficulty of establishing a direct causal link between a patient's health status and the antecedent care he received; the complexity of measuring many outcomes; and the problem, even when poor outcomes are plainly evident, of knowing what practical steps can be taken to prevent them in the future.

In spite of these difficulties, many attempts have been made to evaluate health and medical care using outcome measures that reflect judgments about the effects that services ought to be producing. In the field of primary prevention the intended outcome is, at least in principle, readily apparent – the reduction in the incidence (and, ideally, the total elimination) of the target disease without any deleterious side-effects attributable to the intervention. In the case of immunisation, for example, the introduction of immunisation against diphtheria in 1942 and poliomyelitis in 1957 has been effective in reducing (though not totally eliminating) the incidence of these diseases in children, whilst programmes of immunisation against such diseases as measles and whooping cough have been somewhat less effective (see table 3.8). Screening for the presence of presymptomatic disease may also be an important means of secondary prevention if effective early treatment can be offered to those who are detected in screening programmes. An illustration of a study to evaluate the outcome of one particular form of screening has been reported from Scotland by MacGregor and Teper.[43] The study sought to assess the impact of a systematic approach to the screening of women for cancer of the cervix in two regions of Scotland (Grampian and Tayside), and it took the form of a comparison between these two regions and the rest of Scotland in the age-specific death rates from the disease following the widespread introduction of the screening programmes. In the period before their introduction (1968-70) the death rates per million women of all ages above 35 were higher in both Grampian (211) and in Tayside (183) than in the rest of Scotland, but by 1971-3 they were lower in these two regions than elsewhere, and the improvement had been maintained by 1974-6. The results were not quite so consistent within each of the three age groups. They were best in the middle age group (55 to 64), where both regions experienced a dramatic fall in the death rate between 1968-70 and 1974-6 at a time when it was actually rising in the rest of Scotland, whilst among the younger and the older women the gains were less apparent. Nevertheless, using age-specific death rates as outcome criteria in the evaluation of this particular form of screening, MacGregor and Teper concluded from the study that 'trends in these regions compared with those for the rest of Scotland support the benefit of cervical screening.' Similar conclusions have been reported from other studies, but in the absence of a randomised controlled trial (see chapter 11) they must be regarded with some caution. The point has now been reached, however, at which a full trial is most unlikely to be authorised because of the ethical objections to withholding from the control group a procedure that is *believed* to be effective in reducing the death rate from cancer of the cervix.

Outcome measures for services that aim to cure people of their diseases are, for reasons already discussed, often difficult to apply, but examples of the use of outcome measures to evaluate curative services are readily found in the literature. An early illustration is the study by Ferguson and MacPhail of 705 unselected men discharged after treatment in the medical wards of four acute hospitals in the west of Scotland between 1950 and 1953.[44] The men had been admitted for a variety of conditions. On leaving hospital, 83 per cent of the men were classified by the senior doctors as 'cured' or 'improved', 16 per cent as 'unchanged', and 1 per cent as 'worse'. When the men were visited in their own homes three months after leaving hospital, the proportion who were regarded as 'cured' or 'improved' had fallen to 55 per cent, whilst 20 per cent remained 'unchanged', 14 per cent were 'worse' and 10 per cent had died. Ferguson and MacPhail were careful to point out that the findings did not necessarily reflect badly upon the care given by either the hospital or the patients' family doctors, but they concluded that 'on the face of it these findings are disappointing . . . and they certainly call for study to see where improvement can be suggested.'[45]

A more recent illustration of the use of outcome measures in the evaluation of therapeutic hospital care is the data assembled by Morris of case-fatality rates in teaching and non-teaching hospitals in England and Wales, between 1967 and 1970, among people admitted with various conditions.[46] The case-fatality rate was defined here as the proportion of people admitted with each condition who died whilst still in hospital. The figures were selective for age and sex as well as condition, and they were based upon the 10 per cent sample of patients included in the Hospital In-Patient Enquiry. They showed that, for each condition, the case-fatality rates were higher among patients admitted to non-teaching than to teaching hospitals, suggesting that, if the rates for the teaching hospitals were taken as the standard, the performance of the non-teaching hospitals left something to be desired. In an attempt to find out more precisely what was left to be desired, Morris and his colleagues examined one of the conditions in more detail – hyperplasia (enlargement) of the prostate among elderly men admitted to two teaching and three non-teaching hospitals.[47] As expected, case-fatality rates were higher in the latter hospitals, but particularly in two out of the three non-teaching hospitals. On further investigation it was found that, in these two hospitals, a much lower proportion of unplanned (emergency) admissions were operated upon – a form of treatment that is now regarded as appropriate in most emergency cases of hyperplasia of the prostate. Moreover, these two hospitals also had the least resources in terms of staffing, buildings and equipment – a neat demonstration of the probable links between structure, process and outcome. Morris described the results of the study as 'disquieting' and 'challenging'. 'There could scarcely be a simpler illustration', he wrote, 'of the need for better health-intelligence systems on a population basis, for systematic information on how health services are affecting people's health.'[48]

A final illustration of the use of outcome measures in the evaluation of therapeutic procedures is the account by Reid and Evans of the effect of the introduction of new drugs on the changing mortality from non-infectious diseases in England and Wales.[49] They first pointed out that the only true test of the effectiveness of a new treatment is a controlled trial, but many treatments have, for various reasons, become established in clinical practice without any such evaluation. When this happens, trials may, for ethical reasons, be very difficult to set up, and mortality statistics may be the best available indicator of effectiveness (provided, of course, there are sufficient numbers of cases to draw statistically valid conclusions). However, changes in mortality rates over time may result from many things in addition to the introduction of new treatments. Among them, Reid and Evans drew attention to the effects of improved hygiene, nutrition and housing; refinements in diagnostic techniques; alterations in the definition of diseases or in the conventions governing the recording of the cause of death on death certificates; and the fact that the benefit of a new treatment for a chronic disease may not be reflected in the mortality statistics for some time.

Among the subjects discussed by Reid and Evans is diabetes, and the impact of insulin therapy on diabetic mortality. McKeown has pointed out that the discovery of insulin by Banting and Best in 1921 is regarded as one of the landmarks in the history of medical research, drawing attention to the comment by Dubos that 'insulin enables diabetics to live as long as other persons and to have as many children.'[50] But both McKeown and Reid and Evans concluded that the impact of insulin on diabetic mortality has been by no means clear-cut. The data presented by Reid and Evans show that, following the introduction of insulin therapy, there was an immediate and sustained decline in the death rate from diabetes among both men and women between the ages of 15 and 44. Among children there was no such immediate effect, and it was not until the 1940s that the death rate in children began to decline, probably as a result of improvements in controlling the fluid and electrolyte balances in the body. Among people over the age of 45, death rates declined in the period of the First World War (suggested by some to be due to a reduced diet), but otherwise they remained stable, or even rose in some age groups, through to the end of the 1930s. It was not until after 1940 that death rates from diabetes in men and women over 45 began to fall significantly, and since the mid-1950s the rates have remained more or less stable among women and have actually started to rise again among men. These trends do not provide unambiguous support for the simple assumption that the introduction of insulin therapy in the 1920s 'solved' the problem of early death from diabetes. Reid and Evans concluded that

> only the fall in the diabetic mortality among the young after 1923 can be confidently attributed to the introduction of insulin . . . The impact of insulin on the total problem of diabetes was slight, since there was little benefit at older ages when most diabetic deaths occur. In fact the national standardised mortality rate for diabetes rose uninterruptedly from 1919 to 1938 for women, while the male rate showed only a temporary reduction of about 8% in the six years following the introduction of insulin.[51]

The explanation of this rather paradoxical picture lies in the complexity of the syndrome known as diabetes and its increase among elderly people. The age of onset and severity of this commonest of the endocrine disorders (with a prevalence of perhaps 1 per cent of the population) varies widely. Insulin has vastly improved the outlook for the juvenile form of the disease, but the commoner variety in elderly patients may need other forms of treatment. Diabetes is chronic, and although control of the disease is common, the average expectation of life is still rather less than for non-diabetics, probably because more diabetics live long enough to die of the cardiovascular complications of the disease.

The final example of the use of outcome measures in the evaluation of health care concerns the social dimensions of outcome. Standards of achievement in health care are not defined exclusively in clinical terms of recovery and restoration of normal functioning; they also incorporate social dimensions such as the acceptability of treatment and the quality of life that people can enjoy after treatment. Standards relating to these social dimensions are often as difficult to set as those concerning clinical outcomes, but they cannot be ignored, and they may certainly form the basis of evaluative judgments. An obvious example occurs when questions arise about the quality of life that can be expected by severely handicapped people. In these cases, decisions not to prolong the lives of such people may be regarded by some as good care, although there will be others who regard the preservation of life, wherever that is possible, as an absolute imperative. An interesting illustration of this tension is found in Weatherall and White's study of the survival of children born with spina bifida and/or hydrocephalus (a congenital abnormality in which the skin fails to close properly over the malformed spine and fluid accumulates in the brain cavity).[52] Until the early 1960s, about a fifth of all live-born children with these abnormalities died within the first week of life, about two-fifths had died within the first month, and up to four-fifths within the first year. In the early 1960s, however, a new operation was developed to drain the accumulating fluid from the brain cavity (the so-called 'shunt' operation) together with the closure of the skin defect over the spine, and for several years thereafter the proportion of these children surviving the first week, month and year of life increased substantially. By 1970, for example, the proportion of children dying within the first week of life had fallen to 12 per cent, and within the first year of life to 42 per cent. A leading paediatrician commented that 'the pendulum has now swung too far: there are now many children with dreadful handicaps who a short time ago would have died.'[53] In 1971 the pendulum did indeed appear to start swinging back, with a sudden increase in the proportion of children failing to survive the early weeks and months of life. Why? Weatherall and White discussed a number of possible explanations, only to dismiss them. The reversal of the trend could not, in their view, be explained by a change in the recording of the cause of death or by an increase in the incidence of other lethal conditions in the children. The real explanation, they concluded, was a change in the treatment of the children with these conditions, and this in turn resulted from a change in attitudes about the desirability of preserving the lives of severely handicapped children.

> There was a reversal in the trend observed throughout the 1960s [they wrote], and it occurred only after both doctors and the public had aired their misgivings about the policy of keeping severely handicapped children alive at any cost. We conclude that the change in opinion has led to a change in the management of children with severe defects of the central nervous system.[54]

How that change is evaluated will depend upon the evaluator's own standards about an acceptable quality of life.

Chapter 13

Quality control in health care

The previous chapter attempted to address the question: what is to be evaluated in health care? This chapter focuses on two related questions: who is actually involved in the evaluation of health care, and what can be done when, as a result of an exercise in evaluation, things are found to be wanting?

A partial answer to the first of these two questions has already seeped through from the previous chapter. A host of different individuals and groups are constantly engaged in the business of setting standards (that is, making statements about how things *ought* to be) and of evaluating performance in the light of them. The government sets standards for evaluation whenever the DHSS issues norms or guidelines to the NHS about the structures or processes of care. Parliamentary institutions (such as the Commons Select Committee on Social Services, the Public Accounts Committee and the Comptroller and Auditor-General) make evaluative judgments about current trends and developments in the service. Regional health authorities evaluate the performance of district health authorities, and they in turn may evaluate the performance of district health management teams. Individual officers in the NHS set standards for, and evaluate the performance of, those for whom they are managerially responsible. The professions formulate collective judgments about good standards and practices, and may in certain circumstances evaluate the behaviour of individual members of the professions. Clinicians may make judgments about the quality of the work of colleagues (peer review) and of themselves (self-audit). Senior nurse managers practise job performance reviews. The Health Advisory Service evaluates the caring structures and processes in long-stay institutions. The General Medical Council has available to it the means of evaluating the quality of medical education. Community health councils make evaluative judgments about all aspects of care within their districts. So too do politicans within their constituencies.

Managers and administrators make continuous assessments, as part of their job, of the quality of the services for which they are responsible. Consumer organisations and individual patients are vocal in expressing opinions about the adequacy and shortcomings of local services. The media formulate and disseminate jugments about most aspects of health care, and so too do academics and research workers. And the list could be extended still further.

In short, the expression of opinions about standards, and the evaluation of performance in the light of them, is a continuous activity that is done by different people in different places for different purposes using different assumptions and with different degrees of influence in getting their viewpoints heard by those with the power to effect change. At worst, evaluative judgments may be misinformed, misdirected and misleading. At best, they may be made by responsible people, using good information, and exerting a strong influence over the behaviour and attitudes of individuals or groups of workers whose performance is being evaluated.

An important illustration of a good process of evaluation in the National Health Service is the Confidential Enquiry into Maternal Deaths.[1] Since 1952 most cases of maternal death in England and Wales have been investigated individually, and responsibility has been apportioned. The form of the enquiry is worth describing in some detail. A maternal death is defined as the death of a woman during, or as a consequence of, pregnancy or labour during a period of twenty-one months from conception. The causes of death are divided into those that are due directly to pregnancy or childbirth and those that are thought to be associated with pregnancy or childbirth. Participation in the enquiry is voluntary on the part of the different professions involved, but the proportion of maternal deaths investigated has risen steadily from 77 per cent in 1952-4 to 99 per cent by 1976-8.[2,3]

An enquiry originates with the notification to the district medical officer (DMO) of the occurrence of a maternal death, following which the DMO gathers as much information as he can from the woman's general practitioner, midwife and (if relevant) social worker about her social and domiciliary background. These details are entered onto a standard form, and further information is sought from the consultant obstetrician in charge of the case about the clinical details of the woman's condition, including the antenatal care she received, any operations that were performed, and the status of the hospital doctors undertaking operative and anaesthetic procedures. A post-mortem examination is carried out and these results are also entered on the form.

The form then passes to a regional assessor in obstetrics who examines the evidence and records his opinion about the causes of death and whether any avoidable factors occurred in the clinical or administrative management of the case. The assessor (who is an experienced consultant obstetrician) may seek further information from the GP, the hospital medical staff or the DMO, and, if there is a possibility that the death was associated with the administration of anaesthesia, the regional assessor in anaesthetics may also review the information. The form next passes to the Chief Medical Officer of Health for England and Wales and, following the removal of all names and addresses, it goes to the DHSS's two central assessors in obstetrics and the central assessor in anaesthetics. They in turn record their opinions about the causes of death and about the presence of any avoidable factors. An avoidable factor is one that, in the opinion of the assessors, is 'a departure from the accepted standard of satisfactory clinical and administrative care which *may have* played a part in the ensuing death'. The words 'may have' in this definition are important: the presence of an avoidable factor does not mean that death could have been prevented, merely that the risk of death might have been less but for the effect of the avoidable factor.

Every three years all the cases are discussed by the central and regional assessors, and the findings are published. The ninth triennial report, published in 1982, showed some interesting trends since the beginning of the enquiry.[4] At first sight the trend appears to be encouraging: the number of maternal deaths *directly* due to pregnancy or childbirth in which avoidable factors occurred fell from 472 in 1952-4 to 132 in 1976-8, and the number of such deaths *associated* with pregnancy and childbirth fell over the same period from fifty-three to twenty-nine. However, the decline in the number of deaths directly due to pregnancy or childbirth in which avoidable factors occurred was more than accounted for by the reduction in the *total* number of direct deaths, from 1,094 in 1952-4 to 227 in 1976-8. In other words, although there were numerically fewer direct deaths with avoidable factors in 1976-8 than there had been in 1952-4, they actually constituted a higher proportion of all such deaths, rising from 43 per cent at the beginning of the period to 58 per cent at the end. The good news from these figures, then, is that the overall maternal mortality rate has fallen appreciably (from 0.54 deaths per 1,000 total births in 1952 to 0.10 by 1978); the bad news is that among those deaths which still do occur, an increasing proportion are associated with avoidable factors.

The triennial report also showed the distribution of avoidable factors in the 1976-8 series among those who were judged responsible for them. The time of death is divided into the antenatal period, the period of labour (including any operations performed at this time), and the period following the birth of the child or an operation. The major responsibility in each of the three periods rested with the staff of the consultant obstetric unit: they were responsible for 41 per cent of all avoidable factors, this proportion being somewhat higher during labour and the postnatal period than in the antenatal period. Patients themselves were judged to be responsible for 23 per cent of all the avoidable factors, and for 36 per cent of such factors in the antenatal period. Hospital anaesthetists accounted for 15 per cent of all avoidable factors (most of these occurring during the period of labour or during an operation); GPs accounted for 13 per cent; and midwives, medical officers and administrative staff each accounted for less than 3 per cent of the factors.

In his assessment of the Confidential Enquiry into Maternal Deaths, Tomkinson has noted that the whole procedure is unique in several respects.[5] No other area of medical care has its worst possible outcome (death) analysed and probed in such detail. No other country has such an impartial and confidential enquiry into each case of maternal death. And few other forms of audit identify avoidable factors as explicitly as this enquiry, or allocate responsibility for them. Audits have been reported in which avoidable factors have been investigated in connection with, among other events, perinatal mortality[6] (that is, still births and deaths within the first week of birth) and deaths from malignant hypertension.[7] But they do not approach the extent of coverage or the depth of analysis that characterise the Confidential Enquiry into Maternal Deaths, partly because of the much greater frequency with which they occur.

Tomkinson has suggested that one reason for the success of the enquiry is the rigorous observance of confidentiality. As he has put it, 'to avoid recrimination, the opinions expressed . . . are never passed back down the line of communication from the regional and central assessors to the consultant or family doctor or midwife.'[8] The assurance of confidentiality also protects the doctor against the threat of litigation. The published triennial reports scrupulously avoid all possibility of identifying individual doctors, patients or others involved in each case. The main purpose of the enquiry is to promote the local review of obstetric care, not to identify and discipline individual errors. Sir George Godber, a former Chief Medical Officer for England and Wales, has suggested that, although there can be no certainty that the enquiry has been responsible for the large decline in the maternal mortality rate over the last twenty-five years, the general measures advocated in the published reports have probably contributed to the reduction in deaths from certain causes, particularly those resulting from errors in the administration of anaesthesia.[9]

Nevertheless, the anonymity that pervades the Confidential Enquiry into Maternal Deaths highlights the issue of personal accountability in health care. In what sense, if any, are doctors and other health care providers accountable for their actions and judgments? And to whom, if anyone, are they accountable? Before attempting to provide some answers to these questions, it is illuminating to look at the way in which doctors themselves might respond to these questions when asked to do so. Not surprisingly, relatively few such occasions are reported for public scrutiny, and the Medical Defence Union (which exists to provide advice and assistance to medical and dental practitioners in all matters to do with professional principle, practice and character as well as to promote higher standards of practice through the publication of films and booklets and through cautionary tales in its annual reports[10]) tends to discourage its members from entering into debate on particular cases, not least because of the fear that evidence might emerge which could subsequently be used in civil, criminal or professional proceedings. An interesting illustration was, however, made available to the public in the report of the Committee of Enquiry at St Augustine's Hospital, near Canterbury, which was published in 1976 (see chapter 12).[11] At one point in the enquiry, the Committee was trying to establish the degree of responsibility that the Medical Executive Committee in the hospital (that is, a committee consisting mainly of senior doctors, concerned with the organisation of medical work in the hospital and with the giving of advice to the District Management Team) felt it had towards the care of patients. In this extract from the report, Counsel for the Committee of Enquiry is questioning a former chairman of the Medical Executive Committee, Dr A.[12]

> *Counsel*: Did the Medical Executive Committee collectively, in your view, have an overall responsibility for the care of patients in the hospital?
> *Dr. A*: More individually than collectively. As far as policy decisions are concerned, collectively their major decisions influence the care of patients.
> *Counsel*: I do not understand the answer. Is it not capable of a clear answer? Did the Medical Executive Committee have an overall responsibility for the care of patients in the hospital?
> *Dr. A*: I am sorry, but I cannot answer that more clearly. The Consultant has responsibility for the care of his patients.
> *Counsel*: I am trying to find out where the buck stops. In your view, who had responsibility for the overall care of patients in the hospital?
> *Dr. A*: If you have got to accept that any body or person had overall responsibility for other consultants' work, then clearly you can say the Chairman or the Medical Secretary or the Medical Executive Committee. But I do not understand this concept.
> *Counsel*: You do not understand the concept of an overall responsibility for the care of patients in the hospital?

Dr. A: Not for clinical care, no.
Counsel: You feed in the phrase 'clinical care'. Would you define to me where clinical care ends and other care begins?
Dr. A: In the overall circumstances which contribute to the patients' well being and care, obviously the Medical Executive has a large responsibility. What I am trying to get over is that it is not responsible for an individual consultant's treatment of his patients. Perhaps I am misunderstanding or being very obtuse, in which case I am sorry.
Counsel: I am sorry if I have not been making myself clear. Suppose a visitor comes to the hospital and asks you: 'Who or what is responsible for the overall care of patients in the hospital?' Is that capable of an answer which will be meaningful to him?
Dr. A: I think it is a difficult question to answer meaningfully, quite honestly.

In this extract, Dr A appeared to be wishing to draw a distinction between decisions about general matters of hospital policy affecting patients and decisions about the clinical management of individual patients: the former was the responsibility of the Medical Executive Committee, the latter of the individual consultant. Counsel, on the other hand, did not seem to understand or accept this distinction (which perhaps is understandable in view of the fact that many of the allegations which the Committee of Enquiry was investigating were alleged to have stemmed as much from management failures as from treatment errors), and was consequently unable to identify the locus of responsibility.

The Committee of Enquiry returned to the issue later on when it questioned the consultant member of the District Management Team, Dr CT. The Committee apparently wished to find out the degree of responsibility that the consultant felt he had for decisions of the team, and the assistance he needed in discharging that responsibility. Initially he said that he did not feel the need for help in, for example, dealing with the management problems of a psychiatric hospital, even though he himself was an anaesthetist. The following dialogue then took place between Counsel and Dr CT.[13]

Counsel: You never feel a need to call for an objective view from someone with experience in the speciality you are looking at, and indeed managing?
Dr. CT: No, I don't think so.
Counsel: Some people might find it very surprising that you can manage something – I will not say about which you know nothing, because that would be a gross exaggeration – but about which your knowledge is certainly limited?

Dr. CT: Yes, but the medical practice in British hospitals is that all consultants are regarded as equals in the clinical sense, and that consultants go through a very long process of training. They have to sit higher exams set by the Royal Colleges who have no connection with the health service, who are only interested in maintaining the standards of their particular speciality, so one assumes that by the time someone has gone through this long period of training and elimination that they are competent to carry out their duty.
Counsel: Really it comes to this, does it not, Dr. CT, that it is inconceivable that a consultant will be appointed in the present system who does not, for the remainder of his working life, carry out his job to the highest imaginable standards?
Dr. CT: Yes.

Commenting on the evidence it heard about the accountability of the hospital doctors, the Committee of Enquiry had this to say.

> It has been said that the consultant is accountable to his patient for his performance, but this is no safeguard if the patient is not in a position to call his consultant to account. At St. Augustine's this is no safeguard whatsoever, and we doubt its efficacy elsewhere, for doctors must know that with the present complicated nature of much medical treatment in all spheres of medicine, many of their patients are quite unable to judge their doctor's competence, or the wisdom of his decisions. Neither will a consultant's conscience save his standards from falling. Most of the problems arise because the consultants are unaware, whether through forgetfulness or overwork or ignorance of what needs doing, and not because they deliberately turn aside from their duty.[14]

The question of responsibility and accountability in health care is, then, by no means clear-cut, and the conventional view that the doctor is accountable primarily to his patient raises difficult issues when patients try to enforce it. There are, however, a number of institutional mechanisms through which specific courses of action may be taken if the quality of care and of services is judged to be unsatisfactory.

First, as noted in the previous chapter, various statutory bodies oversee the quality of professional education and training, and they have certain powers of corrective action if things are found wanting. The General Medical Council has various powers of control over the basic undergraduate education of doctors, although as the Merrison Report on the Regulation of the Medical Profession noted, the Council is much more concerned nowadays with the promotion of excellence than with the enforcement of minimum standards.[15] The United Kingdom Central

Council possesses similar powers of control over the education of nurses. Central Councils for Postgraduate Medical Education have responsibility for monitoring standards of postgraduate education and Joint Committees on Higher Training have the power to inspect, and if necessary withdraw the recognition of, postgraduate training posts, and to award certificates of accreditation to those who have successfully completed their training.

Second, mechanisms exist for enabling the caring professions to deal with their own members whose behaviour transgresses the acceptable standards. The General Medical Council, for example, has a range of disciplinary powers that it may use against errant doctors, including the ultimate sanction of removing a doctor's name from the register of qualified medical practitioners. The more common types of offence or misconduct that have been regarded as grounds for disciplinary proceedings include disregard of personal responsibilities to patients; the abuse of alcohol and controlled drugs; the illegal termination of pregnancy; the abuse of professional position for sexual purposes; the abuse of professional confidence; offences involving dishonesty, indecency and violence; advertising; the issuing of false certificates or documents; and improper financial transactions. A doctor whose name has been removed from the register may appeal to the Judicial Committee of the Privy Council, and he may, within ten months of the erasure, apply to the General Medical Council for reinstatement. The number of disciplinary cases dealt with by the Council's staff and committees appears to be increasing. The Merrison Report found that 135 such cases occurred in 1973, but by 1982 it had risen to 770.[16] The increase occurred particularly in cases of alcohol abuse, dishonesty and advertising and canvassing.

An equally serious problem is that of the doctor who is too ill or too incapacitated to practise properly, but who has not necessarily committed an offence or been guilty of misconduct. There are no reliable statistics from which to gauge the precise size of the problem, but the Merrison Committee noted that 'from the evidence we received it is not small.'[17] The Committee documented cases of doctors suffering from various forms of mental illness, alcoholism, personality disorders, and physical disease and disability.

> There *are* very sick doctors [the Committee observed], and by no means all of them have enough insight into their condition to retire from practice before they endanger their patients. Those who do continue to practise can be completely stopped from doing so only if they commit a criminal offence or do something which constitutes serious professional misconduct. That is not a rational way of ordering matters.[18]

The Committee recommended that, as a way of dealing with the problem of sick doctors, the GMC should establish a Health Committee to hear evidence about a doctor's alleged unfitness to practice, with the power, where appropriate, to suspend registration or to make continuing registration conditional upon seeking effective treatment. The recommendation was implemented following the passage of the Medical Act in 1978.

The Merrison Committee felt the need to recommend a new role for the GMC in dealing with sick doctors because it regarded the local NHS machinery for controlling doctors' actions as insufficient to cope with the problem. That machinery does, however, constitute a third channel through which action may be taken if the quality of care or services is judged to be unsatisfactory. It is different for general practitioners and hospital doctors. In the case of general practitioners, family practitioner committees (FPCs) are required to set up service committees with the power to hear allegations or complaints about the failure of doctors to comply with the terms of their contracts. For example, a GP's contract with the FPC requires him, among other things, to give his patients any necessary or appropriate medical care of the kind usually provided by general medical practitioners, and failure to do this is a breach of contract. If the allegation is upheld the FPC may take action against the doctor by warning him, by requiring him to compensate the patient for expenses incurred as a result of the breach of contract, or by withholding part of his remuneration. In rare cases a GP's name may be removed from the FPC list by the NHS Tribunal, effectively preventing him from practising as a GP within the NHS, though as noted above, it is only the General Medical Council that has the power to remove a doctor's name from the list of qualified medical practitioners.

In the case of hospital doctors, guidelines were issued by the DHSS in 1981 on the procedures to be followed by health authorities in dealing with complaints about both non-clinical and clinical matters.[19] Complaints about non-clinical matters should be investigated by the appropriate senior members of staff, and the complainant should be notified of any action that has been taken. In difficult cases the district management team and the district health authority may be involved, and if the complainant remains dissatisfied he should be advised of his right to take the matter to the Health Service Commissioner (see below). Complaints about clinical matters are subject to more elaborate procedures, depending upon the extent to which the complainant is prepared to take his grievance. Whenever possible, all such complaints should be dealt with locally by the consultant in charge of the case, but if this proves impossible or is unsatisfactory to the complainant, the matter may be referred to the regional medical officer (RMO) who will discuss the case with the consultant and search for a reasonable solution. If the complainant still remains dissatisfied, and if the point at issue is unlikely to be taken to court or to be the subject of formal disciplinary action, the RMO may arrange for two independent consultants to review the whole case, discussing it with both the original consultant and the patient. If these 'second opinions' come to the conclusion that there had been no irresponsibility or irregularity in the consultant's management of the case, they should try to remove the patient's anxiety by explaining exactly what happened, and why. If, on the other hand, they feel that something was left to be desired in the consultant's handling of the case, they should report to the RMO on the action they feel should be taken to prevent a similar occurrence in the future. The complainant should be told in broad terms of the outcome of the matter, but no details should be provided.

Perhaps unsurprisingly, these procedures have been described by patients' organisations as 'a kind of Star Chamber arrangement' and as a 'charter to protect the doctor'.[20] The British Medical Association, on the other hand, gave an overwhelming approval to them when they were announced by the DHSS.[21] They are unlikely to allay the suspicion that, on the occasions when things go seriously wrong, corrective action may take a long time to materialise.[22] In 1981 a woman was awarded damages of £414,000 in the high court against a London area health authority.[23] Owing to a mistake during the administration of an anaesthetic when she was about to give birth, the woman became permanently crippled and in almost constant pain. During the course of the hearing in the high court it emerged that the AHA not only took two-and-a-half years to admit liability for the negligent treatment of the woman, it also tried to obstruct the woman's legitimate (and, as it turned out, successful) claim. The judge, Mr Justice Taylor, commented on the behaviour of the authority in strong terms: 'Having heard the history and the consequences to the plaintiff, it ought to be publicly stated that the conduct of the defendants was nothing short of scandalous.'

The Health Service Commissioner (or Ombudsman) for England and Wales, created by the 1973 National Health Service Reorganisation Act, represents a fourth channel through which action may be taken if the quality of services is judged to be unsatisfactory. The Commissioner may not examine matters that involve the exercise of clinical judgment, and he is empowered to consider only those cases that have already been investigated by the health authorities (albeit unsatisfactorily from the complainants' point of view). He may, however, investigate complaints about administrative failures on the part of the health authorities, and these often cause a good deal of unhappiness or hardship to patients. In 1981/2 the Commissioner received 686 complaints, of which 407 were investigated and 37 per cent were found to have been justified.[24] The number of complaints about non-clinical aspects of medical care rose from ninety-three in 1980/1 to 136: those connected with nursing care fell from 125 to 107 over the same period; and those due to administrative error fell from seventy-nine to seventy-three. Included in the scope of the Commissioner's work are instances of bad communication, delay in the provision of necessary services, inadequate facilities, unsatisfactory accommodation, inconsiderate public relations, and so on. It is difficult to judge the precise impact of the Commissioner's work on the quality of care in the service. He has no direct authority to empower change, but the annual reports of his work are widely publicised and read, and his strictures appear to command respect. At the very least, the Commissioner (and his counterpart in Scotland) represent a valuable additional channel for the constructive criticism of certain aspects of the quality of care in the NHS.

As a last resort, patients may seek redress from the courts for what they regard as negligent treatment. Following a ruling of the House of Lords in 1980, the law now appears to recognise a distinction between negligence and an error of clinical judgment: an error would amount to negligence only if it would not have been made by a reasonably competent professional person claiming to have the standard of skill that the defendant regarded himself as having. In general, it is by no means easy to take successful legal action against doctors, hospitals or health authorities. In spite of the publicity given to a number of cases in recent years in which large sums of damages have been awarded, the total cost of indemnity payments by the medical defence societies in the United Kingdom was estimated to have risen by no more than 7 per cent per year between 1974 and 1980, reaching some £5 million in the latter year.[25] The widespread use of litigation in the United Kingdom is generally seen as undesirable, giving rise to the practice of 'defensive' medical care (that is, care which can stand scrutiny in a court of law) rather than optimum care that reflects the doctor's judgment about the best interests of his patient. A more promising development might be the introduction of a national compensation scheme for injuries and disabilities, regardless of their cause. A no-fault accident compensation scheme has recently been introduced in New Zealand,[26] where it is envisaged that diseases as well as accidents might eventually be included.[27] In the United Kingdom, the Royal Commission on Civil Liability and Compensation for Personal Injury rejected a no-fault scheme as financially and administratively impossible, but it did recommend the introduction of strict liability for injuries resulting from all products, including drugs.[28] This would mean that the injured person would not have to prove negligence on the part of the drug manufacturer, merely that his injuries were caused by the drug which the manufacturer produced. It remains to be seen whether the increasing involvement of the law in these different ways will exert a beneficial effect on the quality of care in the health services.

Postscript

The National Health Service is subject to constant change in response to the assorted pressures exerted upon it from the environment, and since completing this book a number of policy developments have occurred in several of the areas covered in the book. Early in 1983 the government announced that nearly £100 million of growth money would be available for the NHS in 1983-4, to be allocated through the RAWP machinery. The average regional increase was about 1.2 per cent; but since the DHSS indicated that 0.5 per cent would have to come from increased efficiency, and since the 1983 public expenditure white paper estimated that an annual increase in spending of 0.7 per cent would be needed simply to meet the increased demands resulting from demographic changes, it was apparent that real improvements in the service would be limited. Whilst the health authorities were developing their plans for using the extra resources, the cabinet agreed, in July 1983, to a reduction of £500 million in public expenditure in the current financial year, of which £140 million was to be borne by the NHS. The cash reduction amounted to 1 per cent in the revenue expenditure and 2 per cent in the capital expenditure of the health authorities, and the authorities were also asked by the secretary of state for social services, as an entirely separate exercise, to reduce their manpower by 1 per cent by March 1984. Later, in November 1983, the secretary of state announced increased cash allocations that effectively restored the spending plans to what they had been before the cabinet's July reductions.

Life was not only erratic for the health authorities, which had been forced to implement cuts in services (particularly for the elderly and handicapped) following the July measures, it was also complicated for those who were trying to understand the trend in expenditure on the service.

The government argued that the additional £800 million allocated for the NHS in 1984-5 would allow an overall growth of 1 per cent, enabling the service to keep pace with increasing demands resulting from the ageing of the population. Opposition spokesmen argued that the 1 per cent growth claimed by the government could be achieved only on the unrealistic assumption that salary increases would be limited to 3 per cent and other price rises to 5 per cent, and that no allowance was made for technological innovation, demographic change or the increasing demand on the family practitioner services. Underlying these political exchanges was the interesting issue of whether, in assessing expenditure over time, it is proper to adjust the figures to allow not only for price inflation (as was done in table 4.1), but also demographic change, trends in demand, and innovations in the technology of care. If this is done (using as a basis the information provided in the DHSS's booklet *Health Care and its Costs*, published in the summer of 1983), then the annual increase in expenditure in the latter years of the 1970s, shown in table 4.1, actually becomes a decrease of about 1 per cent per year.

In addition to the fluctuations in government allocations to the NHS as a whole, hypothecated allocations have been made to enable the health authorities to develop initiatives in particular areas of service provision. Some £3 million has been set aside for each of the years 1983-4 to 1985-6 for schemes to help mentally handicapped children leave hospital for care in the community; some £9 million has been allocated over four years to improve primary health care in inner cities; and £0.7 million has been made available to selected bone marrow transplant centres in an attempt to reduce the numbers of deaths among children who are refused operations through the lack of facilities.

Arguments about the funding of the service have taken a number of different turns. On the one hand, the flurry of government enthusiasm about the transition from a tax-funded to an insurance-based service has abated, and the secretary of state has reaffirmed that his government has no plans to dismantle the NHS. On the other hand, moves to encourage health authorities to contract many of their ancillary services out to the private sector have gained in strength, and may represent a major area of change in the future. In September 1983 the DHSS issued a circular requiring health authorities to submit all their catering, cleaning and laundry services to competitive tender in the private sector, and further encouragement to use the private sector came with the simultaneous decision by the government to allow authorities to claim back VAT on a wide range of services bought in privately.

Other decisions by the secretary of state have also reflected a degree of ambivalence towards the boundaries between the public and private arenas. In November 1983 he announced that, in future, a charge would be made for NHS-collected blood used in private hospitals and clinics;

and in the following month it was announced that the target level of profits permitted to pharmaceutical companies supplying drugs to the NHS would be reduced from 25 per cent to 21 per cent, and also that permitted expenditure on the promotion and sales of drugs would be reduced from 10 per cent of companies' turnover to 9 per cent. These measures, which represented an income to the NHS of about £40 million per year at current prices, suggested a measure of determination by the secretary of state to protect the NHS from the predations of the private sector, but such determination was rather less in evidence in the decision to introduce legislation to abolish the supply of spectacles through the NHS and to end the monopoly held by professional opticians over their sale.

The politics of the prevention of disease (and to a lesser extent the positive promotion of health) have become a little more prominent on the agenda of public debate. In November 1983 the Royal College of Physicians published its fourth report on smoking and health, summarising the current state of knowledge about the risks of smoking and drawing together material on two less well publicised aspects of the problem – passive smoking and smoking in Third World countries. In reply to the question of why yet another report was needed on the dangers of smoking, the *British Medical Journal* observed that 'the answer lies in the obdurate refusal of the Government to recognise the force of the evidence and in the urgent need for new initiatives to stem the growing numbers of smokers among schoolchildren and young adults'. Earlier in the year a new pressure group (Action on Alcohol Abuse) was formed to work politically to reduce Britain's alcohol problems. In reply to the question of why political action was necessary, the *Lancet* observed that 'political action, such as increasing tax on alcohol and curbing advertising, is not a panacea for alcohol problems, but . . . the political response is at least as important, and probably more important, than the medical or social one'. In October 1983 the National Advisory Committee on Nutrition Education published a long-awaited report setting out proposed guidelines and goals for healthy eating. Whilst being widely welcomed as a useful contribution towards positive health for the nation, the NACNE report, like the RCP report on smoking and health, raised issues about action that transcended the individual concern with health education and challenged the role of government and industry in promoting a sensible national food policy.

Within the NHS, the transition from the area health authorities to the district health authorities has been less traumatic than many had feared, and there were some early signs that the members of the new DHAs may be willing to be more involved in policy decisions than their counterparts on the old AHAs had been. At the same time, however, accountability and control was being increased. The 1983 Public Expenditure White Paper announced the introduction in 1984 of a new system of monitoring the efficient use of manpower by the health authorities; the performance reviews of the regional and district health authorities were getting under way; and early in 1983 the secretary of state appointed a team under the leadership of Mr Roy Griffiths (the managing director of Sainsbury's) to enquire into the efficiency of the service. The team's report, published in October 1983, found a number of structural factors promoting inefficiency in the NHS; and, based upon the assumption that management problems in the NHS were much more similar to those in private industry than had commonly been recognised, it recommended the establishment of a general management capability at all levels, from the DHSS down to the units within each district. In particular, the Griffiths report recommended the appointment at district level of a general manager (who may or may not be an existing member of the district management team) with the power to take decisions on matters where there is disagreement, and to be personally responsible for ensuring that speedy and effective action is taken in implementing decisions. Inevitably in a brief report on such a complex theme, the Griffiths report contained ambiguities, contradictions and opacities, and it scarcely began to spell out the implications of its recommendations for the consensus management approach that has dominated the NHS since 1974, for clinical freedom, for the chairmen and members of the DHAs, or for the institutional ethos of the service. In spite of such inevitable lacunae, the 'spirit' of the report seemed to be widely accepted, and the secretary of state announced his intention to implement the recommendations after appropriate consultations. It remains to be seen, at the time of writing, how comprehensively the Griffiths recommendations can be implemented. For example, in its formal response to the report in January 1984 the British Medical Association observed that 'whilst such appointments (as a general manager) may be necessary and desirable in trade and commerce, they can have no place in the health service', and the Association warned the secretary of state that 'it should be clearly understood that the profession would neither accept nor co-operate with any such arrangement'.

In sum, the NHS remains the beast it was at the beginning of this book: a large, complex, vibrant institution; pursuing diverse and sometimes disparate goals; subject to intense and often conflicting pressures and expectations; responsive to the political, social and economic forces of its environment; and striving as best it can to improve the health and wellbeing of the nation. The NHS is, and probably always has been, more open to critical analysis and comment than to adulation and praise, but that perhaps is merely a sign of its resilience. It has changed and developed over thirty-five years in remarkable ways, yet it has retained many of the essential and benign characteristics that distinguish the NHS from other systems of health care delivery. There are grounds for optimism that the NHS will prove to be equally resilient during the next thirty-five years.

Notes

Chapter 1 An organising framework: the health services system

1 Powell, J.E. (1966), *A New Look at Medicine and Politics,* London, Pitman Medical, p. 16.
2 *Oxford English Dictionary* (1933), vol. 10, London, Oxford University Press.
3 Maxwell, R. (1980), *International Comparisons of Health Needs and Services,* London, King's Fund Centre, Project Paper no. RC9, p. 17.
4 Benjamin, B. and Overton, E. (1981), 'Prospects for mortality decline in England and Wales', *Population Trends,* vol. 23, pp. 22-8.
5 Leete, R. (1971), 'Trends in the marital composition of the population since 1961 and projections to 1991', *Population Trends,* vol. 10, pp. 16-21.
6 Butler, J.R. and Morgan, M. (1977), 'Marital status and hospital use', *British Journal of Preventive and Social Medicine,* vol. 31, pp. 192-8.
7 Acheson, E.D. (1982), 'The impending crisis of old age: a challenge to ingenuity', *Lancet,* vol. 2, pp. 592-4.
8 Treasury (1979), *The Government's Expenditure Plans 1979-80 to 1982-83,* Cmnd 7439, London, HMSO, p. 143.
9 Morris, J.N. (1975), *Uses of Epidemiology,* Edinburgh, Churchill Livingstone.
10 Office of Health Economics (1972), *Medical Care in Developing Countries,* London, OHE, p. 3.
11 Knox, E.G. (ed.) (1979), *Epidemiology in Health Care Planning,* Oxford, Oxford University Press.
12 McCarthy, M. (1982), *Epidemiology and Policies for Health Planning,* London, King's Fund.
13 Paul, B.D. (ed.) (1955), *Health, Culture and Community,* New York, Russell Sage Foundation.

14 Medical Services Study Group of the Royal College of Physicians of London (1978), 'Deaths under 50', *British Medical Journal,* vol. 2, pp. 1,061-2.

15 Mason, W.B., Bedwell, C.I., Van der Zwagg, R. and Runyon, J.W. (1980), 'Why people are hospitalized', *Medical Care,* vol. 18, pp. 147-63.

16 Draper, P., Best, G. and Dennis, J. (1976), *Health, Money and the National Health Service,* London, Unit for the Study of Health Policy, Guy's Hospital Medical School, p. 28.

17 Lewis, C.E. and Lewis, M.A. (1977), 'The potential impact of sexual equality on health', *New England Journal of Medicine,* vol. 297, pp. 863-8.

18 Stolley, P.D. (1977), 'Lung cancer: unwanted equality for women', *New England Journal of Medicine,* vol. 197, pp. 856-87.

19 Jahoda, M. and Rush, H. (1980), *Work, Employment and Unemployment, Occasional Paper number 12,* Brighton, Science Policy Research Unit, University of Sussex.

20 Brenner, M.H. (1979), 'Mortality and the national economy', *Lancet,* vol. 2, pp. 568-73.

21 Gravelle, H.S.E., Hutchison, G. and Stern, J. (1981), 'Mortality and unemployment: a critique of Brenner's time-series analysis', *Lancet,* vol. 2, pp. 675-81.

22 Fagin, L. (1981), *Unemployment and Health in Families: Case Studies Based on Family Interviews,* London, Department of Health and Social Security.

23 Maxwell, R.J. (1981), *Health and Wealth: an International Study of Health Care Spending,* Lexington, Mass., D.C. Heath, p. 35.

24 Mackenzie, W.J.M. (1979), *Power and Responsibility in Health Care,* London, Nuffield Provincial Hospitals Trust.

25 Titmuss, R.M. (1974), *Social Policy,* London, Allen & Unwin, pp. 30-1.

26 Royal Commission on the National Health Service (1979), *Report,* Cmnd. 7615, London, HMSO, p. 294.

27 Le Grand, J. and Wiles, P. (1982), Letter, *The Times,* 11 October, p. 11.

28 Klein, R. (1982), 'Reflections of an ex-AHA member', *British Medical Journal,* vol. 284, pp. 992-4.

29 Draper, P. (1972), 'Some technical considerations in planning for health', *Journal of Social Policy,* vol. 1, pp. 149-61.

30 Rose, G.A. (1981), 'Strategy of prevention: lessons from cardiovascular disease', *British Medical Journal,* vol. 282, pp. 1,847-51.

Chapter 2 Health, health services and politics

1 Dixon, B. (1978), *Beyond the Magic Bullet*, London, Allen & Unwin, pp. 33-5.

2 Inglis, B. (1965), *A History of Medicine*, London, Weidenfeld & Nicolson.
3 Dixon, op. cit., pp. 33-5.
4 Ibid., p. 1.
5 McKeown, T. (1979), *The Role of Medicine*, Oxford, Blackwell, p. 3.
6 Kennedy, I. (1981), *The Unmasking of Medicine*, London, Allen & Unwin.
7 Illich, I. (1976), *Limits to Medicine*, Harmondsworth, Penguin.
8 McKeown, op. cit., p. 3.
9 Powles, J. (1973), 'On the limitations of modern medicine', *Science, Medicine and Man*, vol. 1, pp. 1-30.
10 Dollery, C.T. (1978), *The End of an Age of Optimism*, London, Nuffield Provincial Hospitals Trust, p. 1.
11 Beeson, P.B. (1980), 'Changes in medical therapy during the past half century', *Medicine*, vol. 59, pp. 79-89.
12 Morris, J.N. (1980), 'Are health services important to people's health?', *British Medical Journal*, vol. 280, pp. 167-8.
13 Dollery, op. cit., p. 31.
14 Inglis, op. cit., p. 156.
15 Dubos, R. (1951), *Louis Pasteur: Freelance of Science*, London, Gollancz.
16 Doll, R. and Petoe, R. (1981), 'The causes of cancer: quantitative estimates of avoidable risks of cancer in the United States today', *Journal of the National Cancer Institute*, vol. 66, pp. 1,191-308.
17 Department of Health and Social Security, Office of Population Censuses and Surveys, Welsh Office (1981), *Hospital In-Patient Enquiry: Main Tables*, Series MB4, no. 12, London, HMSO.
18 Cutler, S.J., Myers, M.H. and Green, S.B. (1975), 'Trends in survival of patients with cancer', *New England Journal of Medicine*, vol. 293, pp. 122-4.
19 Anonymous (1977), 'Adjuvant therapy of lung cancer: now sits expectation in the air', *British Medical Journal*, vol. 1, pp. 187-8.
20 Stott, H., Stephens, R.J., Fox, W. and Roy, D.C. (1976), 'Five-year follow-up of cytotoxic chemotherapy as an adjuvant to surgery in carcinoma of the bronchus', *British Journal of Cancer*, vol. 34, pp. 167-73.
21 Brent, G. (1969), 'Earlier diagnosis and survival in lung cancer', *British Medical Journal*, vol. 4, pp. 260-2.
22 Doll and Petoe, op. cit., pp. 1,191-308.
23 Doyal, L. and Pennell, I. (1979), *The Political Economy of Health*, London, Pluto, p. 81.
24 Department of Health and Social Security (1982), *On The State of the Public Health for the Year 1980*, London, HMSO, pp. 142-3.

25 Office of Population Censuses and Surveys (1981), *Cigarette Smoking, 1972 to 1980,* Monitor GHS 81/2, London, Government Statistical Service.

26 Doyal and Pennell, op. cit., p. 81.

27 Raphael, A. (1981), 'Tobacco barons and the health reshuffle', *Observer,* 15 November, p. 1.

28 Bostock, Y., Jacobson, B., White, P. and Seymour, L. (1982), 'Ad-man's bullseye; researcher's blank', *The Health Services,* 9 July, pp. 12-13.

29 Marks, L. (1982), 'Policies and postures in smoking control', *British Medical Journal,* vol. 284, pp. 391-4.

30 Ferriman, A. (1981), 'Tobacco lobby has 100 MPs, lecturer claims', *The Times,* 17 November, p. 3.

31 Anonymous (1981), 'Antismokers under attack', *British Medical Journal,* vol. 283, p. 1,281.

32 Wood, N. (1982), 'New sports sponsorship deal will claim 250 lives a year', *Times Health Supplement,* 12 March, p. 6.

33 Anonymous (1981), *British Medical Journal,* vol. 283, p. 509.

34 Anonymous (1981), *British Medical Journal,* vol. 282, p. 1,407.

35 Lin-Fu, J.S. (1982), 'Children and lead: new findings and concerns', *New England Journal of Medicine*, vol. 307, pp. 615-16.

36 Geiger, H.J. (1980), 'Addressing apocalypse now: the effects of nuclear warfare as a public health concern', *American Journal of Public Health,* vol. 70, pp. 958-61.

37 Eastwood, M. (1981), 'The medicine of nuclear warfare: a clinical dead-end', *Lancet,* vol. 1, pp. 1,252-3.

38 International Physicians for the Prevention of Nuclear War (1982), 'An appeal to the President of the United States of America and the Chairman of the Presidium of the USSR Supreme Soviet', *Lancet,* vol. 1, p. 900.

39 Independent Commission on International Development Issues (1980), *North-South: a Programme for Survival,* London, Pan, p. 55.

40 Doyal and Pennell, op. cit.

41 Waitzkin, H. (1978), 'A Marxist view of medical care', *Annals of Internal Medicine,* vol. 89, pp. 264-78.

42 Elling, R.H. (1981), 'The capitalist world-system and international health', *International Journal of Health Services,* vol. 11, pp. 21-51.

43 Navarro, V. (1976), *Medicine Under Capitalism,* London, Croom Helm.

44 Townsend, P. (1981), 'Towards equality in health through social policy', *International Journal of Health Services,* vol. 11, pp. 63-75.

45 Navarro, op. cit., pp. 82-97.

46 World Health Organization (1979), *Controlling the Smoking Epidemic,* Technical Report Series, no. 636, Geneva, WHO.

47 Deitch, R. (1981), 'Marketing of breast-milk substitutes in developing countries', *Lancet*, vol. 1, pp. 566-7.
48 Taylor, R. (1979), *Medicine Out of Control*, Melbourne, Sun Books, pp. 233-4.
49 Lipton, M. (1977), 'From protective health to national recovery', *Institute of Development Studies Bulletin*, vol. 19, pp. 54-62.

Chapter 3 Some epidemiological trends in the United Kingdom

1 Eisenberg, L. (1977), 'Disease and illness: distinctions between professional and popular ideas of sickness', *Culture, Medicine and Psychiatry*, vol. 1, pp. 9-23.
2 Helman, C.G. (1981), 'Disease versus illness in general practice', *Journal of the Royal College of General Practitioners*, vol. 31, pp. 548-52.
3 Kennedy, I. (1981), *The Unmasking of Medicine*, London, Allen & Unwin, pp. 18-25.
4 Bloch, S. and Reddaway, P. (1977), *Psychiatric Terror*, New York, Basic Books.
5 Anonymous (1968), 'Compulsive gambler', *British Medical Journal*, vol. 2, p. 69.
6 Cassell, J.E. (1978), *The Healer's Art: a New Approach to the Doctor-Patient Relationship*, Harmondsworth, Penguin.
7 Parsons, T. (1951), *The Social System*, London, Routledge & Kegan Paul, pp. 436-9.
8 Koos, E.L. (1954), *The Health of Regionville*, New York, Columbia University Press.
9 Stacey, M. (1977), 'Concepts of health and illness: a working paper on the concepts and their relevance for research', in Social Science Research Council, *Health and Health Policy*, London, SSRC.
10 World Health Organisation (1980), *International Classification of Impairments, Disabilities and Handicaps*, Geneva, WHO.
11 World Health Organisation (1961), *Constitution: Basic Documents, 15th Edition*, Geneva, WHO.
12 Office of Population Censuses and Survey (annual), *Mortality Statistics*, series DH, London, HMSO.
13 Office of Population Censuses and Surveys (1978), *Occupational Mortality 1970-72: Decennial Supplement*, series DS, no. 1, London, HMSO.
14 Department of Health and Social Security (1976), *Sharing Resources for Health in England*, London, HMSO.
15 Office of Population Censuses and Surveys (1971), *Handicapped and Impaired in Great Britain*, pt 1, London, HMSO.
16 Benjamin, B. (1968), *Health and Vital Statistics*, London, Allen & Unwin, pp. 78-83.
17 Anonymous (1981), 'Uncertain Certificates', *Lancet*, vol. 2, pp. 22-3.

18 Benjamin, op. cit., p. 81.
19 Department of Health and Social Security, Office of Population Censuses and Surveys, Welsh Office (1980), *Hospital In-Patient Enquiry: Preliminary Tables,* series MB4, no. 11.
20 Common Services Agency for the Scottish Health Service (1982), *Scottish Health Statistics, 1980*, Edinburgh, HMSO.
21 Department of Health and Social Security (1980a), *In-Patient Statistics from the Mental Health Enquiry for England, 1977,* Statistical and Research Report Series, no. 23, London, HMSO.
22 Office of Population Censuses and Surveys (1974), *Morbidity Statistics from General Practice 1970-71,* Studies on Medical and Population Subjects, no. 26, London, HMSO.
23 Royal College of General Practitioners, Office of Population Censuses and Surveys, Department of Health and Social Security (1979), *Morbidity Statistics from General Practice,* Studies on Medical and Population Subjects, no. 36, London, HMSO.
24 Butler, J.R. (1980), *How Many Patients?,* London, Bedford Square Press.
25 Royal College of General Practitioners Birmingham Research Unit (1976), *Trends in National Morbidity,* Occasional Paper 3, London, *Journal of the Royal College of General Practitioners.*
26 Royal College of General Practitioners (1979), *Trends in General Practice*, London, *British Medical Journal* for the Royal College of General Practitioners.
27 Department of Health and Social Security (annual), *On the State of the Public Health,* London, HMSO.
28 Department of Health and Social Security (annual), *Health and Personal Social Services Statistics for England*, London, HMSO.
29 Last, J.M. (1963), 'The Iceberg', *Lancet,* vol. 2, pp. 28-31.
30 Stocks, P. (1949), *Sickness in the Population of England and Wales in 1944-1947,* Studies on Medical and Population Subjects, no. 2, London, HMSO.
31 Office of Population Censuses and Surveys (1973), *The General Household Survey, Introductory Report,* London, HMSO.
32 Dunnell, K. and Cartwright, A. (1972), *Medicine Takers, Prescribers and Hoarders,* London, Routledge & Kegan Paul.
33 Wadsworth, M.E.J., Butterfield, J.H. and Blaney, R. (1971), *Health and Sickness: the Choice of Treatment,* London, Tavistock.
34 Hannay, D.R. (1979), *The Symptom Iceberg,* London, Routledge & Kegan Paul.
35 Parsons, op. cit.
36 Taylor, P.J. (1979), in Gardner, A.W. (ed.), *Current Approaches to Occupational Medicine,* Bristol, John Wright & Sons.
37 OPCS (1971), op. cit.

38 Department of Health and Social Security (1978), *Physically Disabled People Living at Home: a Study of Needs and Numbers,* Report on Health and Social Subjects, no. 13, HMSO.
39 Department of Health and Social Security (1980b), *On the State of the Public Health for the Year 1979,* London, HMSO.
40 Cochrane, A.L., St Leger, A.S. and Moore, F. (1978), 'Health service input and mortality output in developed countries', *Journal of Epidemiology and Community Health,* vol. 32, pp. 200-5.
41 St Leger, A.S., Cochrane, A.L. and Moore, F. (1979), 'Factors associated with cardiac mortality in developed countries with particular reference to the consumption of wine', *Lancet,* vol. 1, pp. 1,017-20.
42 Registrar General (1937), *Statistical Review of England and Wales, 1935,* London, HMSO.
43 Maxwell, R. (1980), *International Comparisons of Health Needs and Services,* Project Paper no. RC9, London, King's Fund Centre.
44 DHSS (1980b), op. cit.
45 Doll, R. (1973), 'Monitoring the National Health Service', *Proceedings of the Royal Society of Medicine,* vol. 66, pp. 729-40.
46 Townsend, P. and Davidson, N. (eds) (1982), *Inequalities in Health,* Harmondsworth, Penguin, pp. 177-90.
47 Chilvers, C. (1978), 'Regional mortality 1969-73', *Population Trends,* no. 11, pp. 16-20.
48 OPCS (1978), op. cit.
49 Townsend and Davidson, op. cit., pp. 65-75.
50 DHSS, OPCS, Welsh Office (1980), op. cit.
51 Royal College of General Practitioners (1979), *Trends in General Practice,* op. cit.
52 Smith, T. (1982), 'The risks of doing nothing', *The Health Services,* no. 32, p. 9.
53 Department of Health and Social Security (1982), *On the State of the Public Health for 1980,* London, HMSO.
54 Central Statistical Office (1981), *Social Trends, No. 12, 1982 Edition,* London, HMSO.
55 Office of Population Censuses and Surveys (1981), *General Household Survey 1979,* series GHS, no. 9, London, HMSO.
56 Hannay, op. cit.
57 Taylor, in Gardner, op. cit.
58 Office of Health Economics (1981), *Sickness Absence – A Review,* Briefing, no. 16, London, OHE.
59 Ibid.
60 OPCS (1971), op. cit.

Chapter 4 Spending on health services

1 Central Statistical Office (1982 and earlier years as appropriate), *Annual Abstract of Statistics 1982 Edition*, London, HMSO.
2 Office of Health Economics (1981), *Doctors, Nurses and Midwives in the NHS*, Briefing, no. 18, London, OHE.
3 CSO (1982, etc.), *Annual Abstract of Statistics*, op. cit.
4 Central Statistical Office (1981 and earlier years as appropriate), *National Income and Expenditure, 1981 Edition*, London, HMSO.
5 Ibid.
6 Royal Commission on the National Health Service (1979), *Report*, Cmnd 7615, London, HMSO, pp. 431-3.
7 Ibid.
8 Bevan, G., Copeman, H., Perrin, J. and Rosser, R. (1980), *Health Care Priorities and Management*, London, Croom Helm, p. 283.
9 Levitt, R. (1976), *The Reorganised National Health Service*, London, Croom Helm, p. 175.
10 Central Statistical Office (1981), *Economic Trends, Annual Supplement, 1982 Edition*, London, HMSO.
11 CSO (1982, etc.), *Annual Abstract of Statistics*, op. cit.
12 Royal Commission, op. cit., p. 333.
13 Abel-Smith, B. (1967), *An International Study of Health Expenditure, Public Health Papers number 32*, Geneva, World Health Organization, p. 44.
14 Maxwell, R. (1981), *Health and Wealth*, Lexington, D.C. Heath, p. 39.
15 Ibid., p. 35.
16 Walker, A. (1982), 'Public expenditure, social policy and social planning', in A. Walker (ed.), *Public Expenditure and Social Policy*, London, Heinemann Education Books, p. 5.
17 CSO (1981, etc.), *National Income and Expenditure*, op. cit.
18 Judge, K. (1982), 'The growth and decline in social expenditure', in Walker, op. cit., pp. 27-48.
19 Ibid.
20 Gough, I. (1979), *The Political Economy of the Welfare State*, London, Macmillan.
21 O'Connor, J. (1973), *The Fiscal Crisis of the Welfare State*, New York, St Martin's Press.
22 Ibid., p. 30.
23 Judge, op. cit., pp. 36-9.
24 Judge, K. and Hampson, R. (1980), 'Political advertising and the growth of social welfare expenditures', *International Journal of Social Economics*, vol. 7, pp. 61-92.
25 Maxwell, op. cit., pp. 38-46.
26 Fuchs, V.R. (1974), *Who Shall Live?*, New York, Basic Books, p. 60.
27 CSO (1981, etc.), *National Income and Expenditure*, op. cit.

28 Department of Health and Social Security (1981), *Care in Action*, London, HMSO.
29 Social Services Committee (1982), *Second Report from the Social Services Committee, Session 1981-82*, HC306, London, HMSO.
30 Jenkin, P. (1981), 'Economic constraints and social policy', *Social Policy and Administration*, vol. 15, pp. 233-41.
31 Treasury (1977), *The Government's Expenditure Plans*, Cmnd 6721-1, London, HMSO.
32 Bacon, R. and Eltis, W. (1976), *Britain's Economic Problem: Too Few Producers*, London, Macmillan.
33 Hopkins, W.A.B. and Godley, W. (1980), 'Effects of public spending cuts', *The Times*, 31 October, p. 15.
34 Maxwell, R. (1974), *Health Care: The Growing Dilemma*, New York, McKinsey.
35 Abel-Smith, B. (1980), 'Economics and health policy: an overview', in A. Griffiths and Z. Bankowski (eds), *Economics and Health Policy*, Geneva, Council for International Organisations of Medical Sciences and Sandoz Institute for Health and Socio-Economic Studies, p. 28.
36 Lee, K. (1982), 'Public expenditure, health services and health', in Walker, op. cit., p. 89.

Chapter 5 Financing health services

1 Office of Health Economics (1981), *Compendium of Health Statistics, 4th Edition*, London, OHE, table 1. 5.
2 Le Grand, J. (1982), *The Strategy of Equality*, London, Allen & Unwin, pp. 23-53.
3 Deitch, R. (1982), 'Will the NHS eventually run out of money?', *Lancet*, vol. 1, pp. 405-6.
4 Deitch, R. (1982), 'Insurance-based NHS no longer on the government's path', *Lancet*, vol. 2, pp. 339-40.
5 Stevens, A. (1982), 'Storm over secret think tank report', *Observer*, 19 August, p. 2.
6 Royal Commission on the National Health Service (1979), *Report*, Cmnd 7615, London, HMSO, pp. 339-42.
7 Royal Commission on Gambling (1978), *Final Report*, Cmnd 7200, London, HMSO.
8 Royal Commission on the NHS, op. cit., p. 285.
9 Anonymous (1982), 'Private hospital beds', *British Medical Journal*, vol. 284, p. 520.
10 Central Statistical Office (1981), *Social Trends 12*, London, HMSO, p. 141.
11 Chubb, P., Haywood, S. and Torrens, P. (1982), *Managing the Mixed Economy of Health, Occasional Paper Number 42*, Birmingham, University of Birmingham Health Services Management Centre.

12 Department of Health and Social Security, Scottish Office, Welsh Office (1973), *Private Practice in National Health Service Hospitals,* Cmnd 5270, London, HMSO, p. 2.
13 Anonymous (1981), 'Pay-beds', *British Medical Journal,* vol. 283, p. 443.
14 Royal Commission on the NHS, op. cit., pp. 294-5.
15 Ibid., p. 288.
16 Cairns, J.A. and Snell, M.C. (1978), 'Prices and the demand for care', in A.J. Culyer and K.G. Wright (eds), *Economic Aspects of Health Services,* London, Martin Robertson, p. 100.
17 Torrens, P. (1982), 'Some potential hazards of unplanned expansion of private health insurance in Britain', *Lancet,* vol. 1, pp. 29-31.
18 Quoted in Wood, N. (1981), 'Stem health insurance boom, warns American experience', *Times Health Supplement,* 27 November, p. 4.
19 Royal Commission on the NHS, op. cit., p. 337.
20 Roe, B.B. (1982), 'A challenge to the health insurance industry', *New England Journal of Medicine,* vol. 307, pp. 551-3.
21 Ibid.
22 Greenberg, D.S. (1980), 'Money and health care', *New England Journal of Medicine,* vol. 302, pp. 978-80.
23 Inglehart, J.K. (1982), 'The future of HMOs', *New England Journal of Medicine,* vol. 307, pp. 451-6.
24 Ibid.
25 Torrens, op. cit., p. 30.
26 Anonymous (1981), 'Management costs in the NHS', *British Medical Journal,* vol. 282, p. 1,409.
27 Royal Commission on the NHS, op. cit., p. 338.

Chapter 6 The allocation of financial resources

1 Hardin, G. (1968), 'The tragedy of the commons', *Science,* vol. 162, pp. 1,243-8.
2 Hiatt, H.H. (1975), 'Protecting the medical commons: who is responsible?', *New England Journal of Medicine,* vol. 293, pp. 235-41.
3 Kinston, W. (1982), 'Resource consumption and future organisation of medical work in the National Health Service', *Social Science and Medicine,* vol. 16, pp. 1,619-26.
4 Ministry of Health (1967), *First Report of the Joint Working Party on the Organisation of Medical Work in Hospitals,* London, HMSO.
5 Department of Health and Social Security (1972), *Management Arrangements for the Reorganised National Health Service,* London, HMSO.

6 Treasury (1961), *Control of Public Expenditure*, Cmnd 1432, London, HMSO.

7 Crossman, R.H.S. (1975), *The Diaries of a Cabinet Minister*, vol. 2, London, Hamish Hamilton and Jonathan Cape, pp. 129-32.

8 Treasury (1982), *The Government's Expenditure Plans 1982-83 to 1984-85*, Cmnd 8494, London, HMSO, vol. 1, p. 7.

9 Social Services Committee (1980), *The Government's White Papers on Public Expenditure: the Social Services*, Third Report 1979-80, HC 702-1, London, HMSO.

10 Glennerster, H. (1981), 'From containment to conflict? Social planning in the seventies', *Journal of Social Policy*, vol. 10, pp. 31-51.

11 Jones, T. and Prowle, M. (1982), *Health Service Finance*, London, Certified Accountants Education Trust, p. 64.

12 Logan, R.F.L., Ashley, J.S.A., Klein, R.E. and Robson, D.M. (1972), *Dynamics of Medical Care*, memoir no. 14, London, London School of Hygiene and Tropical Medicine.

13 Ministry of Health (1962), *A Hospital Plan for England and Wales*, Cmnd 1604, London, HMSO.

14 Noyce, J., Snaith, A.H. and Trickey, A.J. (1974), 'Regional variations in the allocation of financial resources to the community health services', *Lancet*, vol. 1, pp. 554-7.

15 Buxton, M.J. and Klein, R.E. (1975), 'Distribution of hospital provision: policy themes and resource variations', *British Medical Journal*, vol. 1, pp. 345-7.

16 Department of Health and Social Security (1976a), *Sharing Resources for Health in England*, London, HMSO, p. 5.

17 Department of Health and Social Security (1980), *Report of the Advisory Group on Resource Allocation*, London, DHSS, p. 2.

18 Maynard, A. and Ludbrook, A. (1980), 'Budget allocation in the National Health Service', *Journal of Social Policy*, vol. 9, pp. 289-312.

19 Jones and Prowle, op. cit., pp. 27-8.

20 Department of Health and Social Security (1980), op. cit.

21 Department of Health and Social Security (1976a), op. cit., p. 8.

22 Treasury (1976), *Public Expenditure to 1979-80*, Cmnd 6393, London, HMSO, pp. 92-3.

23 Department of Health and Social Security (1976b), *Priorities for Health and Personal Social Services in England*, London, HMSO.

24 Anonymous (1976), 'The priorities of health', *The Times*, 25 March, p. 9.

25 Anonymous (1976), 'A policy of despair', *British Medical Journal*, vol. 1, p. 787.

26 Anonymous (1976), 'The priorities of health', op. cit.

27 Department of Health and Social Security (1977), *The Way Forward*, London, HMSO, p. 17.

28 Haywood, S. and Alaszewski, A. (1980), *Crisis in the Health Service,* London, Croom Helm.

29 Snaith, A.H. (1982), 'Health services administration and health services research', *British Medical Journal,* vol. 284, pp. 1,722-4.

30 Butts, M., Irving, D. and Whitt, C. (1981), *From Principles to Practice,* London, Nuffield Provincial Hospitals Trust, pp. 71-2.

31 Department of Health and Social Security (1981), *Care in Action,* London, HMSO.

32 Klein, R.E. (1981), 'The strategy behind the Jenkin non-strategy', *British Medical Journal,* vol. 282, pp. 1,089-91.

33 Social Services Committee (1980), op. cit.

34 Social Services Committee (1981), *Public Expenditure on the Social Services,* Third Report 1980-1, HC 324, London, HMSO.

35 Public Accounts Committee (1981), *Seventeenth Report, Session 1980-81,* HC 225, London, HMSO, p. vii.

36 Blair, P. (1982), 'Fowler forces authorities to act on priorities', *Times Health Supplement,* 22 January, p. 1.

Chapter 7 The allocation of care

1 Judge, K. (1978), *Rationing Social Services,* London, Heinemann, p. 5.

2 Fuchs, V. (1974), *Who Shall Live?,* New York, Basic Books, p. 4.

3 Ferriman, A. (1981), 'Children die as money runs out', *The Times,* 3 December, p. 4.

4 Fuchs, op. cit., p. 60.

5 Taylor, R. (1979), *Medicine out of Control,* Melbourne, Sun Books, pp. 65-86.

6 Bodkin, C.M., Pigott, T.J. and Mann, J.R. (1982), 'Financial burden of childhood cancer', *British Medical Journal,* vol. 284, pp. 1,542-6.

7 Anonymous (1981), 'Allocation of resources in health care', *British Medical Journal,* vol. 282, p. 1,406.

8 Royal Commission on the National Health Service (1979), *Report,* Cmnd 7615, London, HMSO, p. 334.

9 Cooper, M.H. (1975), *Rationing Health Care,* London, Croom Helm.

10 Anonymous (1975), 'Now rationing is official', *Doctor,* 27 February, p. 3.

11 Le Grand, J. and Robinson, R. (1976), *The Economics of Social Problems,* London, Macmillan, p. 33.

12 Royal Commission on the National Health Service, op. cit., p. 294.

13 Titmuss, R.M. (1968), *Commitment to Welfare,* London, Allen & Unwin, p. 191.

14 Quoted in G. Forsyth (1961), *Doctors and State Medicine*, London, Pitman Medical, pp. 26-7.
15 Taylor, op. cit., pp. 249-56.
16 Mechanic, D. (1977), 'The growth of medical technology and bureaucracy: implications for medical care', *Milbank Memorial Fund Quarterly, Health and Society*, vol. 55, pp. 61-78.
17 Field, M.G. (1953), 'Structured strain in the role of the Soviet physician', *American Journal of Sociology*, vol. 58, pp. 493-502.
18 Smits, H.L. (1981), 'The PSRO in perspective', *New England Journal of Medicine*, vol. 305, pp. 253-8.
19 Anonymous (1980), 'Heart transplants', *British Medical Journal*, vol. 280, p. 654.
20 Powell, J.E. (1966), *A New Look at Medicine and Politics*, London, Pitman Medical, p. 38.
21 Cartwright, A. and O'Brien, M. (1976), 'Social class variations in health care and in the nature of general practitioner consultations', in M. Stacey (ed.), *The Sociology of the NHS*, University of Keele, Sociological Review Monograph, no. 22.
22 Parker, R. (1967), 'Social administration and scarcity: the problem of rationing', *Social Work*, vol. 24, pp. 9-14.
23 Foster, P. (1979), 'The informal rationing of primary health care', *Journal of Social Policy*, vol. 8, pp. 489-508.
24 Grey-Turner, E. (1978), 'Maintaining professional standards', *British Medical Journal*, vol. 2, pp. 841-2.

Chapter 8 The structure of the National Health Service

1 Brown, R.G.S. (1975), *The Management of Welfare*, London, Fontana.
2 Brown, R.G.S. (1979), *Reorganising the National Health Service*, Oxford, Basil Blackwell and Martin Robertson.
3 Ham, C. (1981), *Policy-making in the National Health Service*, London, Macmillan.
4 Ham, C. (1982), *Health Policy in Britain*, London, Macmillan.
5 Lukes, S. (1974), *Power: A Radical View*, London, Macmillan.
6 Maxwell, R. (1981), 'On ministers of health', *Lancet*, vol. 1, pp. 1,412-14.
7 Kellner, P. and Crowther-Hunt, Lord (1980), *The Civil Servants*, London, Macdonald Futura, p. 213.
8 Crossman, R.H.A. (1975), *The Diaries of a Cabinet Minister, Volume 1*, London, Hamish Hamilton and Jonathan Cape, p. 21.
9 Ham (1982), op. cit., p. 74.
10 Royal Commission on the National Health Service (1979), *Report*, Cmnd 7615, London, HMSO, pp. 304-5.
11 Regional Chairmen's Enquiry into the Working of the DHSS in Relation to Regional Health Authorities (1976), *Report*, London, DHSS.

12 Owen, D. (1976), *In Sickness and in Health,* London, Quartet, p. 7.
13 Royal Commission, op. cit., p. 304.
14 Ministry of Health (1968), *National Health Service: the Administrative Structure of Medical and Related Services in England and Wales,* London, HMSO.
15 Department of Health and Social Security (1970), *National Health Service: the Future Structure of the National Health Service in England,* London, HMSO.
16 Department of Health and Social Security (1971), *National Health Service Reorganisation – Consultative Document,* London, HMSO.
17 Department of Health and Social Security (1972), *National Health Service Reorganisation: England,* Cmnd 5055, London, HMSO.
18 Anonymous (1982), 'The elephant's friends', *The Health Services,* 15 October, p. 10.
19 Brown, (1979), op. cit., pp. 189-95.
20 Klein, R. (1982), 'Reflection of an ex-AHA member', *British Medical Journal,* vol. 284, pp. 992-4.
21 Royal Commission on the National Health Service, op. cit., p. 324.
22 Department of Health and Social Security (1979), *Patients First,* London, HMSO.
23 Department of Health and Social Security (1971), op. cit.
24 Klein, R. and Lewis, J. (1976), *The Politics of Consumer Representation*, London, Centre for Studies in Social Policy, p. 13.
25 Department of Health and Social Security (1976), *Guide to Planning in the National Health Service,* London, DHSS, p. ii.
26 Brown, R. and Prince, M. (1982), 'Planning, accountability and caution', *Hospital and Health Services Review,* vol. 78, pp. 197-9.
27 Public Accounts Committee (1981), *Seventeenth Report from the Public Accounts Committee, Session 1980-81: Financial Control and Accountability in the NHS,* HC 255, London, HMSO, p. 55.
28 Department of Health and Social Security (1979), op. cit., p. 18.
29 Department of Health and Social Security (1982), *The NHS Planning System,* HC (82)6, London, DHSS.

Chapter 9 The policy-making process

1 Brown, R.G.S. (1979), *Reorganising the National Health Service,* Oxford, Basil Blackwell and Martin Robertson, p. 203.
2 Smith, B. (1976), *Policy Making in British Government,* London, Martin Robertson, pp. 129-73.

3 Stange, P.V. and Sumner, A.T. (1978), 'Predicting treatment costs and life expectancy for end-stage renal disease', *New England Journal of Medicine,* vol. 298, pp. 372-7.
4 Jenkins, W.I. (1978), *Policy Analysis,* London, Martin Robertson, p. 160.
5 Glennerster, H. (1975), *Social Service Budgets and Social Policy,* London, Allen & Unwin, p. 89.
6 Ibid., pp. 18-19.
7 Central Policy Review Staff (1975), *A Joint Framework for Social Policies,* London, HMSO.
8 Hardie, M.C. (1973), 'Practical steps towards comprehensive health planning', *Community Medicine,* 2 February, pp. 325-30.
9 Bennett, A.E. and Holland, W.W. (1977), 'Rational planning or muddling-through?', *Lancet*, vol. 1, pp. 464-6.
10 Department of Health and Social Security (1976a), *Sharing Resources for Health in England,* London, HMSO.
11 Department of Health and Social Security (1976b), *Priorities for Personal Health and Social Services in England,* London, HMSO.
12 Jenkins, op. cit., p. 178.
13 Ham, C. (1981), *Policy-making in the National Health Service,* London, Macmillan, p. 147.
14 Hunter, D.J. (1980), *Coping with Uncertainty,* Letchworth, Research Studies Press, p. 189.
15 Haywood, S. and Alaszewski, A. (1980), *Crisis in the Health Service,* London, Croom Helm, pp. 141-2.
16 Royal Commission on the National Health Service (1978), *The Working of the National Health Service, Research Paper Number 1*, London, HMSO, pp. 83-9.
17 Butts, M., Irving, D. and Whitt, C. (1981), *From Principles to Practice,* London, Nuffield Provincial Hospitals Trust, p. 89.
18 Hunter, op. cit., p. 208.
19 Michael, J. and Adu, D. (1982), 'Dialysis, cuts and district policy', *Lancet,* vol. 2, p. 990.
20 Ferriman, A. (1982), 'Doctors challenge order to turn away dying patients', *Observer,* 14 November, p. 5.
21 Department of Health and Social Security (1978), *On the State of the Public Health for Year 1977,* London, HMSO, p. 14.
22 Royal Commission on the National Health Service (1978), *Management of Financial Resources in the National Health Service, Research Paper Number 2*, London, HMSO.
23 Klein, R. (1982), 'Reflections of an ex-AHA member', *British Medical Journal,* vol. 284, pp. 992-4.
24 Higgins, R. (1980), 'The unfulfilled promise of policy research', *Social Policy and Administration,* vol. 14, pp. 195-208.
25 Lindblom, C.E. (1959), 'The science of muddling through', *Public Administration Review*, vol. 19, pp. 70-88.

26 Etzioni, A. (1967), 'Mixed-scanning: a "third" approach to decision-making', *Public Administration Review,* vol. 27, pp. 305-92.
27 Dror, Y. (1964), 'Muddling through – "science" or inertia?', *Public Administration Review,* vol. 24, pp. 153-7.

Chapter 10 Thinking about outputs

1 Cochrane, A.L. (1972), *Effectiveness and Efficiency,* London, Nuffield Provincial Hospitals Trust, p. 12.
2 Shannon, R. (1968), 'Manpower planning in the National Health Service', in G. McLachlan (ed.), *Problems and Progress in Medical Care, Third Series,* London, Oxford University Press for the Nuffield Provincial Hospitals Trust, pp. 51-62.
3 Butler, J.R. (1980), *How Many Patients?,* London, Bedford Square Press, pp. 18-65.
4 Royal Commission on Medical Education (1968), *Report,* Cmnd 3569, London, HMSO, pp. 127-47.
5 Butler, J.R. (1979), 'Scottish paradox: more doctors, worse health?', *British Medical Journal,* vol. 2, pp. 809-10.
6 Cochrane, A.L., St Leger, A.S. and Moore, F. (1978), 'Health service input and mortality output in developed countries', *Journal of Epidemiology and Community Health,* vol. 32, pp. 200-5.
7 Fox, P.D. (1978), 'Managing health resources: English style', in G. McLachlan (ed.), *By Guess or By What?,* London, Oxford University Press for the Nuffield Provincial Hospitals Trust, pp. 1-64.
8 Le Grand, J. (1982), *The Strategy of Equality,* London, Allen & Unwin, pp. 23-53.
9 Townsend, P. and Davidson, N. (1982), *Inequalities in Health,* Harmondsworth, Penguin, pp. 51-89.
10 McPherson, K., Strong, P.M., Epstein, A. and Jones, I. (1981), 'Regional variations in the use of common surgical procedures: within and between England and Wales, Canada and the United States of America', *Social Science and Medicine,* vol. 15A, pp. 273-88.
11 Lichtner, S. and Pflantz, M. (1971), 'Appendectomy in the Federal Republic of Germany', *Medical Care,* vol. 9, pp. 311-30.
12 Cooper, M.H. (1975), *Rationing Health Care,* London, Croom Helm, p. 50.
13 Challis, D.J. (1981), 'The measurement of outcome in social care of the elderly', *Journal of Social Policy,* vol. 10, pp. 179-208.
14 Royal College of General Practitioners (1979), *Trends in General Practice,* London, British Medical Journal for the Royal College of General Practitioners.

15 Ginzberg, E. (1975), 'Notes on evaluating the quality of medical care', *New England Journal of Medicine,* vol. 292, pp. 366-8.
16 Jennett, B. (1974), 'Surgeon of the seventies', *Journal of the Royal College of Surgeons of Edinburgh,* vol. 19, pp. 1-12.
17 Charlton, J.R.H., Patrick, D.L., Matthews, G. and West, P.A. (1981), 'Spending priorities in Kent: a Delphi study', *Journal of Epidemiology and Community Health,* vol. 35, pp. 288-2.
18 Mooney, G.H. (1977), *The valuation of human life,* London, Macmillan.
19 Hartunian, N.S., Smart, C.N. and Thompson, M.S. (1981), *The Incidence and Economic Costs of Major Health Impairments,* Lexington, Mass., D.C. Heath.
20 Williams, A. (1974), 'Measuring the effectiveness of health care systems', *British Journal of Preventive and Social Medicine,* vol. 28, pp. 196-202.
21 Culyer, A.J. (1976), *Need and the National Health Service,* London, Martin Robertson, p. 43.
22 Rosser, R.M. and Watts, V.C. (1974), 'The development of a classification of the symptoms of sickness and its use to measure the output of a hospital', in D. Lees and S. Shaw (eds), *Impairment, Disability and Handicap,* London, Heinemann Educational Books, pp. 157-70.
23 McCarthy, M. (1982), *Epidemiology and Policies for Health Planning,* London, King's Fund.
24 Williams, op. cit., p. 200.

Chapter 11 The importance of measuring outputs: effectiveness, efficiency and need

1 Treasury and Civil Service Committee (1982), *Effectiveness and Efficiency in the Civil Service,* HC 236-1, London, HMSO, p. 24.
2 Cochrane, A.L. (1972), *Effectiveness and Efficiency,* London, Nuffield Provincial Hospitals Trust, p. 2.
3 Knox, E.G. (1982), 'Good ideas vs. poor results', *Times Health Supplement,* 19 February, p. 15.
4 Schafer, A. (1982), 'The ethics of the randomized clinical trial', *New England Journal of Medicine,* vol. 307, pp. 719-24.
5 Cochrane, op. cit., p. 29.
6 Hiatt, H.H. (1975), 'Protecting the medical commons: who is responsible?', *New England Journal of Medicine,* vol. 293, pp. 235-41.
7 Taylor, R. (1979), *Medicine Out of Control,* Melbourne, Sun Books, p. 32.
8 Mather, H.G., Morgan, D.C., Pearson, N.G., et al. (1976), 'Myocardial infarction: a comparison between home and hospital care for patients', *British Medical Journal,* vol. 1. pp. 925-9.

9 Joint Working Party of the Royal College of Physicians and the British Cardiac Society (1975), 'The care of the patient with coronary heart disease', *Journal of the Royal College of Physicians,* vol. 10, pp. 5-46.

10 Hill, J.D., Hampton, J.R. and Mitchell, J.R.A. (1978), 'A randomised trial of home-versus-hospital management for patients with suspected myocardial infarction', *Lancet,* vol. 1, pp. 837-41.

11 McKeown, T. (1979), *The Role of Medicine,* Oxford, Basil Blackwell.

12 Ibid., p. 70.

13 Ibid., p. 79.

14 Lever, A.F. (1977), 'Medicine under challenge', *Lancet,* vol. 1, pp. 352-5.

15 Beeson, P.B. (1977), 'McKeown's The Role of Medicine: a clinician's reaction', *The Milbank Memorial Fund Quarterly, Health and Society,* vol. 55, pp. 365-71.

16 Illich, I. (1976), *Limits to Medicine,* Harmondsworth, Penguin, p. 11.

17 Gruenberg, E.M. (1977), 'The failures of success', *Milbank Memorial Fund Quarterly, Health and Society,* vol. 55, pp. 3-25.

18 McLamb, J.T. and Huntley, R.R. (1967), 'The hazards of hospitalization', *Southern Medical Journal,* vol. 60, pp. 469-72.

19 Mulroy, R. (1973), 'Iatrogenic disease in general practice: its incidence and effects', *British Medical Journal,* vol. 2, pp. 407-10.

20 Illich, op. cit., p. 138.

21 Department of Health and Social Security (1976), *Priorities for Health and Personal Social Services in England,* London, HMSO.

22 Department of Health and Social Security (1977), *The Way Forward,* London, HMSO.

23 Department of Health and Social Security (1981), *Care in Action,* London, HMSO.

24 Treasury (1982), *The Government's Expenditure Plans 1982-3 to 1984-5,* Cmnd 8494, London, HMSO, vol. 2, p. 45.

25 Social Services Committee (1980), *Third Report from the Social Services Committee, Session 1979-80,* HC 702-1, London, HMSO, p. 10.

26 Hall, M. and Winsten, C. (1959), 'The ambiguous notion of efficiency', *Economic Journal,* vol. 69, pp. 71-86.

27 Williams, A. and Anderson, R. (1975), *Efficiency in the Social Services,* Oxford, Basil Blackwell and Martin Robertson, p. 7.

28 Marsh, G.N. and Kaim-Caudle, P. (1976), *Team Care in General Practice,* London, Croom Helm.

29 Wager, R. (1972), *Care of the Elderly,* London, Institute of Municipal Treasurers and Accountants.

30 Piachaud, D. and Weddell, J. (1972), 'The economics of treating varicose veins', *International Journal of Epidemiology*, vol. 1, pp. 287-94.
31 Beresford, S.A.A., Chant, A.D.B., Jones, H.O., et al. (1978), 'Varicose veins: a comparison of surgery and injection-compression sclerotherapy', *Lancet*, vol. 1, pp. 921-3.
32 Department of Health and Social Security (1976), *Sharing Resources for Health in England*, London, HMSO.
33 Nevitt, D.A. (1977), 'Demand and need', in H. Heisler (ed.), *Foundations of Social Administration*, London, Macmillan, pp. 113-28.
34 Brahms, D. (1982), 'Whether pregnancy should be terminated and a contraceptive device fitted in a girl aged 13', *Lancet*, vol. 1, p. 1,194.
35 Office of Health Economics (1980), *End Stage Renal Failure*, Briefing, no. 11, London, OHE, p. 5.
36 Gould, D. (1971), 'A groundling's notebook', *New Scientist*, vol. 51, p. 217.
37 Haberman, S. (1980), 'Putting a price on life', *Health and Social Service Journal*, vol. 90, pp. 877-9.
38 Davies, B. (1977), 'Needs and outputs', in H. Heisler (ed.), op. cit., pp. 129-62.

Chapter 12 The evaluation of health care

1 Cochrane, A.L. (1971), *Effectiveness and Efficiency*, London, Nuffield Provincial Hospitals Trust, p. 8.
2 Donabedian, A. (1980), *The Definition of Quality and Approaches to its Assessment*, Ann Arbor, Health Administration Press, pp. 5-6.
3 Ibid., p. 82.
4 College of Occupational Therapists (1980), *Recommended Minimum Standards for Occupational Therapy Staff Patient Ratios*, London, College of Occupational Therapists.
5 Royal College of Physicians (1979), *Recommended Minimum Standards for Departments of Clinical Neurophysiology in the National Health Service*, London, Royal College of Physicians.
6 Deitch, R. (1982), 'Standards of obstetric care', *Lancet*, vol. 1, p. 1,476.
7 McLachlan, G. (1976), 'Introduction and perspective', in G. McLachlan, (ed.), *A Question of Quality?*, London, Nuffield Provincial Hospitals Trust, p. 8.
8 Ministry of Health (1962), *A Hospital Plan for England and Wales*, Cmnd 1604, London, HMSO.
9 Ministry of Health (1963), *Health and Welfare: the Development of Community Care*, Cmnd 1973, London, HMSO.
10 Ministry of Health (1962), op. cit., p. 3.

11 Logan, R.F.L., Ashley, J.S.A., Klein, R.E. and Robson, D.M. (1972), *Dynamics of Medical Care,* Memoir no. 14, London, London School of Hygiene and Tropical Medicine, p. 7.

12 Butler, J.R., Bevan, J.M. and Taylor, R.C. (1973), *Family Doctors and Public Policy,* London, Routledge & Kegan Paul.

13 Butler, J.R. (1980), *How Many Patients?,* London, Bedford Square Press, pp. 18-29.

14 Committee of Inquiry into the Regulation of the Medical Profession (1975), *Report,* Cmnd 6018, London, HMSO, pp. 11-15.

15 Ibid., p. 15.

16 Donabedian, A. (1966), 'Evaluating the quality of medical care', *Milbank Memorial Fund Quarterly,* vol. 44, p. 169.

17 Eddy, D.M. (1982), 'Clinical policies and the quality of clinical practice', *New England Journal of Medicine,* vol. 307, pp. 343-7.

18 Shaw, C.D. (1982), 'Monitoring and standards in the NHS: (2) standards', *British Medical Journal,* vol. 284, pp. 288-9.

19 Department of Health and Social Security (1978), *Code of Practice for the Prevention of Infection in Clinical Laboratories,* London, HMSO.

20 Department of Health and Social Security (1972), *Code of Practice for the Protection of Persons against Ionising Radiations arising from Medical and Dental Use,* London, HMSO.

21 Department of Health and Social Security (1970), *Guide to Good Practices in Hospital Administration,* London, HMSO.

22 Medical Research Council Steering Committee for the MRC/DHSS Phenylketonuria Register (1981), 'Routine neonatal screening for phenylketonuria in the United Kingdom 1964-78', *British Medical Journal,* vol. 282, pp. 1,680-4.

23 Anonymous (1981), 'Caesarian childbirth: summary of an NIH consensus statement', *British Medical Journal,* vol. 282, pp. 1,600-4.

24 Royal College of Obstetricians and Gynaecologists (1962), 'Principles and organisation of general practitioner maternity units and their relation to specialist maternity units', in *A Review of the Medical Services in Great Britain,* London, Social Assay, pp. 243-52.

25 British Paediatric Association/Royal College of Obstetricians and Gynaecologists Liaison Committees (1978), *Recommendations for the Improvement of Infant Care during the Perinatal Period in the United Kingdom,* London, BPA/RCOG.

26 Royal College of Nursing (1975), *Improving Geriatric Care: a Handbook of Guidelines,* London, RCN.

27 Department of Health and Social Security (1980), *Organisation and Management Problems of Mental Illness Hospitals,* London, HMSO.

28 International Hospital Federation (1980), *Good Practices in Mental Health,* London, IHF.

29 Royal College of General Practitioners (1981), *What Sort of Doctor?*, London, RCGP.
30 Smits, H.L. (1981), 'The PSRO in perspective', *New England Journal of Medicine*, vol. 305, pp. 253-9.
31 Pippard, J. and Ellam, L. (1981), *Electroconvulsive Treatment in Great Britain, 1980*, London, Royal College of Psychiatrists.
32 Anonymous (1981), 'ECT in Britain: a shameful state of affairs', *Lancet*, vol. 2, pp. 1,207-8.
33 Royal College of Psychiatrists (1977), 'Memorandum on the use of electroconvulsive therapy', *British Journal of Psychiatry*, vol. 131, pp. 261-72.
34 Anonymous (1981), 'ECT in Britain', op. cit.
35 Doney, B.J. (1976), 'Audit of care of diabetics in a group practice', *Journal of the Royal College of General Practitioners*, vol. 26, pp. 734-42.
36 Robb, B. (1967), *Sans Everything: A Case to Answer*, London, Nelson.
37 Department of Health and Social Security (1969), *Report of the Committee of Enquiry into Allegations of Ill Treatment of Patients and Other Irregularities at the Ely Hospital, Cardiff*, London, HMSO.
38 Baker, A. (1976), 'The Hospital Advisory Service', in G. McLachlan (ed.), op. cit., pp. 203-16.
39 Committee of Enquiry, St Augustine's Hospital, Chartham (1976), *Report*, Croydon, South East Thames Regional Health Authority.
40 Ibid., p. 81.
41 Ibid., p. 88.
42 Donabedian (1980), op. cit., pp. 82-3.
43 MacGregor, J.E. and Teper, S. (1978), 'Mortality from carcinoma of cervix uteri in Britain', *Lancet*, vol. 2, pp. 774-6.
44 Ferguson, T. and MacPhail, A.N. (1954), *Hospital and Community*, London, Oxford University Press for the Nuffield Provincial Hospitals Trust.
45 Ibid., p. 136.
46 Morris, J.N. (1975), *Uses of Epidemiology*, Edinburgh, Churchill Livingstone, pp. 86-9.
47 Ashley, J.S.A., Howlett, A. and Morris, J.N. (1971), 'Case fatality of hyperplasia of the prostate in two teaching and three regional board hospitals', *Lancet*, vol. 2, pp. 1,308-11.
48 Morris, op. cit., p. 273.
49 Reid, D.D. and Evans, J.G. (1970), 'New drugs and changing mortality from non-infectious disease in England and Wales', *British Medical Bulletin*, vol. 3, pp. 191-6.
50 McKeown, T. (1979), *The Role of Medicine*, Oxford, Basil Blackwell, pp. 163-4.
51 Reid and Evans, op. cit., p. 194.

52 Weatherall, J.A.C. and White, G.C. (1976), 'A study of survival of children with spina bifida', in Office of Population Censuses and Surveys, *Child Health: A Collection of Studies,* Studies on Medical and Population Subjects, no. 31, London, HMSO, pp. 3-11.
53 Lorber, J. (1971), 'Results of treatment of myelomeningocele', *Developmental Medicine and Child Neurology,* vol. 13, pp. 279-303.
54 Weatherall and White, op. cit., p. 10.

Chapter 13 Quality control in health care

1 Godber, G. (1976), 'The confidential enquiry into maternal deaths. A limited study of clinical results', in G. McLachlan (ed.), *A Question of Quality?,* London, Oxford University Press for the Nuffield Provincial Hospitals Trust, pp. 23-33.
2 Tomkinson, J.S. (1979), 'An assessment of the enquiries into maternal mortality in England and Wales from 1952 to 1975', *Health Trends,* vol. 11, pp. 77-80.
3 Department of Health and Social Security (1982), *Report on Confidential Enquiries into Maternal Deaths in England and Wales 1976-78,* Report on Health and Social Subjects, no. 26, London, HMSO.
4 Ibid.
5 Tomkinson, op. cit., pp. 77-80.
6 Mersey Region Working Party on Perinatal Mortality (1982), 'Confidential inquiry into perinatal deaths in the Mersey region', *Lancet,* vol. 1, pp. 491-4.
7 Dollery, C., Bulpitt, H.J., Dargie, H.J. and Leist, E. (1976), 'The care of patients with malignant hypertension in London in 1974-75', in G. McLachlan (ed.), op. cit., pp. 35-47.
8 Tomkinson, op. cit., pp. 77-80.
9 Godber, op. cit., p. 30.
10 The Medical Defence Union (1982), *Annual Report 1982,* London, MDU.
11 Committee of Enquiry, St Augustine's Hospital, Chartham (1976), *Report,* Croydon, South East Thames Regional Health Authority.
12 Ibid., pp. 110-11.
13 Ibid., pp. 127-8.
14 Ibid., p. 128.
15 Committee of Inquiry into the Regulation of the Medical Profession (1975), *Report,* Cmnd 6018, London, HMSO, p. 4.
16 Anonymous (1982), 'The GMC and professional conduct', *British Medical Journal,* vol. 285, p. 1,440.
17 Committee of Inquiry into the Regulation of the Medical Profession, op. cit., p. 112.

18 Ibid., p. 113.
19 Department of Health and Social Security (1981), *Health Services Management: Health Services Complaints Procedure,* HC(81)5, London, HMSO.
20 Timmins, N. (1981), 'Way found for hospital patients to question a clinical judgement', *The Times,* 7 February, p. 3.
21 Anonymous (1981), 'CCHMS approves draft procedure on clinical complaints', *British Medical Journal,* vol. 282, p. 585.
22 Anonymous (1982), 'What can be done about a chapter of errors?', *Hospital and Health Services Review,* vol. 78, pp. 67-8.
23 Deer, B. (1982), 'Inquiry blames legal adviser', *Times Health Supplement,* 12 March, p. 4.
24 Health Service Commissioner (1982), *Annual Report for 1981-82,* London, HMSO.
25 Murray, W.G.D. (1982), 'Increasing litigation: the size of settlements in professional negligence', *Lancet,* vol. 1, pp. 1,063-4.
26 Smith, R. (1982), 'Problems with a no-fault system of accident compensation', *British Medical Journal,* vol. 284, pp. 1,323-5.
27 Royal Commission of Enquiry (1967), *Compensation for Personal Injury in New Zealand,* Wellington, New Zealand Government.
28 Royal Commission on Civil Liability and Compensation for Personal Injury (1978), *Report,* Cmnd 7054, London, HMSO.

Index